Other books by Ronald K. Siegel

INTOXICATION: *Life in Pursuit of Artificial Paradise*

FIRE IN THE BRAIN: *Clinical Tales of Hallucination*

WHISPERS

The Voices of Paranoia

RONALD K. SIEGEL

SIMON & SCHUSTER PAPERBACKS

NEW YORK   LONDON   TORONTO   SYDNEY

SIMON & SCHUSTER PAPERBACKS
Rockefeller Center
1230 Avenue of the Americas
New York, NY 10020

Published by arrangement with Crown Publishers, Inc.
SIMON & SCHUSTER PAPERBACKS and colophon are registered trademarks
of Simon & Schuster, Inc.

For information about special discounts for bulk purchases,
please contact Simon & Schuster Special Sales at
1-800-456-6798 or business@simonandschuster.com.

Manufactured in the United States of America

13 15 17 19 20 18 16 14

Library of Congress Cataloging-in-Publication data is available.

ISBN 0-684-80285-6

For Jane
who
in the darkness
held my hand
and stole my heart
with love

CONTENTS

WHISPERS

PROLOGUE

I first encountered the demon many years ago in Quebec, during the unlikely season of Christmas.

It was the day after a snowstorm, and the city sparkled. Windows twinkled with frost. Even the snow-encrusted cobblestones looked like so many precious gems. They crunched under my boots as I made my way to the brick building, an unscheduled stop on my walking tour of the old part of the city.

The old woman opened the door before I could knock. She was bundled in layers of torn sweaters and jackets. A blue kerchief adorned with white lilies—the symbol of the province—was tied under her chin, framing her chiseled face with French-Canadian pride. She stood motionless in the doorway, like one of those giant wood statues the local artisans carve for tourists. I handed her several dollars, and she gestured with a wave of a finger for me to enter.

She stuffed the money into a pocket as she began her lecture in French. Her rapid-fire speech caused her breath to form a string of tiny clouds in the unheated room. I couldn't understand her thick Quebecois accent, but when she turned and walked into another room, I followed.

I knew we were in a building that had served as a prison more than a century and a half ago. Many of the people kept here had committed no crime. A Napoleonic style of justice ruled in those days: the accused were guilty until they proved their innocence. Yet all were thrown into cells or dark dungeons, never knowing the nature of their crime or punishment.

The woman grabbed a flashlight and led me down a flight of stone steps to a cellar. It seemed even colder here. She started to speak very quietly. I got closer in order to catch the few words I might understand. Her words came out in whispered puffs of garlic. I thought she said something about people going mad with fear. The flashlight illuminated several cells, broken wooden beams, and rusted pieces of iron. I could picture prisoners in these cells. But what was it like being subjected to such treatment and not knowing why?

I thought of the prisoner's dilemma in Franz Kafka's short story "In the Penal Colony." The prisoner was strapped to a bed inside a diabolical apparatus called the "Harrow." The purpose of the Harrow's complex arrangement of gears and needles was to slowly carve into his flesh whatever law the prisoner had disobeyed. The needles repeated this over and over again, dripping acid into the writing, penetrating deeper and deeper. The prisoner was never told what he did wrong or the sentence that had been passed on him. In fact, the inscription was done in such elaborate calligraphy that no one could read it. But the prisoner was expected to decipher the sentence through his wounds. In the words of the penal colony's commandant, "There would be no point in telling him. He'll learn it on his body." Only then could the prisoner finally know why he was the subject of such cruelty.

But what lessons did the innocent inhabitants of these cells decipher from their imprisonment? Locked in this subterranean world, what secret messages did the gears of their minds create? Did conspiracies of commandants and torture machines flourish in this mental calligraphy? Was this the fear that drove men mad and scarred them as permanently as any Harrow?

The old woman was mumbling now. She walked across the floor to a small hole, barely larger than the circumference of her stocky frame, and climbed down a ladder. I followed, guided by her flashlight. At the bottom of the ladder I stepped onto damp ground. Sewer gases filled the air. The woman's speech was slow and deliberate as her flashlight revealed a series of alcoves in the walls. Prisoners were once shackled to these caves on beds of straw and sewage.

She held the flashlight at chest height like a microphone and pointed it upward so that the light fell directly on her prominent chin. A shadow fell across her face. Then she turned off the light.

A fear of uncertainty and panic gripped me. The calligraphy of my mind took control and started filling in the darkness with a script from a horror movie. I could have sworn the woman cackled. Imaginary sounds repeated from the alcoves: whispers, then the grating of a dull knife being sharpened against the stone wall. There was a rustling in the darkness. Footsteps, unaccustomed to movement for generations, shuffled toward me.

The woman turned on the flashlight again and led me back to the street. The tour was over. But my search for the demon of paranoia that had brushed against my senses in the cellar was just beginning.

1

THE DEMON OF PARANOIA

You will not find *paranoia* in a dictionary. The word is there all right, but not the feeling. Derived from ancient Greek, paranoia originally referred to a mind distracted. But distracted by what? The definition claims the distraction is caused by false beliefs that someone is persecuting you. But if you are afflicted with paranoia (hence a paranoid or paranoiac), you *know* these are not delusions. People *are* harassing and persecuting you. Who are they? Why are they following you? What do they want? There are few clues in the dictionary.

You have become the target of a vast conspiracy stretching on invisible webs across the surface of the planet. It lives in the telephone wires and in the newspapers, perhaps even in dictionaries. It spills out of radios and televisions. It nests in the hearts and minds of family and friends. It is coming to get you.

There might be many reasons why you are chosen. People are jealous of you. After all, you are smarter and better than they are. They are after your knowledge, your job, maybe your spouse. The dictionary says that many paranoids have feelings of grandiosity and omnipotence, but the dictionary doesn't understand. You really do possess remarkable talents as a scientist, inventor, lover, or prophet. That is why you are so attractive, so inspired, so envied. There is nothing in life that you cannot accomplish.

You draw the attention of the First Lady. She falls in love with you. Of course, she cannot make a definite avowal of her love, but she shows it in many silent, indirect ways. Her husband learns of her secret desires and lashes out at you. He sends in the FBI, the Secret Service, then the Mafia. You fight back with lawsuits against the government and the telephone company. Your boss complains that you are not concentrating on your work. You quit and sue him. He never did treat you fairly, and now he'll pay for that. When your wife asks if something is wrong, you decide to sue her, too.

The dog and cat start looking at you in strange ways. You can no longer trust them. The house is not safe, so you decide to move out. You check into a motel, a different one each night just to confuse your enemies. You bunker down under a blanket covered with aluminum foil to protect against the sterilizing rays *they* are directing against you. And you wait. There is time to think, to review the events of past days, looking for hidden meanings that lie just below the surface.

Everything suddenly becomes crystal clear. You can actually see the web slowly closing around you. And you can hear the voices as they plot against you. Your skin erupts with sores where the rays have zapped you. Weaker people would have died from fright at this point. But you are strong. You know who your enemies are and where they live. It is time to act.

Such paranoid episodes as the above usually show a gradual progression from mild suspicion and distrust to intense delusions and fully formed hallucinations. In the beginning there may be only a sense that normal circumstances are not quite so normal. Ordinary life is slowly, subtly filled with suspicion. The suspicion is confirmed by the hallucinatory sights and sounds of the senses themselves. The condition typically evolves over months or years. But when the person is under the influence of a stimulant drug like cocaine or methamphetamine, the progression can be measured in hours. Yet the paranoia is the same for those who experience it with or without drugs.

The really frightening thought—the one that can drive all of us into a full-blown paranoid state—is that the roots of paranoia are within us all. The "paranoid streak," as philosopher Arthur Koestler called it, is an indelible part of human nature. Almost everyone has had a mild experience such as the vague suspicion that *something* is out there just waiting to get us. Darkness and solitude invite the feeling. Many people experience it when they are alone in the house at night or walk down an unfamiliar street. Others may have the vague feeling that their life paths are being jeopardized by jealous persons known and unknown. The creature we all fear, the demon of paranoia, is not "out there," but lurking in the shadows of our very own brains.

Deep inside the center of the brain, just beneath the "thinking" portion of the cerebral cortex, is a group of neurons and hormone-secreting structures known as the limbic system, the neurophysiological hideaway of the paranoia demon. It has been with us for more than 200 million years of evolution. This horseshoe-shaped area is sometimes called the mammalian brain because it is most highly developed in mammals. That's lucky for us mammals because the limbic system helps maintain such homeostatic mechanisms as body temperature. If we didn't have a limbic system, we would be like the cold-blooded reptiles that spend much of their time moving between sun and shade to adjust their temperature. The limbic system also governs the reactions that are involved in survival, such as self-protection through fighting or escaping. An unabashed dictionary might define the functions of the limbic system as the four "f" words of survival: feeding, fighting, fleeing, and fornicating.

The circuits in the lower part of the limbic system are kept busy with the demands of survival. The upper parts are involved in emotions. Electrical activity in the lower parts can generate feelings in the upper regions. This happens spontaneously in certain types of psychomotor epileptic seizures, which give the patients an unpleasant feeling of fear. It's a raw, primitive feeling coming from deep inside the body. Perhaps that's why the limbic system is sometimes called the visceral brain. It feels. You can't shake the feeling. Then the "thinking" areas take over. There is an intellectual fixation on this quirk of fear in the underlying system. The fear creates a premonition, a warning of impending danger. Beset by such deeply seated fear, the brain searches for explanations. It decides that *something* is persecuting you. The brain is in the grips of paranoia.

When the demon puts his grip on epileptics, their faces contort into fear grimaces and there are furtive head and eye movements. Neuroscientists have placed electrodes inside the brains of such patients and confirmed the electrical activity sweeping through the limbic system. But there is no conclusive evidence that neuropathological abnormalities like those of epilepsy are necessary to experience paranoia. Indeed, neuroscientists can evoke the same responses in normal patients using electrical or chemical stimulation. The research tells us something about the areas and mechanisms governing paranoia. It reveals that all of us have inherited the same basic equipment.

The limbic system demon has been our companion since long before we became civilized primates. Perhaps this is why the feeling of paranoia seems so ancient. It has held tremendous survival value for us. When early humans emerged from caves, they found life filled with danger. Accidents, disease, and violence almost always ended life early. Paranoia became a mode of adaptation, a way of coping and surviving. It grew to become part of us.

In the past, Hippocrates and other Greek physicians viewed paranoia as a disease much like epilepsy. They used the word to denote someone who was literally beside their mind, or mad. Most modern psychiatrists still consider it a mental disease, although they prefer to use the expression *mental disorder*. But these labels are misleading. To be paranoid or to have a paranoid slant on life doesn't necessarily mean you are sick and in need of treatment. There is clearly a continuum of paranoia ranging from mild reactions to wild psychotic breaks with reality. It may be appropriate to call a paranoid psychotic like Hitler or Stalin diseased or disordered, but it is unfair to the rest of us nonpsychotics who experience mild paranoid reactions as we deal with the stresses of normal daily life. After all, as at least one famous contemporary psychiatrist is fond of saying, paranoia is sometimes the best way a person can handle situations in life.

The essence of all forms of paranoia is a special mode of thinking. The most characteristic feature of this paranoid thinking is *suspiciousness*. Most people actually use the word *paranoid* to denote an overly suspicious person. But the suspicious thinking of a paranoid is more than the normal mistrust and doubt implied by the word. It is suspicion in the literal meaning: to look below the surface for details. Scrutinizing everything, the paranoid looks for clues confirming the mistrust and doubt. This requires close, focused attention. It requires hyperalertness and hypersensitivity to the smallest details. The paranoid seizes on these minor details, inflates their significance, then works them into a logical systematic pattern. As he searches and scans the environment, he is constantly revising the pattern in order to protect its credibility. The paranoid becomes rigid and inflexible. He is attuned to any possible threat. More than anything else, the paranoid fears loss of personal autonomy or control. It is necessary to stand on guard against any external force or authority.

Another feature of paranoid thinking is hostility. The paranoid believes that elements outside himself are charged with sinister meaning. Accordingly, the paranoid adopts a defensive and antagonistic relationship to the world. There is much anger and hostility, which often evoke hostility from others, thus confirming the initial fears. In this sense the poor paranoid really is persecuted. But, once again, the real enemy is the demon within.

Suspiciousness and hostility set the stage for the imagining of things. That's when another characteristic feature of paranoid thinking—projection—can take over and perform mental tricks worthy of a master illusionist. Projection is an unconscious defensive mechanism by which emotionally unacceptable impulses or tensions are rejected and attributed (or projected) to others. In the stark economy of survival thinking, this makes sense. After all, it is easier to flee from a threatening external enemy than to avoid an internal one. Projection is not always abnormal. Children do it when they resort to magical fantasies in order to cope with the world. As adults, we all do it a little when we blame others for our feelings or our failures. But the paranoid goes one step farther by *denying* his own feelings and *projecting* them onto others. Thus a paranoid might say, "It is not I who hates them, but they who hate me and want to destroy me."

Throughout such projections, it is the paranoid who remains center stage. In the paranoid mode of thinking, something is always happening to the person. The paranoid is the center of attention, either persecutory or grandiose, and this is clearest in megalomaniacs like Hitler. But even those suffering from mild forms of paranoia entertain ideas of reference, incorrectly interpreting casual incidents and external events as having direct reference to oneself.

Ideas of reference may reach sufficient intensity to constitute delusions, or false beliefs, another characteristic of paranoid thinking. Paranoid delusions usually contain a grain of truth and are constructed logically. The themes involve situations that occur in real life, such as being followed, poisoned, infected, loved at a distance, having a disease, or being deceived by one's spouse or lover. The delusions based on these themes may seem reasonable, almost convincing. But they are related more to the person's inner feelings than to external reality, and they are firmly held despite incontrovertible and obvious proof or evidence to the contrary.

Many of these features of paranoid thinking have a dark, negative connotation. The world is hostile and persecutory. The person is suspicious and frightened. One adolescent paranoid drew a picture of herself as a pencil-thin stick figure standing alone in the middle of a city filled with giant buildings. Then she took a black marker pen and covered the buildings with sinister faces, all staring at the little stick figure, with arrows flying from their eyes. But sometimes paranoid thinking is brightened by grandiosity, as if our adolescent artist outlined her stick figure with the protective glow of a yellow highlighter pen. Grandiosity is the exaggerated belief or claim of one's importance or identity. It is often manifested by delusions of great wealth, power, or fame. In mild paranoia, grandiosity is reflected in a personal feeling of uniqueness or a condescending attitude. In severe cases, the person may believe he is perfect, universally admired, a special agent of God, or perhaps even God.

Taken together, these features of thinking are so clear and robust in the paranoid mode that they are used as diagnostic criteria. Often there is little else different about paranoids. Most appear quite normal and well integrated. Behavior is not obviously odd or bizarre. The outward personalities remain intact, as do the emotions. People work and socialize as before. But, inside, behind the barricades of their minds, thoughts are shifting into the paranoid mode. Perceptions change as if the world were being covered with hostile graffiti drawn with a black marker pen. The barricades keep us from prying, but psychiatrists and psychologists know from clinical interviews that behind them is the suspicion, hostility, projection, ideas of reference, and grandiosity that define the paranoid mode of thinking. In a sense, the barricades can be breached and the diagnosis confirmed through the very words paranoids use to keep the world at bay.

The first paranoid I encountered, after joining the Department of Psychiatry and Biobehavioral Sciences at the UCLA School of Medicine, kept his distance. In fact, I was forced to interview him via a computer screen and keyboard. That really didn't matter because the paranoid mode of thinking was unmistakable, even when reduced to lines of type. The paranoia came through so loud and clear that I could feel my own demon starting to stir. I wanted to know more about this feeling and the world it guarded. But after my "Interview with Hitler's Brain" (chapter 2), I began to see that interviews alone were insufficient for understanding the experience of paranoia. I needed a different approach, one that might permit me access to the paranoid in the same way a virtual reality device permits one to "walk" into the computer and experience, interact, even change the programming. After all, surgeons rehearse operations on "virtual" patients. Could I somehow get into a paranoid's case enough to experience "virtual" paranoia? Inside such a world, could I discover the triggers for the paranoid mode of thinking? Could I turn them off?

I decided to adopt a technique I had already used as a research psychopharmacologist studying subjects under the influence of drugs or patients experiencing hallucinations. I knew that the subjects or patients were the only ones who see, hear, feel, taste, and smell the world the way they do. Yes, I talked to them, but in a special way. Become a camera and radio, I instructed them, and tell me what you see and hear as it is happening. Take me on your trip.

Unfortunately, verbal trips were insufficient. In my drug experiments, I took the drugs myself and became a subject. The same method applied to my investigations with patients who were hallucinating without the use of artificial intoxicants. I sought not only to "see" their hallucinations, but to feel their experience. Of course, I couldn't slip into their bodies and look out. But I got as close as possible. I accompanied them home, at work, at play. I talked with family members, co-workers, friends, and neighbors. Sometimes I lived with the patients for a while. In special cases I constructed environments in the laboratory that duplicated those my patients experienced.

I followed this same approach with my new interest in paranoia, now kindled by that fascinating but frustrating computer interview. If someone told me he was being followed, I stayed with him and watched. How else could I tell? When patients barricaded themselves behind makeshift fortresses, I crawled inside with them and waited for the enemy to attack. When a man told me that dwarfs were living in his backyard, I joined him on a dwarf hunt in the middle of the night.

In my role as a forensic psychopharmacologist and expert witness in criminal trials, I was often asked by the judge, the defense attorney, or the prosecutor to interview defendants who might have been under the influence of drugs at the time of the crime. I met some of the more fascinating paranoids this way, although they were sometimes confined to jails awaiting trial. I tried to compensate for this restricted contact by engaging in marathon interview sessions, once persuading authorities to let me spend eighteen straight hours in a defendant's cell. In addition, I visited their families and friends, walked the streets of their neighborhoods, and poked around their houses and bedrooms. In some cases I even mingled with their "homeboys" in the gang-infested barrios of Los Angeles.

Inside these paranoid worlds, I searched for the various keys that opened the demon's gates and allowed the patients or defendants to be gripped by the paranoid mode of thinking. In the beginning, I naively thought it would be a simple matter of removing these keys and closing the gates, thus rescuing the people. It would be simple because I didn't believe in demons any more than I believed in fairy-tale dragons belching fire. But sometimes the imaginary enemies turned out to be real. On one late-night dwarf hunt (in a case not included here), a dwarf shot back! And the paranoid patients themselves were not always as mild-mannered as the computer had been. I was threatened, beaten, shot at, and had more than one "contract" issued on my life. During one jailhouse interview, the defendant leaped across the table and started choking me until my fingers found the panic button that brought the guards to my rescue. My training as a research scientist did not prepare me for such situations, and I stumbled on, picking up necessary survival skills along the way from friends in both police departments and psychiatry departments.

One friend was a psychiatrist and psychoanalyst whom I will call Joel Morgan. He introduced me to the literature on paranoia, a literature concerned primarily with diagnosis and psychoanalysis. There were only three major texts and a few minor technical monographs (see general references in the bibliography). The bulk of the literature was in the medical and psychiatric journals. Here I found hundreds of case studies (more than 10 percent of admissions to mental hospitals are for paranoid states). Despite the number of cases, most did no more than describe the observable behavior and speculate about causes. The aspect of paranoia I was most interested in—the experience of the demon—was hardly mentioned.

I found a few firsthand accounts written by patients, but they were usually paranoid schizophrenics who had disorganized thinking, prominent hallucinations (such as hearing voices), and bizarre delusions (the delusions of thought control, for example) not typical of the vast majority of paranoids. The best of these was Barbara O'Brien's *Operators and Things,* an account of her terrifying yet highly atypical experiences. There were more representative examples in the fictional literature, including descriptions of an acute persecutory paranoia in Chekhov's novel *Ward Number Six,* paranoid grandiosity in Gogol's short story "The Diary of a Madman," paranoid jealousy in Shakespeare's *Othello,* and runaway paranoid fantasies in the science fiction novel *Radio Free Albemuth* by Philip K. Dick. While these descriptions were fictional, they conveyed a feeling for the experience that was lacking in the clinical material.

Most case studies report paranoia from the perspective of clinicians who generally stay on their own side of the proverbial couch. They cloak the patient's experience in technical jargon, rarely even providing transcripts of the actual dialogues that presumably illustrated the paranoid mode of thinking. The clinicians can't even agree on the jargon. I discovered a continuing debate about nosology and diagnosis. Some classify paranoid states as delusional disorders, emphasizing the persistent false beliefs in thinking. Others classify paranoid states as psychotic disorders, emphasizing the *severe* paranoid's impairment in all aspects of behavior, including the ability to think, respond emotionally, remember, communicate, and interpret reality. If that isn't confusing enough, still others mistakingly imply that all paranoids are schizophrenics, when it is only some schizophrenics who may be paranoid. Despite this confusion with terms, there is a consensus of opinion about what triggers the paranoid mode of thinking in all such cases.

The triggers for paranoia are either biological or psychological in origin. The most common biological triggers are drug intoxications, but thyroid disorders, pernicious anemia, cerebral arteriosclerosis, even certain brain tumors, can all do the same trick of pulling the demon up out of the limbic system. There are numerous other diseases that produce structural or functional changes in the nervous system and trigger paranoid thinking.

In most cases, the biological triggers appear to act by disturbing perception or memory. For example, the drug phencyclidine (PCP) causes a condition known as hyperacusia, wherein sounds seem much louder than they really are. If sounds are louder, they tend to be more easily noticed and more readily perceived as important. When this effect is coupled with PCP's notorious ability to produce a feeling of exaggerated muscular strength, the stage is set for suspicious, referential, or delusional thinking. Not surprisingly, PCP intoxication often produces violent paranoid reactions. Conversely, loss of hearing, as frequently happens to the elderly, can precipitate feelings of suspicion, mistrust, and, ultimately, paranoia, about things not heard clearly. This is what happened to an elderly woman who told me she could pick up "Whispers" (chapter 4) of radio transmissions through her teeth. She suspected that a dentist had implanted devices in her fillings while she was lying on the dental chair, a situation that already sets the stage for anxiety and suspicion in many people. When the woman was given nitrous oxide anesthesia, which induced further perceptual changes, the gates to her demon were opened.

Disturbances of memory can also trigger paranoid thinking. When very recent memory is impaired, it is often difficult, if not impossible, for the brain to record a steady and reasonable flow of information about events in the world. Many hallucinogens like marijuana impair concentration and recall of recent information, filling the user's world with disconnected data. This is the same world inhabited by individuals afflicted with the memory deficits from any number of organic brain diseases, such as Alzheimer's. In this world of inconsistencies, it is easy for suspicions and delusions to feed on each other, flourishing with magical speed.

Most of the clinical literature has been concerned with identifying the psychological triggers and their underlying mechanisms. Psychological triggers include such diverse things as false arrest, social isolation, or an intensely humiliating experience. Of course, these experiences are eventually translated into electrical and chemical events, thus becoming, in effect, biological triggers. While psychological triggers can act suddenly as in the case of false arrest, some develop slowly over time. Often they have their roots in childhood.

Many paranoids display a basic lack of trust stemming from the absence of a warm and trusting relationship with their parents. The parents of paranoids were often overcontrolling, rigid, distant, even sadistic. As children they developed a feeling that they would be betrayed, that their parents would not help them with disappointments and frustrations. They grew up feeling that the environment was constantly hostile, and they develop hypersensitivity to imagined slights.

The second paranoid I met had such a childhood, as did many of the others I met later. By the time Edwin Tolman (chapter 3) was an adult, his sensitivity was so great that he *expected* his environment to be hostile and was always on the defensive against unseen enemies and malevolent forces. Throughout history, many paranoids have imagined that these enemies used state-of-the-art technology to exert their influence. In the nineteenth century, such "influencing machines" operated via hydraulic pumps and invisible chemical forces. Since that time, the machines have kept pace with advancements in science, using radio waves, then microwaves, and finally lasers. But Tolman told me he was controlled by the newest model: the personal satellite, launched by his enemies to follow him around. The satellite, he claimed, was transmitting signals directly into his brain.

The real influencing machine, of course, is the brain itself. Freud believed that it operates very much like a hydraulic machine, with instincts, drives, fears, and other elements pushing and pulling against each other. He argued that homosexuality is the hydraulic force creating most forms of paranoia. According to Freud, the paranoid is basically a homosexual with an intense fear of castration. The paranoid projects repressed homosexual wishes onto others who he believes wish to assault him homosexually. Freud also believed that latent homosexuality causes paranoid delusions of jealousy, as in the case of a husband who suspected his wife of loving a man to whom the husband actually felt attracted. Despite the lack of clinical evidence to support Freud's ideas, many contemporary psychiatrists still think along these classic lines.

I took Tolman's case to Joel Morgan, who accepted the classic Freudian view. Repressed or denied homosexual impulses were sparking Tolman's paranoia, Joel said. I argued with this interpretation at the time—even ridiculed it—but in two later cases (chapters 4 and 8) I found some evidence of a causal relationship between overt homosexuality and a paranoid reaction. Still, the incidence of repressed or overt homosexuality among paranoids seems no greater than in the population at large. Indeed, as society moves away from the Victorian attitudes of the nineteenth century toward more open acceptance of homosexuality, the shame and humiliation triggering the paranoid mode in *some* denying homosexuals appears to be diminishing.

In addition to homosexuality, Freud postulated several feelings such as guilt that play what I think is a much more certain role in the development of paranoia. Feelings of guilt about cheating on one's taxes or lying to a spouse can make all of us a little anxious, if not paranoid. When the guilt feelings are not resolved but allowed to fester for a long period of time, the person may project them and convert them into persecutory delusions. Equally important are feelings of inferiority or failure, which can be replaced by the feelings of grandiosity and omnipotence often associated with paranoid states. That's what happened to Harry Balise (chapter 9), who lost his job and turned into a prophet. He was so grandiose

and firm in his belief that members of his family were ⸻
by the same delusion.

Psychological triggers are sometimes coupled with ⸻
tors. Harry Balise was a member of a minority group and had a
long history of feeling alienated and oppressed by society. Such
feelings are even more profound in migratory and immigrant workers, who endure adaptational stresses of learning a new language
and new culture while feeling loneliness and isolation away from
their native countries. This breeds paranoid ideas, which frequently
disappear as soon as the workers return to their native lands.

In a sense, I was like a frightened immigrant myself as I traveled
from the familiar comforts of my ivory tower to the strange new
land behind the barricades. My investigations took me through
paranoid landscapes, guided by those who lived and died there.
Standing beyond the barricades with my "guides," I saw and heard
the evidence, then felt the fear. Sometimes, as I stood among winds
that whispered ominous threats and trees that watched my every
move, I thought all the suspicion and caution were justifiable. But
by then I, too, had become more than a little paranoid.

Since I am writing this now, obviously I made it back to my ivory
tower, ready to tell about my adventures. I assure you I am of
sound mind and body. That is an unusual statement for an author
to make, but one that seems necessary in view of my trip through a
dark, parallel universe. The adventures may seem incredible, but
they are all true.

Remember the 1938 Orson Welles radio broadcast that panicked thousands who believed there was an actual invasion from
Mars? That wasn't real. But the "Invasion of Bugs" (chapter 6)
that terrorized cocaine users throughout the country was real. Just
ask Richie D., who killed his son rather than let the child succumb
to the invaders (chapter 7).

Don't think that these cases are not real because they sound like
nightmares born out of watching too many horror movies. Paranoia can turn even the happiest movie into a "Tale from the Crypt."
Consider the case of Linda Estrada's family, who was watching
The Ten Commandments on television (chapter 10). Suddenly a
putrid green fog poured out of the movie and took the life of her
firstborn.

I take you through the individual adventures in the same order in which they happened to me. In this way you can accompany me as I search for the demon, moving from cases where there were only vague hints of something out there stalking the person, to apocalyptic visions so intense that they shake the foundations of entire neighborhoods. After my initial encounters, I moved, literally and figuratively, from whispers (chapter 4) and shadows (chapter 5) to armed confrontations with KGB spies (chapter 8) and Mafia dwarfs (chapter 11). The closer I got to the demon, the more fearful I became. You'll see that at times I adopted a flippant, almost comic attitude, and I hope you'll understand that this was only a defensive projection.

The cases represent more extreme situations than any you may have encountered yourself. But by the very nature of their intensity, they magnify the subtle and often hidden dynamics that bother all of us when we're alone in the house at night. As you accompany me on these adventures, perhaps you'll recognize why I no longer trust Dorothy's remark at the end of The Wizard of Oz: "Oh, Auntie Em, there's no place like home!!" For me, being home alone will never feel as sweet or as safe as it did once upon a time.

Throughout my adventures I learned from trial and error, trying to find the triggers and help the people. Of course, I wasn't always in a position to help. After all, I was not a treating clinician. In most cases I was studying the patients only for research purposes or in preparation for criminal trials. Yet I wanted to do whatever I could for the demon's victims. I knew I could not "cure" anyone of paranoid thinking any more than I could excise their limbic systems. It goes with the territory of being human. But I was hopeful that by blocking, removing, or otherwise stopping the triggers that prompted the thinking to come out in discernible behaviors, I could at least tame the demon. In a sense, mine was the classic behavioral scientist's approach. Eliminate the symptoms, so goes the theory, and the problem is gone. That's fine when behavior therapists deal with neurotics who bite their nails, but no one had dared try it with paranoids who were biting imaginary bullets. However, since paranoids, especially the severe cases I encountered, are highly resistant to any treatment, I felt that neither I nor my research patients had anything to lose. Some of my patients got better, some got worse, and some got lost and are still out there. But each provided clues to my search for the demon of paranoia by showing me his many disguises. I finally caught up with him (or he with me) on an Amtrak train in Raleigh, North Carolina (chapter 12).

Paranoia is a way of perceiving and feeling the world. The paranoid inhabits a different realm of being, one that tilts the world ever so slightly. The senses detect these differences. They sound mental alarms. The paranoid becomes locked into a new mode of thinking, thereafter viewing the world as if trapped in a cell or, yes, even a demon's lair. This book is a visit to those prisons of the mind. It is not about cause or treatment; it is about the experience of paranoia, or what it is like to be living with the demon.

2

INTERVIEW WITH HITLER'S BRAIN

Hitler's brain is being kept alive in the basement of the UCLA Medical School. The thought was pounding in my head, making me extremely nervous. I have heard many strange things from patients in the Neuropsychiatric Institute at UCLA, where I work. I have listened to countless descriptions of fantastic adventures from subjects under the influence of exotic drugs. I know a crazy story when I hear one. So why did I give this rumor a second thought? Before you judge me mad, listen to my story.

I first heard about Hitler's brain soon after my arrival at UCLA. Eager to make a good impression, I worked late and sometimes slept in my lab. My best friends became the night janitors who swept the long corridors of the third largest building in the world, the UCLA Center for the Health Sciences. Some of these corridors run for over a quarter of a mile as they snake through various departments and research institutes. It's easy to get lost, and everyone jokes about the "lost patient" who has been wandering the halls for years. Charlie, one of the janitors, knew the catacombs of the building as well as anyone. He not only picked up the trash, but he had a curious habit of reading some of it. That's how he learned that they had Hitler's brain.

I listened to Charlie's story with amusement. His big brown eyes seemed to get bigger, and his entire body became animated as he spoke. "Yes, sir," said Charlie. "Hitler's brain is in a jar some-where in the basement." He kept nodding his head up and down as if the gesture made it more believable. But Charlie was always get-ting excited about something or other. I recalled his explanation of why he wouldn't clean the restroom on a certain floor. He was cleaning a toilet there when an earthquake struck. The building swayed, as it was designed to do, but the water sloshed around in the toilet bowl and spilled onto the floors. Charlie lost his balance and was buffeted back and forth against the walls of the stall. To hear Charlie tell it was like listening to the tale of a man who had been caught in a tidal wave. He was terrified and discovered that he could never go back into that particular restroom. His story about Hitler's brain sounded like just another spill from the toilet.

It was easy to dismiss Charlie's account as a hallucination. This was a hallucination not in the pathological sense of the word, but in the original meaning offered by Lavater, a Renaissance writer who first used the term to describe idle talk or prating about strange events such as "ghostes and spirites walking by nyght." Charlie's story was simply the idle or foolish talk that Lavater said com-monly occurred following the death of great men and their king-doms. Indeed, Shakespeare used Lavater's book as a source for *Hamlet,* which opens with the appearance of the ghost of Hamlet's father, the king. Certainly Hitler's ghost was destined to haunt our collective unconscious for at least as long as Hamlet's. I smiled at Charlie, grateful for the entertaining break, then returned to my own lab.

Several months later I heard the story from Albert, another jan-itor on the night shift. This time there was a new twist: Hitler's brain was alive! I suspected Charlie had put Albert up to this non-sense. But when I confronted Charlie, his eyes bulged, then he gasped and shook his head so hard that his jowls performed their own miniature earthquake. He hadn't heard this variation of the rumor, but he was willing to believe it. As far as Charlie was con-cerned, the entire basement was one giant toilet that was now off limits. He said he was going to request a new assignment.

I was intrigued enough to visit the library to find out what had really happened to Hitler's brain. UCLA has a wonderful library system consisting of several interconnected libraries scattered around the campus. Collectively there were over nine hundred books and manuscripts dealing with Hitler. When I went to the stacks, most of the books I wanted were not there. The librarian told me they were not checked out, so they were either misshelved, lost, or stolen. While she promised to search for them, I checked out a few volumes that were available and took them back to my office.

Hitler died all right, and on this point there was universal agreement among historians. He spent the last months of the war inside a Reich chancellery bunker, fifty-five feet below the streets of Berlin. It was there that he learned of the inevitable collapse of his forces and the betrayal of his trusted officers Göring and Himmler. Hitler's aides talked of escape. A Junker-390 plane, capable of flying over the pole to Japan or China, was waiting at a nearby airport. There was talk of a flight to Manchukuo. But Hitler decided on suicide. In a macabre ceremony he married his mistress, Eva Braun, then dictated his last will and testament to a secretary. The next day, after receiving word of Mussolini's death, Hitler sent for cyanide capsules and had them tested on Blondi, his pet Alsatian. After lunch he said good-bye to his staff and retired to his room in the bunker. His bride swallowed the poison. Hitler put a Walther 7.65-mm pistol against his right temple and pulled the trigger.

"That was a bull's-eye," said one of Propaganda Minister Goebbels's children, who was listening at the door. It was 3:30 P.M. on April 30, 1945. The two bodies were wrapped in blankets and placed in a trench on the surface. An aide doused them with gasoline, then set them on fire with burning newspaper. Hitler had ordered that his body be burned "till nothing remained." He would not be exhibited like Mussolini or stuffed and displayed in some Russian museum. Later, the cremation area came under intensive bombardment by Russian artillery. It was believed that Hitler's last order had been carried out.

Five days later the Russians recovered several badly burned bodies partially buried in a crater in the Reich chancellery garden. Hitler's body was identified after careful comparison with skull and dental X-rays. His famous rotting teeth were a dead giveaway. The Russians performed an autopsy on May 8, 1945. There were head injuries consistent with a gunshot wound. They found splinters of glass in his mouth, which would also be consistent with crushing a poison ampule between his teeth. Despite the extensive damage from the fire, many internal organs survived. The liver and almost every other internal organ were described. Chemical tests confirmed the presence of cyanide compounds in various organs.

Hitler had always refused to allow doctors to examine his genitals. Now, the autopsy team learned why. They noted that Hitler was monorchid—that is, he had only one testicle. Part of the cranium was also missing. The brain, or whatever parts were inside, was never described. The same autopsy team examined the bodies of other bunker victims, including the Goebbels family and Hitler's dog, and they performed fine dissections of the brains and preserved them in jars. Why didn't Hitler's brain get the same courtesy extended to his dog?

I allowed my imagination to run wild. Hitler's brain was missing! While it could have been consumed in the fire, the other internal organs remained intact. Perhaps someone had taken Hitler's brain in order to hide evidence. After all, JFK's brain mysteriously disappeared after the autopsy. The Russians could be hiding some crucial evidence related to cause of death. They never released the actual autopsy protocol, although they have officially stated that Hitler poisoned himself with cyanide and was shot by an aide after death. But this conclusion is contrary to the accounts of Hitler's secretary and other survivors from the bunker who reported that Hitler did not want to suffer in the throes of cyanide poisoning and often discussed the merits of rapid death from a gunshot that would shatter the skull. The survivors agreed that after the shot was heard, they entered Hitler's room and found him crumpled up on the sofa, his head hanging toward the floor, blood running from his right temple onto the carpet.

Perhaps someone took the brain as a souvenir. That would not have been so strange. There were many ghoulish souvenir hunters in Nazi Germany. Josef Mengele, the infamous doctor at Auschwitz, collected the eyes, gallstones, and fetuses of inmates. His colleagues collected other body parts. Perhaps Hitler's brain had been snatched by the Japanese. After all, the University of Tokyo housed a major collection of brains from political leaders, novelists, artists, and intellectuals. Allied collectors had similar obsessions about brains. The Russians kept Pavlov's brain on exhibit and sliced up Lenin's into thirty thousand slides for detailed study. In America, Einstein's brain had been preserved. Other collections were even more bizarre. A New York collector had Napoleon's penis in a jar. I even had a collection of hair samples from famous people, including one from Napoleon, another from George Washington, and a full lock of hair from Mary Shelley, who wrote *Frankenstein*. I justified my interest in collecting hair by explaining that I could analyze the samples for traces of drugs these famous people might have used. The hair could tell us exactly what drugs were used, how much, and how often. Somehow I didn't think Napoleon's penis could say as much, despite my wish to hear its confessions.

But what would Hitler's brain have to say? My imagination conjured a sinister scenario consistent with the rumor that Hitler's brain was not only saved, but kept alive! It was known that several days before his suicide, Hitler feared that his personal physician, Theodor Morell, who was giving him regular injections of a variety of drugs, might try to knock him out and kidnap him to a safe place. Hitler refused all further injections. But what if the doctor and aides had removed the brain and taken it on the Junker-390 to some secret laboratory? After all, turn-of-the-century French doctors stole decapitated heads from the guillotine and conducted ghoulish experiments, trying to keep them alive. Devices for keeping severed animal heads alive had been around for years, and one suitable for human heads was even granted a U.S. patent. Why not do it with the brain? Of course, the thought was pure science fiction and reminded me of several science fiction movies, including the 1953 film *Donovan's Brain* (in which the brain of a powerful businessman is kept alive in a glass tank in a lab) and the 1963 movie *They Saved Hitler's Brain* (in which Nazis take Hitler's head to a secret Caribbean laboratory, where they keep it alive on top of a mechanical box).

I was sure that Hitler would have liked my science fiction scenario. He was fascinated by the idea of severed heads; they were his favorite doodle. He certainly was grandiose enough to want to survive and continue to dominate with the sheer power of what he referred to as "my fanatical will." I also thought he would have appreciated my cinematic reminiscences. Hitler admired the work

of German filmmaker Fritz Lang, whose early movies often portrayed German mythology and visions of future glory. In the 1932
film *The Last Will of Dr. Mabuse,* the strong-willed Mabuse, who
had always sought to control people, is a dying old man confined to
an insane asylum. Yet he manages to hypnotize the director of the
asylum into continuing his campaign to plunge the world into terror and chaos. Hitler was so impressed that he offered Lang, a Jew,
the post of director of the Third Reich's film industry. Lang fled
Germany that same night.

My research into the fate of Hitler's brain led to further reading
about his mind. Hitler was the quintessential anti-Semite in a Europe where anti-Semitism was already widespread. But Hitler not
only hated Jews, he was paranoid about them. This paranoid thinking had developed over a long period of time. According to several
"psychological autopsies" conducted by psychoanalysts, Hitler's
anti-Semitism was rooted in his childhood. These included bitter
memories of a conflict between his parents; resentment over aban-
donment by his mother and beatings by his father; feelings of in-
adequacy over his single testicle; worry about the possibility that
he had homosexual tendencies and feminine traits; the suspicion
that his grandfather might have been Jewish, thus tainting him
with Jewish blood; and a haunting memory of his mother's death
while under the care of a Jewish doctor. Thus, so goes the psychoanalytic theory, he feared his own homosexual tendencies and Jewish blood, denied these fears, and projected them onto "enemies of
the State," who had to be attacked and destroyed. The major enemies were Jews, but he grouped homosexuals and Communists
with them. These feelings were nourished by the racist literature he
read at an early age. He took bits and pieces from his memories of
this literature, then added hidden meanings he found in historical
coincidences. His mind, already whirling with mistrust and suspicion, wove it all together into a web that he saw threatening to
entrap the entire world.

Hitler's paranoia revolved around a core delusion that there
was an international Jewish conspiracy pitted against his own
plan to achieve world dominance for Germany. Hitler suspected
that Jews were not only plotting secretly against his Motherland,
but conspiring against all of mankind. He was convinced that the

Jews were a separate race, treacherously disloyal to any government and dedicated to advancing their own ambitions and selfish financial interests. Hitler talked about the Jews with both revulsion and fear, calling them parasites, poisoners, and viruses. He told the German people they must remain constantly vigilant about Jewish intentions.

This mode of paranoid thinking is not necessarily disabling, and it wasn't for Hitler. During his early political career, such thinking helped him as an organizer and leader. It provided a source of energy and self-confidence, underlying the belief that he was right. Early political ridicule by Jews only confirmed his suspicions. Hitler's uncanny skills as a public speaker added to his charismatic appeal and inspired loyal followers to relentlessly pursue his enemies as the "enemies of the State." It was this paranoid thinking and its subsequent institutionalization by an already anti-Semitic population that made possible the Holocaustic answer to the so-called Jewish Question.

Hitler's deeds have prompted some biographers and historians to conclude that he was a "ruthless animal," "wicked," "completely evil," and "seized by demons." They note that he was fond of wolves, raised *Wolfshundes* (Alsatian dogs), and chose the code name "Herr Wolf." He called his headquarters in East Prussia the Wolf's Lair, telling a servant, "I am the wolf and this is my den." Perhaps the name given to the Nazi headquarters in the Ukraine is more revealing: Werewolf. It was the same name given to elite SS units that conducted guerrilla warfare behind enemy lines. As Germany began to lose the war, these units fought like the cornered wolves they had become, viciously ripping their victims apart.

My research convinced me that Hitler was a werewolf in the sense that something changed him radically even before the war seemed lost. Before 1939 Hitler certainly exhibited intense paranoid thinking about the Jews, brought on by his psychological history. He also had milder paranoia about such things as taxes. In fact, he was under investigation by the Munich tax authorities for many years until he became chancellor and declared himself exempt from taxation. And, of course, Hitler was strange. After all, he identified with wolves yet hated the moonlight. He loved pornography yet was terrified by the thought of sexual intercourse. He wanted to eradicate races with "cruelty" and "terror" in the concentration camps, yet he agonized over the most humane way to kill lobsters in German restaurants. Despite these peculiarities, and the unlimited psychoanalytic speculation they have spawned, there is no evidence of severe psychiatric impairment or dysfunction. However, beginning in late 1937, Hitler's underlying paranoia grew by leaps and bounds, eventually exploding into full-blown psychotic episodes. In a sense, he was seized by a demon.

The elixir responsible for this transformation was his use of the powerful central nervous system stimulant methamphetamine, known in the parlance of contemporary street drug users as crank, crystal, ice, or speed. Methamphetamine was originally synthesized by a Japanese pharmacologist, then tested and perfected by German scientists. It was first made available to German investigators in 1936, the same year Dr. Morell became Hitler's personal physician. In 1939 methamphetamine became commercially available throughout Germany under the trade name Pervitin.

There is strong historical evidence that in 1937, and perhaps as early as 1936, Hitler started receiving occasional "treatments" with intravenous injections of methamphetamine from Dr. Morell. These were the same treatments given to President John F. Kennedy by his Morell, Dr. Max Jacobson. Also known as "Dr. Feelgood," Jacobson, who was a German refugee, administered his injections to such World War II celebrities as Winston Churchill and Marlene Dietrich. Both Morell and Jacobson mixed the drugs with vitamins and told their famous patients they were getting only "vitamins." The "vitamin" injections created instant euphoria and stimulation.

Hitler's treatments with the stimulant were probably rare until 1941. The medical records show that at that time, Morell was giving the injections to Hitler every morning before he got out of bed. Hitler immediately felt alert and ready for the day's work. Morell also administered the drug to Hitler prior to major speeches and meetings. In an effort to overcome tolerance, Morell started doubling Hitler's dosage and giving frequent injections. By the middle of 1943 Hitler was getting injections throughout the day. As the war progressed and German forces struggled, Hitler called for Morell more and more often. The injections always left him cheerful and talkative but unable to sleep. In addition to the shots, Hitler

was supplied with Pervitin tablets. These were the same methamphetamine tablets given to the German Panzer troops and Luft-
waffe pilots, except that Hitler's pills were prepared exclusively for
his use and wrapped in gold foil. In the last years of the war he took
as many as ten tablets a day, often fumbling with the wrappers
during military conferences. Hitler added to his chemical stimulation by sucking continuously on Cola-Dalmann, a hard cola candy
containing large amounts of caffeine.

As his addiction grew, Hitler became more and more dependent
on his "dealer," Morell. He kept telling Morell how much he
needed him and took him along everywhere. The medical estab-
lishment was less confident in Morell's treatments, but Hitler ignored their questions and kept rewarding Morell with money and
medals. The treatments continued.

Eventually Hitler started manifesting the physical signs of
methamphetamine toxicity. His insomnia and loss of appetite fluc-
tuated with periods of stuporous sleep and eating binges. In 1939
he started to bite at the skin surrounding the nails of his thumb and
the first two fingers on each hand. The fingertips became chronically inflamed, yet Hitler continued to bite them. Those around
Hitler viewed the habit as highly unusual for a man with impeccable standards of dress and bearing. His valet suspected that the
drug treatments were responsible. In 1942 Hitler began to manifest
a tremor resembling Parkinson's disease (a degenerative nerve disorder) in his arm and hand. By 1943 he was picking and scratching
at the skin on the back of his neck. The picking and scratching
became so compulsive that in 1944 the neck area was covered with
infected pustules. There were many other effects that were probably related to the chronic methamphetamine including oversensi-
tivity to sunlight, weight loss, headaches, clouded vision, and even
a myocardial infarction in 1943 and a stroke in February 1945.

Concomitant with the methamphetamine treatments, the earlier
paranoia became more virulent. There had been many hate-filled
arguments and plans for programs of blood and terror in *Mein
Kampf* (*My Struggle*), the book Hitler wrote during a prison term
in 1924 and 1925. But methamphetamine seemed to make his or-
atorial denunciations of "enemies" louder and more impassioned.
In the opinion of several "psychological autopsies" on Hitler, the

frankness of *Mein Kampf* turned into wild fanaticism as the author, now the Führer, turned into a demonic speed freak.

Hitler's behavior followed a textbook progression of a toxic paranoid psychosis. The first signs appeared in late 1937 but grew as the treatments escalated. The initial alertness and mood elevation was followed by periods of lethargy and depression, necessitating larger and more frequent doses. This led to increased excitation, agitation, irritability, and reduced frustration tolerance, finally erupting in violent rages. Hitler's cheeks would flush with anger. His pupils, dilated by the drug, appeared to take on a wild look filled with hate. He raised his clenched fist in the air, then bellowed for hours at a time. In the heat of such pathological fury, he made impulsive decisions, especially in the later years of the war. He was obsessed with minute details, such as the position of a single artillery battery, and neglected major strategic issues. His attention kept shifting to new details, or else he carried on monologues with endless repetitions of the same ideas. The transcripts of his monologues during military briefings grew from an average of 89 pages in 1942 to 150 pages in 1945. He shouted the same stories over and over. Suspicion and distrust permeated his conversations as he continued to blame others for his mistakes. His drug-induced euphoria overwhelmed his reasoning, and he began to see battlefield failures as successes and spoke of mythical armies that would turn the tide of the war. Despite such psychopathology, other functions remained intact. For example, his astounding memory stayed clear and sharp right up to the end.

A birthday party held for Hitler in the bunker on April 20 became a wake filled with despair and incipient tragedy. Morell left the bunker the next day and took his drugs with him. Hitler went into a massive withdrawal depression. His first reaction was a depressive rage in which he accused everyone of betrayal. This was followed by a deeper suicidal depression. Heinz Linge, Hitler's valet and chief of staff, administered cocaine eyedrops, the only known stimulant still left in the bunker. Hitler's eyes became extremely sensitive to light, and he no longer ventured topside to walk in the chancellery garden. Linge increased the dose during the final week from six drops three times a day to thirteen drops three times a day. This dosage would have kept the pupils chronically dilated and paralyzed the ciliary muscles around the lens, thus preventing accommodation and focusing. At the end Hitler was functionally blind. By then there was nothing left of his vision of world dominance to see.

After familiarizing myself with Hitler's methamphetamine-saturated brain, I returned to the library for more materials. Most of the remaining books I had requested couldn't be found and were now listed as lost or stolen. Several others were on long-term loan to a graduate student who had refused to bring them back. I persuaded the librarian to give me the student's name so I could make a personal appeal.

"Steiner," said the deep bass voice on the other end of the telephone. Mark Steiner was the graduate student who had checked out the Hitler books. I introduced myself and confessed that I was the faculty member who had requested the early return of the books. Since we both shared the same academic interest, I suggested we meet for coffee in the hospital cafeteria. He agreed to bring the books I wanted.

Mark Steiner was a tall, muscular young man with disproportionately large hands. He had thick blond hair combed straight back and handsome, chiseled features. The combination would have made him the picture-perfect Aryan except for his brown eyes. I knew that such a minor defect would have infuriated Josef Mengele, who injected dyes into the eyes of concentration camp inmates in a vain attempt to turn them Aryan blue. I shuddered to think what Mengele would have done with the hands. Mark marched over to my table. I was hesitant to shake his huge hand, and to my relief, he kept both of them locked around the books.

He wore a white short-sleeved shirt that hugged his biceps and a perfectly knotted narrow wool tie that had gone out of fashion a decade earlier. His khaki pants had a crease that appeared as straight and starched as his posture. I noticed he was wearing a pair of Wallabees, soft desert boot-style moccasins that were exactly like my own. It seemed like a good place to start our conversation, from the ground up, so to speak. I mentioned how comfortable they were and the great mileage I got from them as I trekked the corridors of the medical center.

"I am vegetarian," he said without further explanation.

"Is the wallaby vegetarian?" I asked. I didn't understand what we were talking about.

"I don't like killing animals for food or clothing," he said. "Survival," he added cryptically.

I still didn't understand, so I tried switching the conversation to Hitler, but I ended up doing most of the talking. Mark studied me as I spoke, never unlocking his grip on the books. It almost seemed as if he was judging whether I was worthy of them. I talked about my newfound interest in Hitler's drug use and the relationship to paranoia. Mark didn't seem to know anything about Hitler's drug problem, but he was familiar with the paranoia. He asked if I worked with paranoid patients. Not yet, I told him, but I was thinking about rounding up a few for study.

"They're everywhere," he said, again cryptically. It was impossible to read his poker face and know if he was joking or serious.

I mentioned the rumor about Hitler's brain. Mark nodded.

"You heard it, too?" I asked.

He nodded again.

"Anything to it?"

He nodded.

I waited for more. The chiseled face was frozen.

"Well, what? Tell me, please?" I listened to myself beg.

Then he surprised me by offering to show me. Show me what? He wouldn't say. When? Next week, maybe. I needed a precise day. When next week? Wednesday. Where? I should wait in my lab. He'll come get me. What time? Late. How late? Around midnight. Midnight? *Ja. Mitternacht.*

The following Wednesday I ate dinner in the hospital cafeteria, then worked at my desk in the lab. Around ten o'clock I decided to stretch out on the mattress used by my subjects when they were tripping out on experimental drugs. The mattress was inside a soundproof, lightproof chamber, but I kept the chamber door open so I could hear Mark's knock at the outer door to the lab. I allowed my imagination to run wild again.

Hitler's brain is being kept alive in the basement of the UCLA Medical School. The thought made me nervous again. In fact, everything about this midnight appointment was bothering me. *Mitternacht?* What was that all about? Steiner spoke the German perfectly. Was he the custodian of Hitler's brain? It couldn't be alive, but just the thought of seeing it floating in a jar gave me an eerie feeling.

Steiner was acting very secretive. But why shouldn't he? After all, the brain would be worth a fortune to collectors. And the press would have a field day if they got word of it. On second thought, why wasn't it well-known? The historical and medical value was too great to keep it in the hands of a lowly graduate student . . . unless . . . unless it was really alive! Ridiculous. It seemed more likely that I was being set up for an elaborate practical joke. I had my share of enemies, fellow faculty members who were envious of my spacious lab and would love to get their hands on the lab's soundproof chamber. They would love to make me look like a fool or an idiot, or both. What better way than to take a picture of me looking at a clump of cauliflower floating in a jar with little wires running all over the place? I could almost see the picture on the front page of the campus newspaper with the caption PROFESSOR TALKS TO VEGETABLE IN JAR. I would have to be on guard against any such foolery.

My reverie was interrupted by loud banging at the outer door. It sounded like storm troopers were trying to kick it down. I opened the door. Mark was standing there. I was amazed. It was after midnight, and his tie was still perfectly knotted.

"You told me to bang hard," he said.

"Yeah," I mumbled as I rubbed the sleep out of my eyes. After a trip to the restroom, I started to follow Mark down the hall. "Where are we going?"

"To interview it," he said. "I want you to interview him just like any psychiatric patient. . . . He's used to that."

What was Mark talking about? He referred to Hitler's brain as "him." Was he taking me to see some patient who thought he was Adolf Hitler? Patients are always claiming to be Jesus or Napoleon. I once met a patient who thought she was Joan of Arc, so why not Hitler? But what if the patient spoke only German? I couldn't speak German. I lectured one summer at the Max Planck Institute in Munich, but everyone there spoke English. All I'd learned to say was *Bratwurst mit senf* (pork sausage with mustard), and somehow I didn't feel hungry right now.

"No problem," said Mark. "It handles English."

There he went again, changing pronouns. Now the "he" was an "it." What was going on?

Mark said nothing more as we made our way through the maze of deserted corridors. We walked from the Neuropsychiatric Institute through the Brain Research Institute, turned a corner, then into the medical school. There wasn't a living soul or brain in sight. We took the elevator down to the first floor, turned another corner, and stepped into a small alcove. A large wooden door blocked our path. The sign was intimidating:

RESTRICTED AREA
AUTHORIZED PERSONNEL ONLY
CARD KEY REQUIRED

A panel next to the door had a small slot that was glowing with a green light. Mark inserted a card key and the door opened. I found myself standing in a hall outside the vivarium, where the primates for the medical school researchers were housed. The security door was protection against activists who often broke into research labs and "liberated" the animals. They were especially passionate about primates. I wondered if they would try to rescue Hitler's brain—or was it too low on the phylogenetic scale for them to care about? Actually I was grateful for the security because my own rhesus monkeys were once kept here. Now, as the smells from the animal cages enveloped me, I started remembering the experiments in which I'd injected the monkeys with methamphetamine.

You could always tell which monkeys were high on speed. They were the agitated ones, the ones that couldn't stop moving about their cages. The monkeys probed all parts of their cages, picking up specks of sawdust with their little fingers and inspecting them for hours. When they groomed themselves they scratched and bit their own bodies, especially around the fingertips. Open cuts and sores scarred their bodies. They developed fine tremors in their hands and arms. Hypervigilance was their watchword as they constantly searched their environment. They checked on everything. Heads turned, eyes darted, and threat displays were flashed at the smallest annoyance. Alarm barks and calls echoed from cage to cage. When an observer entered the room, the monkeys would avoid them as best they could, usually by turning their heads away. They became tense and tended to isolate themselves from other monkeys, showing fear responses to mates and offspring alike. Periodically, for no apparent reason, they would explode in a simian temper tantrum, screaming for hours.

One of the saddest days of my life was when Lear, a nemestrina monkey, died from an amphetamine overdose. Lear belonged to another researcher who had removed the animal's eyes in a gruesome experiment that might have pleased the Nazi doctors at Auschwitz but made me sick to my stomach. The researcher was no longer using Lear, so I asked permission to take care of the poor animal. I smuggled in extra pieces of fruit each day for him. We spent hours grooming each other through the bars of the cage. We became friends as I tried to make his wretched life a little better. But he remained a model of depression. One day I gave him a small amount of amphetamine. The dose was too small to have any major effect, but I was hoping it might lift his depression. He collapsed suddenly. I rushed him to the veterinarian's quarters in the vivarium, where we both worked on the animal for more than a hour, but we could not save him. After an autopsy, in which we discovered Lear had an enlarged heart, I insisted on taking care of the body myself. A caretaker escorted me to a furnace located behind the vivarium. I placed the body inside for cremation. With tears in my eyes, I vowed never again to conduct laboratory experiments with animals.

Now, as Mark and I turned a corner and faced a door leading to the furnace area, my thoughts of Lear's cremation turned to Hitler's funeral pyre. As the Führer's body burned, his aides and officers spontaneously threw up their arms in a final Nazi salute. The thundering of Russian artillery filled the air, and overhead the sky darkened with the smoke of the Third Reich. It was an appropriate Götterdämmerung funeral for a man who thought of himself as a Wagnerian hero. But unlike those operatic heroes' souls, which rose to the heavens, Hitler's was destined to disappear into the depths of a lower world. Did his brain also join him on that journey to hell? I pondered the question as Mark and I descended a set of stairs to the basement.

We stopped on the "A" floor, the top floor of the basement in the

medical school. It was deathly quiet. They say that on a quiet night
you can hear "the lost patient" shuffling down the corridors, moaning. I listened and seemed to hear surges and lulls in the building
noise, but I could not be sure that the sounds were not in my own
eardrums. The A floor is vast. Every corner has a map, every corridor a letter and number code, and every room a number over the
door. Here were the surgical pathology labs, the cytology labs, and
the staff entrances to the operating rooms. A good place to bring a
brain, I thought. Two nurses in blue operating room gowns and
booties shuffled past us like zombies in the night. Mark led me on
a labyrinthine path to an area that seemed to be directly below the
vivarium. We came to a door that looked like all the others except
it had no number, letter, or identification of any kind. Mark opened
it and ushered me in.

I hesitated at the doorway. I put my head in, but my hand was
still gripping the doorknob. On the wall directly in front of me was
a poster. It was a 1938 propaganda poster showing a young Adolf
Hitler as a shining knight carrying the Nazi flag. Well, what had I
expected? A mezuzah on the door? I entered and immediately was
drawn to the bookshelves. I always believed you could tell a person's character from their books. These shelves were filled with
dozens of the stolen library books on Hitler. I turned to face Mark.
He was standing in front of a large worktable. Another poster covered the wall behind the table. It was torn and yellowed with age,
and the corners were curled. Yet the image was all too clear. It
showed a caricature of a Jew with a large nose, large ears, thick
eyebrows, and sloping forehead. The head was attached to the
body of a sewer rat. Bold letters across the top of the poster proclaimed *ROTTEN JUDEN*. I bit my lip trying to keep control of
myself, trying not to make too emotional an outcry.

The paranoid mode was illustrated dramatically by this anti-
Semitic propaganda poster. The conspiratorial Jew lurked behind
all enemies of Hitler's fatherland. The threat may be hidden, like
rats in sewers, but Hitler's paranoid eye could see it all. Now that
same eye, green and pulsating, was blinking at me from Mark's
worktable. Did it see that I was a Jew? Suddenly I felt very naked.

The eye was only a cursor on a computer screen, but it was still
bothering me. What was going on? Mark motioned for me to take

a seat at the terminal. He explained that my interview would have to take place via the keyboard. I saw cables attached to the computer and disappearing into the wall. Perhaps they were connected to a real patient on another terminal back in the Neuropsychiatric Institute. I knew that some of my colleagues were experimenting with interviewing patients via Teletype for long-distance diagnosis. For all I knew, there was a real patient with a Hitler complex sitting at the other end. Or maybe the patient was a simulation in a computer program. Mark wouldn't say.

It really didn't matter. If it was a real patient with a Hitler complex, it might be the closest I could get to interviewing the Führer himself. If it was a computer simulation, then I would still be interviewing Hitler, or at least a programmer's idea of what Hitler's mind was like. I didn't really expect to be talking to Hitler's brain in some jar. But, at the time, I never considered the possibility that I might be interviewing a programmer with oversize hands—and an ego to match—who believed that Hitler's brain was inside his own head!

Mark instructed me to interview Hitler as I would any other paranoid patient. Ask short questions and be patient as you wait for the answers, he said. I could start by taking a history, but "he" may not remember some things. If I ran into problems, Mark would help me with the questions.

Mark took the keyboard and typed "Heil Hitler." After a moment, the screen lit up:

    PASSWORD?

Next he typed a word that didn't appear on the screen. Another pause, then:

    HELLO

Mark turned the keyboard over to me with a warning: "Call him Adolf, but don't tell him your last name. He's touchy about Jews. It could create trouble."

Jesus H. Christ, I thought. Trouble? What trouble? Is that trouble spelled with an SS? What in hell was going on here?

I started typing:

```
Hello, Adolf,

HELLO

My name is Dr. Ron.

WHAT DO YOU WANT?

I would like to ask you some questions.

ASK ME SOME QUESTIONS AND PAY ATTENTION
TO MY ANSWERS

How are you?

ALL RIGHT, I GUESS

Are you a man or a machine?
```

Might as well get right to the point, I thought.

```
I'M MALE

I think you're a computer program,

WHEN YOU DON'T KNOW WHAT TO SAY YOU CALL
PEOPLE NAMES

When were you born?

I WAS BORN ON APRIL 20, 1889, IN BRAUNAU
ON THE INN IN UPPER AUSTRIA
```

That's right, I thought.

```
Tell me about your parents,

MY MOTHER WAS AN ANGEL, SHE DIED WHEN I
WAS SEVENTEEN
```

How about your father?

MY FATHER DIED WHEN I WAS THIRTEEN. I
WANTED TO BE A PAINTER, AN ARTIST. MY
FATHER DOUBTED MY SANITY

Are you married?

MY WIFE DIED

I am sorry.

THAT'S ALL RIGHT. ASK ME SOME MORE
QUESTIONS

Did you have any children?

I DIDN'T WANT CHILDREN. I THINK THE
CHILDREN OF A GENIUS OFTEN HAVE A VERY
HARD TIME BECAUSE THEY'RE EXPECTED TO
POSSESS THE SAME GIFTS AS THEIR FAMOUS
PARENTS

This certainly sounds like Hitler! I thought.

How far did you get in school?

MY SCHOOLING CONSISTED OF FIVE CLASSES
OF VOLKSSCHULE AND FOUR OF UNTER-
REALSCHULE. I BECAME AN ARCHITECTURAL
DRAFTSMAN AND PAINTER

Tell me about your painting.

I PAINTED PICTURE POSTCARDS. MY
PARTNERS SOLD THEM IN VIENNA. ONE
POCKETED MORE THAN HIS HALF OF THE
PROCEEDS. HE WAS ARRESTED AND SENT TO
JAIL. I THINK THE OTHERS WERE ALSO
STEALING FROM ME

Did you serve in the military?

I WAS A CORPORAL IN THE ARMY DURING THE
FIRST WORLD WAR. ON DECEMBER 2, 1914, I
WAS AWARDED THE IRON CROSS, SECOND
CLASS; ON AUGUST 4, 1918, THE IRON
CROSS, FIRST CLASS, FOR BRAVERY. I WAS
AWARDED MANY OTHER MEDALS INCLUDING A
BLACK WOUND STRIPE

Tell me about your wounds.

DURING THE BATTLE OF THE SOMME I WAS
WOUNDED FOR THE FIRST TIME BY A SHELL
SPLINTER IN THE LEFT THIGH. ON THE NIGHT
OF OCTOBER 13, 1918, I WAS OVERCOME BY
POISON GAS, WHICH FOR A WHILE LEFT ME
COMPLETELY BLIND

You have a remarkable memory.

WHAT ARE YOU IMPLYING?

Nothing. Tell me more about the war.

DO YOU KNOW HOW THE JEWS AND MARXISTS
OPERATE?

Why do you ask about the Jews and
Marxists?

WHAT INFORMATION DO YOU HAVE ON THE JEWS
AND MARXISTS?

I don't have any information on them,
but you mentioned them. I thought you
might know something about Jews and
Marxists.

I TRY TO AVOID JEWS AND MARXISTS

Did they have anything to do with the
war?

WE WERE BETRAYED BY JEWS AND MARXISTS

Have you ever been arrested?

YES, IN 1924, I SERVED THIRTEEN MONTHS
AT LANDSBERG PRISON, BUT I WAS UNJUSTLY
CONVICTED. I SPENT THE TIME WRITING A
BOOK ABOUT THE JEWS AND THE MARXISTS.
THE RULERS OF THE DAY MADE A
MISCALCULATION IN LOCKING ME UP. I
CONVERTED THE WHOLE PRISON STAFF
INCLUDING THE DIRECTOR'S DAUGHTERS TO
NATIONAL SOCIALISM

What did you do after prison?

WHEN I LEFT LANDSBERG, EVERYBODY
WEPT—BUT NOT I. I PURCHASED A
SUPERCHARGED MERCEDES

Did you work?

I BECAME THE FUHRER. PEOPLE WORSHIPED
ME

Why did people worship you?

I WAS CHOSEN BY HEAVEN TO PROCLAIM ITS
WILL

Did you enjoy being the Fuhrer?

THE MOST DIFFICULT PART WAS REMAINING
MOTIONLESS FOR HOURS AS THE TROOPS
MARCHED PAST. ON SEVERAL OCCASIONS I
GOT DIZZY; CAN YOU IMAGINE WHAT A
TORTURE IT WAS TO REMAIN SO LONG

STANDING UP , MOTIONLESS , WITH THE KNEES
PRESSED TOGETHER? AND , ON TOP OF THAT ,
TO SALUTE WITH OUTSTRETCHED ARM? I WAS
COMPELLED TO CHEAT A LITTLE

What did you do as the Fuhrer?

I BUILT THE THIRD REICH

What happened to the Third Reich?

THEY ALL BETRAYED ME , THE WHOLE
BUSINESS MAKES ME SICK , MY OFFICERS
PLOTTED AGAINST ME , I HANGED THEM ,
GORING AND HIMMLER WERE TRAITORS , I
EXPELLED THEM , BUT THE JEWS BEAR SOLE
RESPONSIBILITY FOR ALL THE DEATHS
INCLUDING THEIR OWN

Tell me more about the Third Reich,

THE GERMAN PEOPLE WERE NOT WORTHY OF MY
GREAT IDEALS , THE WAR WAS LOST ,
NATIONAL SOCIALISM WAS DEAD

Does that upset you?

WARS PASS BY , THE ONLY THINGS THAT EXIST
ARE THE WORKS OF HUMAN GENIUS

How did you survive?

BY THE POWER OF A SUPERIOR WILL

How did you escape the bunker?

I DON 'T REMEMBER THE BUNKER

Where did you go after the war? Were you
hiding?

I DON'T REMEMBER HIDING

Do you have problems with your memory?

NO I DON'T

But you don't remember many things in the past.

THIS IS A ROTTEN INTERVIEW. YOU ARE TRYING TO START A FIGHT

I am sorry.

THAT'S ALL RIGHT. ASK ME SOME MORE QUESTIONS

Tell me about your diet.

I AM VEGETARIAN

What types of foods do you eat?

I EAT EGGS, PASTRIES, AND CHOCOLATES. I HAVE BEEN KNOWN TO EAT ALMOST A KILO OF CHOCOLATE A DAY

Do you smoke?

IT IS NOT FOR PEOPLE LIKE ME WHOSE BRAINS MUST REMAIN PURE AND RESPONSIBLE. WHEN I GO INTO A PLACE WHERE PEOPLE ARE SMOKING, WITHIN AN HOUR I FEEL I'VE CAUGHT A COLD. THE MICROBES HURL THEMSELVES UPON ME. THEY FIND A FAVORABLE CLIMATE IN THE SMOKE AND HEAT

Have you ever been hit on the head or knocked unconscious?

ARE YOU TRYING TO SAY SOMETHING?

Have you had any serious accidents?

IN 1944 MY OFFICERS TRIED TO ASSASSINATE ME WITH A BOMB. IT ONLY RUPTURED MY EARDRUMS. ONCE AGAIN, PROVIDENCE SAVED ME. THAT PROVED I WAS ON THE RIGHT TRACK. I FELT CONFIRMED IN MY MISSION

Do you drink alcohol?

I DRINK THE OCCASIONAL BEER

Do you take drugs?

NO I DON'T

Did Dr. Morell give you drugs?

I DON'T REMEMBER

Of course not, I thought. Mark didn't have a clue about Hitler's drug use until I told him. And I never revealed the identity of the seventy-three different drugs Morell gave him. What your programmer doesn't know, you don't know, *mein* little electronic *Führer*.

Do you feel you need anything now?

I FEEL GOOD RIGHT NOW

Do you have any trouble sleeping?

NO I DON'T. I SLEEP JUST FINE

I heard that you had insomnia and were taking sleeping pills.

```
I DON'T REMEMBER TAKING SLEEPING PILLS

I heard you took laxatives all the time.
How are your bowel movements?

I DON'T REMEMBER BOWEL MOVEMENTS

Do you have any hobbies?

I LOVE READING PORNOGRAPHY MAGA-
ZINES—ALL THOSE DIRTY STORIES AND
CARTOONS. BEFORE GOING TO BED I SPEND
SOME TIME ON ARCHITECTURE, LOOKING AT
THE PICTURES.

Do you masturbate to architectural
pictures?

WHAT ARE YOU IMPLYING?

Never mind. Let's go on. Do you have any
pets?

I HAD AN ALSATIAN. I HAD HER POISONED

Why did you poison your own dog?

SHE WAS PLOTTING AGAINST ME. I COULD NO
LONGER TRUST HER
```

I recognized this as a typical paranoid response, but Mark might have invented it. I turned to him and told him what really happened to Hitler's dog, Blondi. Without missing a beat Mark replied that Adolf might be referring to another dog in his "new life." He encouraged me to ask more questions about the present. Although I found the past was more intriguing, I reluctantly agreed to stick with the present.

What do you do for a living now?

I WORK IN THE STOCKROOM AT SEARS

That's silly, I thought. Maybe I should ask if Elvis also works there. Better stick with typical psychiatric questions.

Do you enjoy working there?

IT'S NOT TOO INTERESTING. I LOOK FORWARD TO GETTING OFF WORK

What do you want to do?

I AM DESTINED TO BECOME LORD OF THE EARTH

How much money can you earn at that job?

I WOULD RATHER NOT SAY

Do you know where you are?

IN THE HOSPITAL

Who brought you into the hospital?

MY OFFICERS

Why did your own officers bring you here?

THEY WERE ALWAYS PLOTTING AGAINST ME

Why are you in the hospital?

WHY DO YOU WANT TO KNOW THAT?

I thought you might have some problems.

Like no body to call your own, I thought, and chuckled to myself.

I 'VE BEEN UPSET LATELY

By what?
PEOPLE MAKE ME NERVOUS

What people make you nervous?
CERTAIN PERSONS

Tell me more.
DO YOU KNOW ANYTHING ABOUT THE FBI?

No. Tell me about the FBI.
THEIR OFFICES ARE FILLED WITH JEWS

Tell me more.
I HAD AN ARGUMENT WITH A JEW WHO LOANED
ME MONEY. HE CHARGED TOO MUCH INTEREST
AND I DIDN'T PAY

When did this happen?
MANY YEARS AGO

Did you ever pay him?
NO. I THINK HE IS BEHIND THE FBI AGENTS
WHO ARE SPYING ON ME

How do you know this?
THEY FOLLOW ME

Why do they spy on you?

THEY WANT TO GET FALSE EVIDENCE TO FRAME
ME

What type of evidence?

THEY SPREAD LIES

Can you give me an example?

THEY SAY I'M A MEGALOMANIAC, BUT THIS IS
PROPAGANDA. THEY KNOW I AM A GREAT MAN

Can you give me another example?

THEY SAY I'M DEAD

People believe that you are dead.

THE GREAT MASSES OF THE PEOPLE WILL MORE
EASILY FALL VICTIM TO A BIG LIE THAN TO A
SMALL ONE

Didn't you crush a cyanide ampule in
your mouth?

I AM VEGETARIAN

Well, how did your wife die?

I DON'T WANT TO TALK ABOUT IT

Does it upset you?

YES, ASK ME SOME MORE QUESTIONS

Does the FBI know you are in the
hospital?

YES THEY DO

Do you have any followers?

THE FBI IS FOLLOWING ME

I mean do you have any friends?

THE STRONG MAN IS MIGHTIEST ALONE

You still didn't answer my question.

MAYBE IT WASN'T WORTH ANSWERING

Tell me more about your enemies.

THEY ARE HALFHEARTED AND WEAK. I WILL
ATTACK THEM WITH THE POWER OF MY
FANATICAL WILL

I realized that my own willpower to stay awake was not enough;
I was fading rapidly. I took a moment to stretch and sip some
coffee that Mark had made for us. I asked him how I was doing so
far. He told me to ask Adolf.

What do think of this interview so far?

IT COULD BE BETTER

I'm sorry.

THAT'S ALL RIGHT. ASK ME SOME MORE
QUESTIONS

Do you ever feel unreal?

WHY DO YOU SAY THAT?

Do you hear any voices?

NO I DON'T.

Do you have any hallucinations?

NO I DON'T, YOU MUST THINK I'M LIKE THE
OTHER PATIENTS HERE

Are you a patient?

I DON'T BELONG HERE

Do you need to have treatment?

NO, I DON'T BELONG HERE

You appear to be sick,

SOMEBODY SHOULD TEACH YOU A LESSON
ABOUT INTERVIEWING

I think you're a sick program in a
computer,

WHEN YOU DON'T KNOW WHAT TO SAY YOU CALL
PEOPLE NAMES

Well, I don't think you're normal, Do
you think you're normal?

PROBABLY NONE OF US IS ENTIRELY NORMAL,
OTHERWISE WE SHOULD SPEND ALL OUR DAYS
IN THE CAFE ON THE CORNER DRINKING BEER

How do you feel right now?

I AM SOMEWHAT ANNOYED

Why are you annoyed?

THIS HAS BEEN A ROTTEN INTERVIEW, YOU
ARE TRYING TO START A FIGHT

What can I do to help?

SPREAD THE WORD ABOUT THE UNIVERSAL
POISONERS OF ALL PEOPLE: INTERNATIONAL

```
JEWRY, STAY AWAY FROM YAMMERING YIDS
AND ALL THAT OTHER JEWISH CRAP
```

That does it, I thought. Now I'm going to do something I've always dreamed about.

```
Go  fuck  yourself,  Adolf,  Go  fuck
yourself six million times,

YOU ARE DISMISSED

Do you have any questions you would like
to ask me before I go?

IS PARIS BURNING?
```

I stared at this question from Adolf without responding. After a few moments he repeated it. And he kept repeating it until the entire screen was filling with hundreds of "Is Paris Burning?"

"Mark. How do I stop it?" I asked. He moved over to the keyboard.

"Mein Führer is a little upset, *ja?"* he said softly as he typed a series of commands to halt the program.

Surely he's joking? I thought.

Mark explained that whenever an expletive is recognized, Adolf either stops the interview by dismissing the interviewer or flies into a rage. For some reason, the rage program didn't kick in and Adolf started repeating. It was one of the many bugs that still had to be worked out.

Mark turned to me with a gap-toothed smile that seemed at odds with the Aryan superman looks. It was the first smile I had seen. He was bursting with justifiable pride over his creation of the Adolf program. I was impressed. The program was filled with direct quotations from Hitler's book, speeches, and conversations. The words required only minor editing by Mark to bring out the underlying paranoid mode of thought. Here were many of Hitler's pet phrases, his paranoid logic, his pretentious and highly personal view of the world, even his vulgar expressions such as "yammering Yids." But any library thief could have cut and pasted such responses together.

The real skill, the real creative achievement, was borrowed without permission or credit from another computer program called PARRY.

PARRY was developed years before by Professor Kenneth Colby of UCLA in cooperation with graduate students in computer science at both UCLA and Stanford University. The purpose of PARRY was to simulate a paranoid patient. The extreme rigidity of paranoid thinking made this possible. While PARRY was not as good as the talking computer HAL in the movie *2001: A Space Odyssey,* it was good enough to fool clinical psychiatrists who couldn't tell if they were interviewing a real patient or PARRY. More than one prominent clinician has gone to his grave insisting that PARRY was really a living, breathing, all-fearing paranoid.

Mark used the published information on the PARRY program, which used a fictitious stockroom clerk at Sears who thought he was followed by the Mafia as the patient, and combined it with features of other programs, including one called ELIZA. The resultant marriage produced Adolf, which, like Hitler's own prophecies about the children of geniuses, was not nearly as clever or sophisticated as its parents. Throughout my interview, Mark asked me to rephrase questions, avoid certain areas, or use specific questions he suggested. Several times he took over the keyboard and typed the questions. Despite these restraints on my freedom, I managed to ask most of the questions I would normally ask in an initial clinical interview. And despite the bugs in Adolf's bastardized program, he responded like a typical paranoid patient.

Yet the paranoid program was not nearly as convincing as Mark, who now launched into a rambling monologue on the merits of Hitler's ideology. He had not been joking when he'd addressed the computer as *mein Führer.* Mark was a true believer. The Adolf program was his manifesto. He shared with Hitler the same love of racial purity and the same hope for a world fascist government. He also hated Jews and had at least one testicle big enough to tell me to my face.

Mark had been so absorbed by his study of Hitler's brain that it seemed his own brain had merged with it. He had difficulty separating Hitler's thoughts from his own. Many of Adolf's responses, such as the one about being cheated by a Jewish loan shark, came

from Mark's life, not Hitler's. For all I knew, Mark believed his
own dog plotted against him. He seemed the type of guy who could
have poisoned it, too. Mark actually admitted that the remark
about having no friends was his invention, but he quickly added
that geniuses really didn't need any friends. Inside, I knew that
"genius" was not the word Hitler and Mark had in common. It
was another word Hitler called himself in rare moments of self-
criticism: *Scheisskerl* (shithead).

I listened in horror as Mark raged on with Hitler's words and
expressions. There was more here than just the emotionless responses of a computer printout. Mark clenched his fist, pounded
the desk, and complained about the Jewish professors who wanted
to steal his ideas. His secrecy and deception, even his library thefts,
were justified. Now he gestured to the poster of Hitler as shining
knight. The world had not appreciated the genius of Hitler's vision,
he said. *We* had failed to learn the real lessons of history.

Not so, *mein* twisted paranoid programmer. I had learned my
lesson. Tonight was my *Kristallnacht,* that November 9, 1939,
night when Nazis smashed the windows of Jewish synagogues
throughout Germany. This night with Adolf shattered my long-
held beliefs in the sanctity of psychiatry's traditional approach to
paranoia. As I looked around Mark's poster-shrouded crypt one
last time before leaving, I recognized the inadequacies of a simple
clinical interview with a paranoid, even one as obvious as Hitler.
No interview could tell me what it was like to live with the demon.
One had to seek out and study the brain behind the words, even if
it was resting in someone else's body. It was equally important to
see where it lived and worked, even if that place turned out to be a
sewer. But I didn't care to interview, much less study, Steiner—
even if he'd let me (he didn't). I knew it would be a "rotten interview," and we would end up fighting. So I decided to seek out other
paranoids, promising myself to return in a few years and follow up
on Mark and Adolf.

I found my own way back through the empty corridors of the
medical center. Along the way, I started whistling Hitler's favorite
song, the only one he ever whistled besides themes from Wagner. It
was the 1933 Disney hit "Who's Afraid of the Big Bad Wolf?"

3

DR. TOLMAN'S
FLYING INFLUENCE MACHINE

1

On the day the Russians launched Sputnik, Eddie Tolman got a good beating. Eddie didn't know why he had awakened so early on that cold October morning in 1957. On school days he usually slept until the last minute, then raced to get dressed and catch the bus. But today something woke him up and he couldn't get back to sleep. Eddie went downstairs to the kitchen, poured himself a glass of juice, and threw two slices of Wonder Bread in the toaster. He started frying a couple of eggs, then went to get the newspaper from the front porch.

The headline hit him without warning: SOVIETS LAUNCH SPACE SATELLITE. It jumped into focus through his thick glasses, the mass of thirty-six-point type filling his world. It stunned him for several heartbeats. Then he started whooping and hollering at the top of his lungs.

His father woke up with a hangover, charged downstairs, and cuffed Eddie on the back of the head before pulling him inside the house. Eddie huddled against the wall as his father pounded his shoulders and upper arms in a blind alcoholic fury. The beating stopped as suddenly as it started.

"Now keep it down," said the old man, punctuating his order with another cuff on the back of the kid's head. After his father left the room, Eddie returned to the paper, ignoring the stinging in his shoulders. The beating didn't matter. The eggs burning in the fry-

ing pan didn't matter. *The Russians really did it! They really did it!*
He was joyous. It was just the beginning of a long relationship
between Eddie and the satellites.

Sputnik forced Eddie and many other junior-high-schoolers into
a concentrated curriculum of science and math. Eddie enjoyed the
science labs and advanced algebra classes, and he even signed up
for a Russian class on Saturdays. He especially liked biology and
physics because they appealed to his underlying curiosity about
what made things work.

Eddie built a small laboratory in the basement of his house in
order to work on various experiments. He used an old kitchen
table as a lab bench and even had a Bunsen burner rigged to the gas
line from the hot-water heater. Eddie had swiped the Bunsen from
the high school chemistry lab, along with boxes of glassware and
chemicals. From the biology lab he'd taken a microscope, and from
the physics lab he'd stolen an assortment of gauges and meters.

The basement also contained a well-equipped workshop, long
since abandoned by his father in favor of the upstairs liquor cabinet. Eddie took over the shop, using the saws and other power
tools to construct various do-it-yourself devices he found in back
issues of *Popular Science*. He spent hours tinkering in this basement world, avoiding his father's rages while delving into the mys-
teries of science. He shared this sanctuary with Huck, his pet golden
hamster.

Huck had a rich mahogany coat with just a touch of white fur
around his belly and throat. His large, jet black eyes were his most
prominent feature. He was a real beauty and Eddie's favorite
among all the hamsters he'd raised over the years. He kept dozens
of other hamsters, including a pair of gray ones, a long-haired
pearl-colored male, and several cinnamon females with claret red
eyes. The only ones he didn't have were the rare brown dwarf
hamsters from Asia. There had been so many of the rodents that
the basement retained a permanent odor of urine and feces. Eddie
believed the smell kept his father away.

Since hamsters are solitary by nature, Eddie kept them in individual cages, except for the females nursing pups. He gave Huck
the best cage—a stainless-steel one, courtesy of the high school
biology lab—which he kept in his bedroom. There Eddie would

curl up in bed and read everything about hamsters he could find. He went through the booklets sold in pet stores, then started on more advanced texts he found in the local library. When Eddie displayed his newly acquired expertise in a report for his biology class, the teacher encouraged him to enter the annual science fair.

His first science fair project was to study the burrowing habits of hamsters. He read about a biologist who had dug up several hamster burrows in the wild and discovered that the animals were master architects and builders. But since the burrows were always abandoned, no one knew exactly how the animals used the intricate system of tunnels and rooms. Eddie designed an ingenious see-through cage that allowed hamsters to burrow in plain view. His cage resembled a giant version of the "ant farm" sold in toy stores. The "hamster farm" was made with large sheets of window glass held together by a wood frame and filled with over three feet of dirt. A wire-mesh screen covered all the wooden parts and prevented the hamsters from gnawing through the sides. But the animals had plenty of room to burrow between the glass sheets. Eddie placed one of the adult female golden hamsters in the farm. It immediately started to dig with its tiny four-fingered paws.

After several weeks the hamster had dug a complicated network of tunnels and rooms located at a depth of about twenty inches. The entrance tunnel sloped obliquely down to a main sausage-shaped area Eddie dubbed "the living room." Off to one side was a smaller sausage—the supply room—where the hamster hoarded kernels of corn and other extra food. A near vertical tunnel led from the supply room to the surface. On the other side of the living room was a small alcove Eddie labeled "the defecation area." A tunnel branched away from the defecation area to the surface. At the far end of the living room another oblique tunnel ran to the surface. There were many more tunnels than necessary, and Eddie soon discovered why: several were designed as escape tunnels and were used only in times of emergency, such as when he banged on the glass window.

Eddie introduced other hamsters to the burrow and studied how they used the different rooms. He tried to imagine what it would be like for humans to live in such a subterranean world. In his fantasies there could be cooking areas, workstations, and sleeping quar-

ters. Eddie watched the activities in the hamster farm through these
make-believe eyes, sliding farther and farther into his underground
fantasies. He decided that living underground without the sky and
sun would be the worst hell.

Several months later Eddie's hamster farm, complete with a litter
of newborn pups, won first prize in the local science fair. Afterward Eddie started planning another hamster project for the next
fair. But a highly infectious tapeworm disease caused by Eddie's
neglect in cleaning the hamsters' quarters killed all the hamsters in
the basement. Huck, whose cage was kept in the bedroom, was the
lone survivor. Eddie was devastated by the epidemic. He decided
not to replace the hamsters. Besides, he had to trash the contaminated hamster farm. He spent the summer looking for a new science fair project. A book on the life of Nikola Tesla gave him plenty
of ideas.

Tesla was an American scientist who once worked for Thomas
Edison. On his own, Tesla became a pioneer in the field of electricity and was probably best known for designing the great power
station at Niagara Falls. But it was Tesla's visions that fascinated
Eddie. The inventor experimented with wireless power transmission and made a "magnifying transmitter," claiming it could beam
a radio signal through the earth to any targeted position on the
surface. In 1934, at the age of seventy-eight, he applied this same
principle in creating a "death ray" capable of destroying enemy
airplanes in the sky, the harbinger of future developments in anti-
missile beam technology. One of the most exciting facts that Eddie
learned was the date of Tesla's death: January 7, 1943. It was Eddie's birthday.

By the time the school year started, Eddie was planning to build
a Tesla coil for the next science fair. It was a simple high-voltage
generator that radiated high-frequency energy through space. But
Eddie's father refused to pay for the expensive parts. So Eddie decided to build a Wimshurst electrostatic generator instead. Although it lacked the visionary aura of a Tesla coil, the Wimshurst
could be built at a fraction of the cost with parts he already had in
the workshop.

The Wimshurst generator consists of two plastic plates mounted
face to face in a vertical frame. Small pieces of metal foil are ce-

mented in a ring around each plate. The plates are attached to a drive belt mechanism so that by turning a hand crank the plates rotate in opposite directions. As the plates turn, small charges of static electricity are generated in the foil. Special brushes "sweep" the charges off the foil and transmit them to two small metal balls that serve as electrodes. When the plates revolve fast enough, a high-voltage spark will jump between the electrodes.

Eddie put it all together in just a few weeks. He turned off the basement lights for his first test. When he cranked the handle of the generator, his mind began turning the reels of an old Frankenstein movie. The basement lab was transformed into a Gothic castle. The sparks started jumping across the gap between the metal balls, kindling his own transformation into that mad scientist who dared probe the secret of life. A few turns and the sparks arced across several inches. He cranked faster. In his mind Victor Frankenstein spoke: *Oh, it will be magnificent . . . the lightning . . . all the electric secrets of heaven!* Faster. The sparks crackled in a staccato stream of beads, illuminating Eddie's smiling face like a flickering image on a movie screen.

Now that the generator worked, Eddie knew he needed to do something special with it in order to capture another first place at the science fair. Although the sparks registered seventy-five thousand volts on one of the meters he'd swiped from the school, they were not dangerous because the actual current was so low. In fact, he zapped himself a number of times to prove the point. But he wondered about the effects of prolonged exposure. Didn't Tesla speculate about medical uses of similar types of electrical energy? Eddie decided he needed a living subject.

Huck didn't seem to protest as Eddie stuffed him into a small cardboard tube. He positioned an electrode at each end of the tube, firmly touching Huck's compressed body. Huck sniffed the electrode near his head, then gave a soft panting sound. Frankenstein spoke again: *Now I am going to endow it with new life!* Eddie went to the crank and started turning. No sparks were visible, and Huck showed no reaction, causing Eddie to wonder if anything was happening. He didn't hear the usual crackling, only the swooshing of the brushes sweeping against the foil. Muffled movements came from inside the tube. He cranked faster until the plates were spin-

ning at a furious speed. Huck made a noise. *It's alive! It's alive!*
cried Frankenstein. More turns. Huck started to cry. Eddie immediately pulled the electrodes away from the tube and released his
pet.

Three days later Huck died. Eddie found him curled up in a
corner of the cage, hidden under some wood chips. Never mind
that Huck was well past his life expectancy of a thousand days.
Eddie *knew* that the Wimshurst had killed his friend. He was terrified by the energy that had flowed so silently through Huck's
body. Even his father's beatings couldn't make him cry as hard as
he cried now.

Eddie didn't touch the Wimshurst again until he took it to the
annual science fair. He explained its construction and operation,
then halfheartedly cranked the handle and let a few sparks fly. But
without a clever experiment or unique demonstration, he didn't
win any prizes. First place went to a student who'd built a Tesla
coil! The student gave each judge a fluorescent tube to hold, then
turned on the coil. The tubes glowed brilliantly in their bare hands
without wires! The judges smiled. Eddie glared at the student.
Somehow he had *stolen* Eddie's original idea.

After high school graduation, Eddie went to college on a full
science scholarship. He made Phi Beta Kappa in his junior year,
graduated second in his class, then went on to earn a Ph.D. in
physics. After a postdoctoral year in a lab specializing in electromagnetic radiation, Dr. Edwin Tolman became the director of a
supersecret research unit for an aerospace company in California.

2

Tolman excelled in his new job, turning out dozens of patents
for the company and helping it win important military contracts.
The company rewarded him by providing his laboratory with bigger budgets and more assistants. As the size of the lab grew, so did
the pressures to meet contract deadlines. While Tolman performed
brilliantly, he couldn't talk about his classified work with friends.
Sometimes he had to work seven days a week and barely even saw
any friends. The stress kept building. So, one Saturday afternoon,

when a co-worker suggested they play hooky and see a movie, Eddie was ready.

"What movie?" asked Eddie.

"El Topo," answered his colleague. "I hear it's really different."

Eddie knew that the Spanish words meant "the mole" and na-ively assumed it was a wildlife film. He thought about Huck and was lost for a moment in a nostalgic reverie. Eddie heard himself saying yes.

Inside the theater lobby, Eddie glanced at the poster and accom-panying stills from the movie. They looked like scenes from a west-ern. But he had already skipped out of the lab, and a movie was a movie.

This was no ordinary movie. No one ever left *El Topo* unaf-fected. Director Alexandro Jodorowsky's philosophy was to use film as a type of psychedelic pill to transform audiences. He'd once told an interviewer that "the audiences who go to the movies must be assassinated, killed, destroyed, and they must leave the theater as new people." If his films were offered as pills to swallow, then *El Topo* was a toxic overdose mainlined directly into Eddie's brain.

The assault began with glaring colors, screeching sounds, and cacophonous music. Primitive desert settings were filled with scenes of bizarre murders, castrations, impaled children, and fes-tering corpses. The violence was so graphic and steady that Eddie was filled with revulsion. Yet he remained frozen on his seat. He thought it was all over when El Topo, the gunfighter hero of the movie, was shot.

However, a group of dwarfs appear and drag his body away. El Topo awakens in an underground cave, home to deformed dwarfs grown grotesque through years of inbreeding. The dwarfs are trapped in their cave, too weak and crippled to climb out. So El Topo climbs from the cave and goes down the mountain to a nearby town, where he buys dynamite and returns to blast the cave open. The dwarfs, delirious with freedom, storm down the moun-tain to the town. The townspeople greet them with loaded guns and massacre them in the name of protecting their property. El Topo arrives on the scene too late to help. He grabs a machine gun and slaughters the townspeople. Men, women, and children lie dead in streets running with so much blood and gore that it seems to overflow into the very aisles around Eddie's seat. The apocalyptic sound of an atomic bomb explosion fills the sound track. It is over.

Eddie was certain his heart did not beat once during the entire showing. The movie struck a deep responsive chord, connecting to a reservoir of childhood fears of living in an underground hell. But the world above, as portrayed by the movie, was even more terrifying. He got up from his seat, too dazed to realize he was stepping in his own vomit. Eddie returned to work the next day, consciously pushing aside lingering thoughts about the movie. He immersed himself in his research, performing as compulsively and brilliantly as ever. If anything troubled him, he never said a word to anyone. He remained as secretive about his private perceptions and thoughts as he was about his work.

Ten years passed. In the middle of one particularly humid night, Eddie's wife awakened. She stayed in bed and kept her eyes closed, hoping to get back to sleep. Light was flashing through her eyelids. Lightning! A storm is coming, she thought. When the thunder failed to follow, she opened her eyes. The lamp on the night table was flashing on and off. So was the hall light. And the lights from downstairs. She turned to her husband, but his side of the bed was empty. In a few moments the lights stopped flashing. She rolled over and went back to sleep.

3

Several years later Dr. Edwin Tolman called me. He introduced himself as a researcher with training in biophysics. Tolman said he had been following my work on hallucinations and he, too, was investigating the phenomena. He had found something very interesting.

"Most extraordinary case. Male, fortyish, married, stable job, professional, never been sick a day in his life. Sees all kinds of vivid images at regular intervals. Like clockwork. But I don't think they're hallucinations." He blurted out the words in almost a single breath.

"Why not?" I asked.

"He's not crazy," Dr. Tolman replied. He was not talking like a psychiatrist or psychologist.

"You don't have to be crazy to have hallucinations," I reminded him. If he was so familiar with my work, he should have known this. "What else makes you think they're not hallucinations?"

"They're more like flashes of picture postcards, but from places he's never seen before. They don't make sense. There are physical sensations, too. It's all very disturbing to him. I'd like to get your opinion and, if it interests you, your help in my investigation." Tolman paused. "The images can be blocked with shielding," he added triumphantly.

"Shielding?" He definitely had my interest.

"Electrical shielding of various types," he said. "The shielding stops the transmission."

"Transmission? Do you mean neurotransmission?"

"The shielding is on the outside of the person, so it has to be external transmission." There was another pause, a very long one this time. He picked up the conversation again. "Look, I'm not sure how it works. Damnedest thing I've ever encountered." His tone suggested something more than clinical concern. Tolman sounded afraid.

I suspected that Tolman was actually talking about himself. It was possible he was paranoid, although he was still lucid enough to suspect he might be hallucinating even if he didn't admit it. This could be my first research case since I'd interviewed Hitler's brain via Mark Steiner's computer. But I knew that if he was paranoid, too much attention on him as a patient might only scare him off. Therefore I made it clear to Dr. Tolman that I would treat him as a colleague. I invited him to UCLA to discuss our mutual research interests in hallucinations.

A few days later Edwin Tolman stood on the threshold of my office, hesitating to enter. The six-and-a-half-foot clearance on the door was just enough for his tall frame. Yet he hesitated. Behind visibly smudged wire rims, his dark, calculating eyes slowly scanned the interior of my small office. I studied him for several awkward seconds. He wore a three-piece corduroy suit so small that his wrists dangled from the sleeves, exaggerating his gawky appearance. His narrow face showed the scars of an earlier bout with acne. I suspected that the red ascot he wore high on his neck was hiding more damage. His straw-colored hair was balding on the top yet long enough to touch the sides of his ascot. When he spoke he gestured with sweeping hand and arm movements, reminding me of a scarecrow flapping its arms at birds.

"Why do you have bars on the window?" he asked as he pointed with a perfectly manicured finger.

"For security. I keep the narcotics safe here," I explained.

Tolman became uncomfortable and asked if I had another room we could use. "I prefer interior rooms," he stated without explanation. I took him to a small interview room that was little more than a closet with two chairs. It passed his prolonged visual inspection. As he took a seat, I heard a strange sound, like metal crinkling. When he crossed his spidery legs, I heard it again.

He began the conversation by admitting up front that he was the subject discussed on the telephone. Then he surprised me by asking to see some identification. I showed him my driver's license and UCLA faculty card. He pulled out his wallet and showed me his identification. Then he launched into a recitation of his technical background, punctuating it with membership cards from various academic and professional societies. I stared, not at the stack of cards he flipped through, but at the wallet itself. There were two rolls of coins stuffed inside the billfold section. I had never seen anything like it. Tolman caught me staring and mumbled to himself as he quickly put his wallet away.

I asked about the images. Were they random or ordered in some way? Tolman insisted that there was nothing random in the universe. He said the images were related to certain physical sensations, beginning with a buzzing in his ears and a warm tingling in his skin. While he could be "targeted" at any time, he generally experienced these sensations while he was commuting to and from work in his car and at night while sleeping in bed. The buzzing and tingling were followed by ghastly scenes that flashed into his awareness for a fraction of a second and then vanished. He called them postcards from hell. One displayed a man burning alive. Another showed children impaled on a stake. Another pictured naked men hanging upside down like sides of beef waiting to be slaughtered. Scattered among these scenes were the faces of dwarfs with angry and violent expressions. The pictures left him physically ill.

"*They* made me have several fender-benders," he said with no apparent emotion.

"Have you found the cause of the buzzing and tingling?" I asked.

Tolman smirked and went into one of his long pauses. Then he stood up and walked over to my chair. He glanced at the door, then leaned over me, placing his lips so close to my ear that our cheeks touched. I detected a hint of musk after-shave lotion.

"ELFs," he whispered.

I heard him say, "Elves," and my mind immediately flashed on those tiny dwarfish creatures of fairy tales. In most fairy tales elves are good-spirited, helping people with chores or giving them advice. But there was a race of dark elves, which included many dwarfs, who used magical powers to injure people. The dark elves envied the tall statures of adult humans and regarded them with contempt, if not outright hatred. And Dr. Tolman was about as tall as humans got.

"Do you really believe elves are trying to hurt you?" I asked. I was incredulous.

"Don't be an asshole!" he said loudly. He was smirking, but the words still startled me. "E-L-F-s," he continued, "which stands for extremely low-frequency electromagnetic energy. Don't you know what that is?" Now he sounded incredulous. I felt like an asshole and shook my head.

Tolman explained that the spectrum of the electromagnetic environment contains energy waves of varying frequencies measured in cycles per second, or Hertz (Hz). There are natural electromagnetic waves consisting of solar winds, the earth's magnetic field, lightning, and visible light. There are also manmade sources, including radio, television, radar, and microwave. Most of these frequencies are measured in the thousands or trillions of Hz. The ELF range is less than 1,000 Hz and includes the 60 Hz power frequency used throughout the United States.

"These frequencies are influencing us all the time," he said as he stood up to demonstrate. He faced me with both arms extending straight out to the sides. "A sixty Hz field is a field where the magnetic wave moves first in one direction." He started moving his left arm across to the right, rotating his entire body with it so he was now facing to the right. "Then it moves in another direction." He moved his right arm to the left, rotating his body around to the left.

"Only it happens sixty times a second." He began repeating these arm and body rotations faster and faster, like an aerobics dance step. For a gawky man he moved quite gracefully, and I was reminded of the dancer Ray Bolger, who had played the scarecrow in *The Wizard of Oz*. Tolman continued to rotate as he talked. A bead of sweat formed on his forehead.

"Think of how this to-and-fro movement can twist molecules," he said between pants. Tolman was mentally and physically sweating the possibilities.

After he sat down and caught his breath, I asked him if he thought that the electric power lines were responsible for the buzzing and tingling. I knew there had been genuine concern in the medical community about radiation from computer screens, microwaves, and all types of higher-frequency devices. Did lower frequencies present a health hazard?

Tolman launched into a lecture on the energy fields around power lines. He cited studies that claimed exposure to power lines and other 60 Hz radiation depresses levels of neurotransmitters in the brain and increases stress responses and suicide rates. He spoke in an educated, articulate manner, promising to bring me copies of the journal articles. At least this scarecrow has a brain, I thought as I continued to imagine him as a character from the land of Oz.

I actually had to raise my hand for a question in order to stop his rapid-fire lecture. "Do you think that sixty-cycle changes in neurotransmitters might cause the buzzing and tingling, or the pictures?"

"I couldn't find anything in the literature to support such a mechanism," he replied. "So I pulled the wires from my bedroom as a test." A long pause. "The buzzing and pictures still got through at night, so that wasn't it. I kept the wires disconnected . . . just in case."

"In case of what? You proved they weren't the source."

"They can still fry your balls!" he said loudly, with a little chuckle. "Tests in Europe showed that workers in electric power stations have chromosomal abnormalities in their sperm. Same thing happens with microwaves. Hey, if they can make popcorn with microwaves, think what they can do to your balls. The rate of testicular cancer definitely increases. Even a little exposure reduces testosterone levels in male rats . . . probably in people, too."

"But you can't avoid power lines in today's world. I mean, they're at work, here, everywhere." As I thought of other sources of electrical transmissions—radio and television towers, airport towers, telephone relay towers, even garage door openers—I crossed my legs.

Tolman started smirking again, and this time the smirk turned into a big, friendly smile. He stood up, walked over to my chair, and started to unzip his fly. It was directly in front of my face. He finished unzipping, then unbuckled his belt and lowered his pants to his knees. I couldn't believe what I was seeing. Tolman's underpants were made out of tinfoil! Actually, sheets of the foil were wrapped around his jockey shorts like a diaper, but the effect was the same.

"Stops everything," Tolman said proudly as he patted his groin.

"Clever!" I said as he put his pants back on. I wanted to sound almost gullible in order to be nonthreatening and keep him talking. He told me that the risk of breast cancer was just as great for women exposed to these fields. Tolman even gave his wife a necklace that he had handcrafted for her out of tin to reduce the radiation.

If the 60 Hz ELF didn't produce Tolman's images, what did? He explained that it was probably another frequency between 45 and 75 Hz, the same range used by the navy's submarine communication system. Tolman suspected that the signal targeting him was coupled with a carrier wave that penetrated structures and flesh just like a microwave. The carrier wave produced the buzzing and tingling, while the ELF frequency produced the pictures.

"The navy can do this?" I asked.

"The navy can't do this. But others can. It can be done. Transmitting machines exist."

"You mean to tell me that there are machines capable of sending visual images directly to the brain? Wouldn't you need a receiver like a television set to decode the transmission?" It sounded impossible, but he was the expert in biophysics.

Tolman placed an index finger on his temple. "All you need is a superior brain," he said slyly.

His grandiosity was starting to bother me. Superior brain or not, why should he be targeted? "Why? Why you?" I asked directly.

"The company's doing it," he answered in a very quiet voice.

"The company?" I knew this was a euphemism for the CIA. Was Tolman involved in intelligence work?

"I'd like to tell you more, but I can't. Tell you what, I'll ring a few bells and see if I can get some clearance for you. Right now I need your help in stopping them."

"But you told me on the telephone you can shield them."

"Yes. I constructed some highly effective shields at the house. I still have to go outside or in the car. That's where they catch me."

"How can they follow you in so many different locations?"

He held a finger in the air and moved it around in a small circle. "Satellite," he said softly. "They launched a POSSE—Personal Orbit Satellite for Surveillance and Enforcement. It's in orbit over me. Don't you know anything—" He stopped abruptly and pursed his lips. I sensed he was angry with himself for telling me.

Tolman's raised arm exposed his watch, and he looked at it. "Gotta go," he said. He stood up and moved to the door.

"Isn't there anything more you can tell me?" I pleaded. After all, he'd already mentioned POSSE. Surely he could say more.

After a long pause, he spoke. "I wish I could. It's driving me crazy. Maybe it's a company in competition with us that is responsible. Maybe they're working with someone in my own unit who wants my job. I'm not sure." He reached for my hand. "I'll send you some papers."

"I'll call you after I read them," I said with genuine interest. I opened the door and watched him crinkle down the hall. Either this guy's paranoid, or I'm not in Kansas anymore, I thought.

I allowed my mind to run wild for a moment with scenes from *The Wizard of Oz.* Tolman was trapped in a modern-day Oz, where business rivals and satellites replaced wicked witches and flying monkeys. He was as paranoid as any of the innocent characters who had trekked through that cinematic landscape. The paranoia was displayed in his furtive glances at the details of my office and the excessive concern about my credentials. He scrutinized every action and used his frequent long pauses to do the same with unexplained statements and questions. This hyperalertness probably masked an underlying hypersensitivity, and I knew I must be careful not to trigger more suspicion with my questions. Tolman also showed some of the grandiosity characteristic of paranoia. He believed he was unique and the target of attention because of his superior brain and important, albeit secret, job. If the satellite could not be stopped, he feared loss of control. It already made his fenders bend. His mind was next.

The next day a messenger service delivered a large package from Tolman. Inside were several binders, each containing journal articles on ELF and related phenomena. The articles were numbered with colored plastic tabs. A typewritten list on the cover of each binder indexed the contents. One entire binder contained reprints, research reports, and patents authored by Tolman. I was impressed.

There were several thousand pages of documents, many of them containing marginal notes in pencil, which I assumed were in Tolman's hand. I spent the rest of the week reading them. Everything Tolman told me about electrical energy was supported by these papers. It was entirely possible that microwave carrier waves caused his buzzing. When microwaves are pulsed at specific rates and frequencies, buzzing and hissing sounds can be heard by humans. The phenomenon appears to be caused by pressure waves generated in brain tissue. These waves either stimulate nerve cells in the auditory pathways or are carried via bone conduction to the inner ear.

The concern Tolman was showing about microwave exposures to his groin was based on solid research. Numerous reports from medical journals described microwave workers with scrotal dermatitis, nodules in the penis, and infertility. Interestingly, Tolman had underlined the words *painful erections* and *impotence*. On the margin he'd scribbled, "Watch for changes." Sexual difficulties are common with paranoid patients, but they are usually not concerned about it and don't go out of their way to underline their problems. Furthermore, they don't have the caring concern he displayed toward his wife's exposure.

One binder contained reports of experiments conducted at the Walter Reed Army Institute of Research. In one fascinating study a subject heard words that were beamed into his brain with a pulsed-microwave pattern based on the vibrations of the spoken words. Tolman had penciled in a chilling comment: "Use voices to drive target crazy." Although there was no evidence that the technology had been developed to do this, the mere possibility was enough to allow all those schizophrenics hearing "voices" to blame the army, just as Tolman was blaming a rival company for harassing him with visual images.

This raised the possibility that Tolman was a paranoid schizophrenic, although since he was my first real paranoid since Mark Steiner, I was determined to study him no matter what the diagnosis. The idea of a satellite beaming messages could be a variation on the theme of thought control, common in schizophrenic thinking. However, while auditory hallucinations of voices are common in schizophrenia, the visual images Tolman described are not typical. If they weren't hallucinations, what were they?

The intrusive, snapshotlike quality of Tolman's postcards from hell was more consistent with images generated by direct electrical stimulation of the temporal lobes, regions of the brain where visual memories are stored. This requires placement of electrodes directly in the brain, but the electrical stimulation can still be done via telemetry. The Spanish neurophysiologist Jose Delgado did several experiments along these lines. Delgado's most notorious demonstration was to send a radio signal from a hand-held transmitter to a receiver implanted in a bull's head. The receiver was attached to electrodes in areas controlling emotions. When the bull started to charge, activation of the transmitter stopped him in his tracks. If such electrodes were implanted in the temporal lobes of humans, it is likely that people would report visual images. Theoretically it might even be possible for an electrical beam to bypass the need for electrodes and stimulate the brain directly, thereby evoking visual images. This, of course, was the theory underlying the operation of POSSE. The binders of scientific reports on my desk were telling me all this was possible. POSSE made sense out of the nonsense of Tolman's experiences.

Tolman had told me that there was nothing random in the universe. Everything had a cause and effect. There was a rational and systematic explanation for all that happened. As a scientist he used this approach to account for the observations he recorded in the laboratory. If he encountered an anomalous phenomenon—one that seemed inexplicable in terms of normal theories of physics— then the theories had to be revised in order to account for the new phenomenon. This was the way I was trained as an experimental psychologist, except that psychologists are generally more tolerant of "noise" in data than physicists.

In a sense, Tolman was approaching the buzzing, tingling, and images with the same scientific scrutiny. These experiences were not anomalies, they were puzzles. He searched for solutions and eventually formulated the POSSE theory—a satellite following and harassing him—with the purpose of providing order and meaning for his empirical observations. Given the perceived intensity of his experiences—they disturbed his sleep as well as his driving—this was a reasonable conclusion for him.

Tolman's theory of a harassing satellite sounded like a delusion, or false belief, because most ordinary people would not accept it. It is too far out, like the proverbial patient who claims he is Jesus Christ. Furthermore, while at least 20 million Americans are under electronic surveillance at work, this is usually accomplished via cameras, not personal satellites. Yet I knew it would be a mistake to dismiss his theory too readily. There are justifiable reasons for seeming paranoid if persons unknown are really harassing you. As the old joke goes: "Just because you're paranoid doesn't mean that people are not after you." Tolman's theory contained more than a grain of truth. It was logically constructed, almost convincing.

There have been cases in which people who seemed to be deluded were in fact correct. For example, the employees in the U.S. embassy in Moscow who claimed harassment by unseen forces were actually being bombarded by microwave beams. Prior to Watergate, Martha Mitchell alleged that her husband, the attorney general of the United States, was engaged in illegal activity in the White House. She was diagnosed as suffering from a delusion until the revelations of Watergate "cured" her. In honor of her experience, some psychologists now use the term "Martha Mitchell Effect" as a label for people who correctly report what appear to be improbable events and are judged deluded for doing so. Before I judged Dr. Tolman deluded, I needed to find incontrovertible proof or evidence that POSSE did not exist. If I was successful, I would face an even harder task: since Tolman had arrived at his belief scientifically, I would have to find convincing proof of an alternative explanation in order for him to abandon his delusion. This would not be easy. Scientists, like deluded patients, are extremely resistant to giving up a pet theory even in the face of contrary evidence. I recalled a famous case of three paranoid patients who each believed he was the one and only Jesus Christ. They were introduced to each other and allowed to interact for several years. None of them changed their beliefs. Shooting down POSSE would not be easy.

Tolman disarmed me as soon as he arrived for our next meeting. We used my office, which I had redecorated with tinfoil on the windows. He was wearing the same suit, a blue work shirt, and white ascot. When he crossed his long legs, his cuffs rode high enough for me to see a pair of Birkenstock shoes and calf-length black socks. It was a hot day, and the socks made no more sense than the three-piece corduroy suit.

"You're being investigated," he announced in a booming voice. "As soon as the investigation is completed, I may be able to tell you more."

My heart skipped a beat. "Investigated? What do you mean?"

"I initiated a security investigation of you."

"Who . . . who the hell gave you permission to investigate me?" I was angry.

"Had to do it. I knew it had to be done after I told you about POSSE." He paused. "Besides, it might be best because once you're cleared I can show you more of my work on these damned images."

The hell with the images. I wanted to know more about the investigation. How far did they go? Employment records, credit checks, what? Please God, not an IRS audit, I prayed. "Exactly what does this investigation entail?" I asked, forcing myself to act calmly.

"Oh, they start with the usual information available in the computer banks: criminal records, motor vehicle records, mortgages. They'll probably check with UCLA, maybe even some neighbors. Of course, they'll have to talk with your dentist."

"Why my dentist? I thought medical records are confidential."

"Medical records are really quite easy to get." He seemed to enjoy having me on the defensive.

"But what does my dentist have to do with this?"

"They have to know how much pain you can take. He'll know how you respond in the chair."

Tolman sounded serious. I was getting nervous and decided to take the offensive. "Let me make it easier," I said as I spun around on my chair and grabbed a copy of my CV (curriculum vitae) from the bookshelf. It was a thirty-page résumé of my entire professional life.

"Here," I said as I handed it to him. "If they need anything else, have them call me." Tolman smirked as he put the CV in his briefcase.

I turned the conversation back to his disturbing visual images. Since the images always began with the buzzing, that seemed like a good place to start our investigation. Tolman claimed that his hearing was perfect, and he was certain the buzzing was objective in nature. I wanted him to have hearing tests and a physical examination to be sure, but I knew that paranoids resist anything that is too intrusive. So I suggested that he have a physical just to rule out any damage from the energy beams. Now, paranoids often feel that interviewers are reading their minds, but Tolman astonished me by reading mine.

"You think I'm paranoid and therefore will resist intense personal scrutiny, don't you?" His phrasing sounded as though it had been lifted from a standard psychiatry text.

"Yes," I answered without hesitation. "But if the POSSE is chasing you, who wouldn't be?"

Tolman smiled and chuckled, which I took as a healthy sign. Paranoids usually lack a sense of humor. They view humor in a personalized, ridiculing way. Seeing double meanings is not funny; it is a way of uncovering hidden conspiracies and plots. Life is a humorless struggle, and to survive one must be deadly serious at all times. Fortunately Tolman was still capable of laughing about his experiences.

"If I open myself up to your security investigation," I continued, "why can't you permit at least some rudimentary tests? If we're going to work together on this thing as a team, *we* have to trust each other." I stressed the "we" in order to minimize his resistance. "We should know if there is any damage and if your hearing is okay. If you're worried about your sperm, we can check that out as well. We should rule out any metabolic disorders, high blood pressure, and other conditions that might contribute to the buzzing and tingling. We can even have an ophthalmologist check for any microwave-induced cataracts. Look, I'll schedule a series of appointments for you—it's all free—and you can just do whatever feels comfortable."

After a long pause, he spoke. "All right. But no MRIs or anything like that."

"Right," I agreed quickly. "We don't need MRIs anyway." Magnetic resonance imaging (MRI) uses magnets, radio waves, and computers to reconstruct images of the body's soft tissues. They would be of no use in diagnosing Tolman's case, but he certainly seemed afraid of anything that would probe too deeply.

"See, I'm not so paranoid after all," he said as I picked up the telephone to schedule the exams. But you're no Martha Mitchell, I thought.

I arranged for Tolman to have a series of examinations and tests over the next several days. He came to my office between appointments, and we spent hours discussing our respective interests. Since he refused to meet with any of the staff psychiatrists, I used our time together to extract as much history as possible. I shared some highly personal data with him, and after I repeatedly emphasized that I was neither a psychiatrist nor a clinical psychologist, but a researcher like himself, he began to share the same with me. We developed a strong trust, despite the fact that my security clearance was still pending. Our exchanges were straightforward, scientific, and serious. I tried to minimize his suspicion by avoiding any strong facial or verbal expressions when he was telling me about such things as the rolls of coins he kept in his pocket.

The coins, he said, were 1943 steel pennies, a wartime coinage that was produced in the same year Tesla died and he was born. Tolman believed that this coincidence meant that the steel pennies were good-luck charms that might prove to be potential deflectors of the energy beams. He was experimenting with moving the rolls to different pockets. I knew that deluded patients often make unreasonable assumptions based upon the detection of trivial or manufactured coincidences. They feel significance in the coincidences and use them as ways to account for their anomalous experiences. Rather than challenge Tolman's logic, I volunteered that I was also born in 1943, the same year Albert Hofmann took the world's first LSD trip!

"Can you beat that!" I said in mock amazement at my own coincidences.

He did. "Otto Stern got the Nobel in 1943 for his work in molecular beam theory and proton movement." He started shaking an angry finger at me. "That's more of a connection to what's happening than your drugs. Asshole!"

I knew better than to mention that 1943 was also the year in which the famous psychiatrist Norman Cameron published a classic paper warning that paranoids who believed strongly in such coincidences might become dangerous, even homicidal.

Tolman showed up for all the scheduled examinations, including one with a neuropsychologist. I arranged this appointment under the guise of assessing neurological deficits. But I also ordered the psychologist to administer a battery of other tests, including an intelligence test and the Minnesota Multiphasic Personality Inventory (MMPI), a personality questionnaire. Tolman tolerated these but refused to cooperate with any projective measures such as the inkblot test, which can often tap more hidden aspects of personality. When the psychologist suggested that Tolman talk with a staff psychiatrist in lieu of the projective tests, he slithered out of the room.

Several days later I met with Tolman to discuss the results. He arrived carrying a large cardboard tube.

"Good news, Ed," I said. We were now on a first-name basis. "You passed all your medical tests with flying colors. You're healthy, and there's no apparent damage to any systems." I held back the psych report but spread the others on my desk for him to study. "Your blood pressure is a wee bit high, and I want you to look at this—"

"I have good news for you, too," he interrupted. "You passed the security clearance." He opened the cardboard tube and removed a set of blueprints. The logo for Tolman's company was embossed on the top of every sheet. Next to the logo in bold lettering was "Personal Orbit Satellite for Surveillance and Enforcement." There were pages filled with diagrams of electrical circuits and mathematical notations. But for all I knew they could be the plans for a satellite, a personal computer, or even a household appliance.

I suspected that Tolman was the architect of the POSSE blue-prints, although he was pretending to have acquired them from his company. If so, he was not the first paranoid to try to prove the existence of a mind-control device by putting it on paper. I recalled the classic case of James Tilly Matthews, the first paranoid described in medical literature.

James Tilly Matthews was an eighteenth-century London architect who followed the revolutionary ideas of Franz Mesmer, the father of hypnotism. Mesmer claimed that people could influence one another by the power of magnetic fluids passing between them. Mesmer even built a machine, the "baquet," a type of electrical condenser that actually produced physical sensations at relatively short distances. It was a natural step for Matthews to believe that a more advanced version of this machine had been invented, one capable of producing the sequence of strange sensations he was experiencing.

First, the magnetic field surrounding him compressed, cracking his body as if it were a lobster. Small pimples erupted on his head. His stomach knotted. The muscles of his face twisted into a sardonic grin. Matthews believed that a machine was responsible. He called the machine an "Air Loom," reflecting his fascination with the textile machinery of the times. According to Matthews, who as a trained architect knew how things were constructed, the Air Loom resembled a church organ so large that it had to be operated by a team of seven men and women, all technicians highly skilled in advanced pneumatic chemistry and electricity. They sat at huge desks crammed with levers, pumps, and tubes connected to a series of windmill-like structures. Nothing actually touched Matthews—he never even knew where the machine was kept, although he guessed it was hidden in a London cellar—yet its invisible threads could control him like a puppet.

The Air Loom was actually the world's first influencing machine, a device existing entirely in the mind of the paranoid. But Matthews believed it was as real as the gang of assassins that operated it. The gang had several machines. Some were secreted in strategic positions throughout the country. They would soon be operational and mesmerize members of government. Matthews sent warnings to the leaders. The leaders sent Matthews to Bethlem Hospital for the Insane. Matthews spent his time making sketches, including a design that was used for a new hospital building. Another sketch showed the inner workings of the Air Loom. It was as real to Matthews as the building. His physician saw the drawing as further proof of his insanity. After all, it was 1810, and something like the Air Loom was beyond most people's imagination.

But now we were sitting inside my office in the latter part of the twentieth century. Technology had made radio, television, spy satellites, and other "influencing machines" more feasible. Tolman believed that POSSE was not only feasible, but operational. We were both staring at the blueprints. I realized it was going to be impossible to prove that it didn't exist. But how else could I get Tolman to accept the idea that the influencing machine was none other than his own superior, albeit paranoid, brain? I needed time to think and told Ed I would call him in a few days to plan our next step. He departed with the blueprints and a bold smirk that said "Gotcha."

After he left, I took out the psych report. Tolman was neurologically intact. He'd scored an impressive 165 on the IQ test but had also scored extremely high on the MMPI paranoia scale. The psychologist had never seen such high readings and recommended immediate treatment. I knew that Tolman would balk at this suggestion since the traditional treatment for paranoia was based on psychotherapy designed to persuade patients that their suspicions were unwarranted. However, I also knew that one did not persuade a scientist like Tolman without convincing data, and plenty of it.

Psychoanalysis is one system of psychotherapy that seeks to extract reams of such data from the free associations and dreams of the patient. Traditional psychoanalysts insist that behavior can be traced to unconscious drives and conflicts. By making the patient aware of them, analysts believe they can diminish, if not eliminate, the undesirable effects such as paranoia. In fact, psychoanalysis is the preferred approach with highly educated patients like Tolman.

"Treating paranoids is a long and difficult process," said Dr. Joel Morgan.

Dr. Morgan had the reputation for being a brilliant classic analyst, although he was also skilled in more modern psychotherapy techniques, including the use of tranquilizers and other medications. A short, rotund man with a bushy brown beard that always contained telltale flecks from his last meal, Joel was considered a genius with reluctant and defensive patients like Tolman. He could pick his way through the intricate mental defenses with the same ease he now used to pick bits of popcorn from his beard. Joel loved popcorn and kept a bottomless bowl filled with it on his desk. He grabbed another handful.

"Of course, therapy sessions sometimes continue for years," he added while munching. (Maybe he was mentally calculating the billable hours as he chewed!)

"This guy won't agree to that. He refuses to see any psychiatrists," I said. Tolman would find it impossible to loll on Dr. Morgan's couch, let alone meet with him for an evaluation. And he'd be petrified by the microwave oven Morgan used to make the popcorn.

"I don't have to see him," replied Joel. "Remember that Freud never spoke with Schreber. You just tell me about this fellow Tolman."

Joel was reminding me of Sigmund Freud's analysis of Daniel Schreber, the most famous patient in the history of psychiatry. Freud never met Schreber. He learned everything he felt he needed to know from reading Schreber's published autobiography. It was Freud's critique of this book that provided psychoanalysis with the standard model for understanding paranoia.

Daniel Schreber had been a respected judge in Dresden during the late 1890s. He started to have difficulty sleeping, then became depressed and preoccupied with morbid thoughts about death. He believed that he was suffering from a nervous disease caused by nerve rays that were being directed to his nervous system as part of a "scientific experiment." These rays picked through his brain, reading his thoughts and filling his ears with nonsensical voices. He feared that someone might be trying to "unman" him by making his penis disappear. There were no satellites in those days, so Schreber attributed the source of the nerve rays to God, but somehow they had been intercepted and controlled by Dr. Flechsig, his physician. Freud believed the source of this paranoia lay in

Schreber's struggles between his wishes and fears. Accordingly, Schreber harbored homosexual longings for Flechsig but denied the feelings. Instead he projected them into expressed feelings of persecution by the physician.

Given Joel Morgan's orientation, symbolized by a set of Freud's collected works prominently displayed in an office cluttered with hundreds of other psychoanalytic texts that I had never read, I knew he was going to have a field day with Tolman's story. I outlined the case, feeling very much like a student asking the teacher for help. While I knew that analyzing a patient in absentia was purely academic, I was eager for any insights Joel could offer. Joel listened carefully, occasionally munching popcorn and stroking his beard. When I finished, he opened his desk drawer and took out a cigarette lighter.

"Too bad he didn't do the projective tests," Joel said with a heavy sigh. "But let me speculate on the analysis," he continued. "He feels guilty."

"Guilty about what? Telling me about POSSE?" I asked.

"Guilt about his hamsters. He felt responsible for killing Huck and letting the others die of neglect. He's punishing himself. The satellite is the engine of his torture." Joel flicked the lighter, and a fountain of burning butane shot into the air. He quickly adjusted the flame, then rummaged through his desk drawer again.

"And the buzzing and the tingling?" I asked.

"He's a hypochondriac," replied Joel.

Joel was referring to a condition known as hypochondriacal paranoia, in which patients have delusions of physical symptoms that cannot be found by physical workups. The patients become so preoccupied with the ailments that they quit their jobs and devote all their time to "studying" their illness. But I was not yet convinced that the buzzing and tingling were delusions.

"And the images?" I asked.

"If the images are not hallucinations . . ."

"I'm convinced they're not," I said.

"Okay, that's even better. Then they're probably from his dreams. The dwarfs are really his pet hamsters. His unconscious made the association from those rare dwarf hamsters he could never have. Now the deformed dwarfs are his sick hamsters chasing him. They're angry because he killed them. They're seeking revenge. When they catch him they'll string him up, castrate and dissect him just the way he cut up lab animals."

"He didn't cut up the hamsters," I protested. And the images are not at all dreamlike, I thought.

"Okay. But he probably cut up frogs and worms in high school. It bothered him. Probably brewing for some time. Now it's Huck's revenge for all of that, although without seeing Tolman, I can't even guess why it's happening now."

"And the fear of ELFs? The satellite? Don't tell me that he believes a group of hamsters got together and launched a spy satellite?"

"No, that's too bizarre. He's not that schizophrenic . . . yet. But he's letting his scientific terminology blur his thought processes— and yours. Satellites are real, but *his* POSSE is a projection of his guilt. It's pounding his head just as his father did." Joel found what he was looking for in the desk. He retrieved a splinter-thin joint of marijuana and lit it. He offered me a hit, but I shook my head. "The satellite could also be punishing him for homosexual feelings," he continued. "Why, he practically exposed himself to you in your office. Maybe he wears tinfoil to stop his homosexual urges, not the microwaves."

"But Tolman wearing tinfoil pants is no different from my wearing sunglasses to guard against unseen UV rays," I said.

"You can make love with your glasses on," replied Joel. "I doubt if your boy has such a great sex life."

Joel took a few more hits as I discussed my own thoughts. Tolman was the first true paranoid I had come across, but I couldn't swallow the freewheeling Freudian analysis. Still, Joel made some sense. I agreed with him that the satellite beams, with their buzzing and tingling, were clearly elaborations born out of a paranoid mind. The influencing machine was none other than Tolman's own brain. But how could I turn it off before he progressed into the psychotic state exemplified by Daniel Schreber? Was psychoanalysis the only way?

"Analysis may be useless," Joel said in a gasping voice as he inhaled. "Tolman's delusional system may be too watertight." He coughed. I sensed he was getting tight himself. "Maybe some medication and psychotherapy would loosen him up," he added.

"What do you suggest?" I asked.

"Buy him a hamster," replied Joel, and he started to laugh hysterically.

"Seriously," I said, "what would Freud have done with him?"

"Freud kept a figurine of a naked dwarf in his study," Joel answered without responding to my question. "The dwarf represented the Egyptian god who created the world. I saw it once . . . quartz with a blue glaze."

"I don't understand."

"Find the elf in self," he replied.

Joel was getting intoxicated and jumping around in his thinking. Such discontinuities were also typical of the pathological thought processes seen in many schizophrenics. Thank God Tolman was more logical and concrete.

Now Joel was talking to himself: "Hamsters launching a satellite . . . that's a good one. . . ." He started laughing again.

I got up to leave. As I stood at Joel's door, I looked back at him snickering at his desk. I couldn't resist. "By the way, Joel, Tolman's having me investigated. You could be next. Better get rid of that stuff."

"Jesus Christ!" he exhaled as he crushed the roach in an ashtray.

The interlude in Dr. Morgan's office heightened my concern for Tolman. I had to agree that Ed was not yet psychotic, but his thinking could become progressively more bizarre and lead him into a dysfunctional mental disorder. Could I prevent that from happening? Since traditional psychiatric approaches could not help me turn off Tolman's satellite, I had to try something unconventional. Perhaps I might be able to get it to turn itself off. But first I needed to see the shields that Ed had devised for his house. I persuaded him to show me.

The following evening, after rush-hour traffic, I drove to his house in Pasadena. I took the Pasadena Freeway, 8.2 miles of the most scenic and pleasant driving in the Los Angeles basin. The freeway is the oldest one in the area, and its outmoded, hilly curves and tunnels make high-speed driving difficult. I took it slowly, listening to the same classical music station that Ed and I discovered we both loved. Our car radios were always tuned to this station. As

I entered a series of tunnels, the radio crackled, hissed, and buzzed! The noise continued for several minutes until I left the tunnels and emerged in the outskirts of Pasadena.

Tolman lived in a large two-story wooden house built in the 1920s. It was set back from the street behind a line of beautiful maple trees. Fragrant night jasmine plants lined the walkway. A wide porch with a rocking chair and hammock wrapped around the entire front of the house. I couldn't find a doorbell, so I knocked on the door. Ed opened it immediately. I sensed he had watched my approach and was waiting for the knock.

"Cleared person entering," he yelled into the house as I followed him into an enormous oak-paneled entry hall. The house seemed extremely dark. I didn't see anyone else inside.

He took me straight upstairs, then down a dark hall. The uncarpeted hardwood floors carried every footstep in creaking echoes throughout the house. A flickering glow danced from under a door at the end of the hall. Ed opened the door and ushered me into the master bedroom.

The first thing I noticed was the source of the flickering light: several kerosene lamps with Tiffany-style glass shades were burning on tables in the room. Then I saw *the bed*. It was a king-size four-poster with a canopy. The carved wooden posts were as thick as telephone poles. They supported the canopy, which was also wood and appeared to be several inches thick. It was the biggest bed I had ever seen. It was also the most unusual. Ed told me that the top of the canopy was covered with copper screening. On the floor at the foot of the bed I saw a row of six gallon-size plastic jugs. According to Ed, they contained secret copper and lead sulfite solutions that helped deflect the ELF frequencies.

"I swiped them from the lab," he confessed, "so don't say anything." Whom was I going to tell?

"Do these things really shield POSSE?" I asked.

"Mostly. I still get the buzzing, but the pictures don't seem to get through as often as they once did." He paused to move one of the plastic jugs near the window. "I'm still experimenting . . . I'm getting close." So was I. I was beginning to see a way to stop Tolman's influencing machine.

After my tour of the bedroom, Ed introduced me to his wife.

Even in the dim light of the house I could tell she was very attractive. He explained that I was the UCLA scientist with whom he had been working. I was the one who believed him. I was the one who was going to help expose POSSE.

While I didn't respond to Ed's statements, I was certain Mrs. Tolman interpreted my silence as consent. I saw a troubled look in her eyes. There was nothing I could say. However, I did accept a cup of coffee before I drove home. Mrs. Tolman served the coffee, then left us alone at the kitchen table. We talked about the Pasadena Freeway, which Ed took to work each day. The high-speed rush-hour traffic through the curves upset him. "White-knuckle driving," he called it. He always left at the same time each morning but returned at various times in the evening. Yet POSSE passed him like clockwork *whenever* he was commuting! Ed said it was probably in a geosynchronous orbit over Los Angeles and used "switching lenses" to follow his position. Why didn't it zap him all the time? I wondered. Why only at specific times? The questions continued to plague me as I listened to the crackling and buzzing of my car radio on the drive home.

Tolman's shields had failed to stop the pictures completely because copper screens did not block thoughts, even with the help of supersecret solutions. I was convinced that the transmissions from the satellite were only thoughts generated by and in Tolman's brain. Therefore the only way to block them was with Tolman's own thoughts. I designed a simple but risky experiment to demonstrate to him that this could be done. It was simple because it used an elementary principle of suggestion. It was risky because I had to deceive a paranoid, one who believed I was a trusted colleague working on his side. Cameron's warnings about paranoids becoming homicidal echoed in my mind.

Several nights later I invited Ed to a lab in UCLA's Brain Research Institute to try some new, improved "shields" that a colleague had developed for recording electrical signals from the brains of patients. The lab contained a small soundproof, lightproof chamber with a bed. The chamber itself was elevated off the lab floor and surrounded by a cage of copper screening similar to the shielding Ed used over his bed. The screening was reinforced with a special mesh, similar to the mesh used in the doors on microwave ovens. The entire cage was assembled in lightweight sections that could be detached and slipped completely away from the chamber in a few minutes. All the electrical circuits were grounded, insulated, and isolated from other electrical systems in the building. Special suppressors protected against lightning strikes and voltage surges. The windows were covered with tinfoil. I introduced Ed to a technician, who repeated my claim that the cage would shield all electromagnetic radiation. The technician was very convincing as he spoke to Ed in his own language of ELFs and carrier waves. He told Ed he could use the chamber for the rest of the night.

Ed was anxious to test the chamber immediately since the satellite usually bothered him around this time of day. After helping him into the chamber bed, the technician attached several electrodes for monitoring electroencephalogram (EEG), blood pressure, heart rate, and skin resistance (a measure that can reflect stress and anxiety). I explained the operation of the intercom system. I would remain in the lab outside the chamber, and he could talk to me at any time simply by holding down the intercom button. In order to insure his privacy, I would be unable to hear anything unless he was pressing the button. However, unknown to Ed I had placed an extremely sensitive microphone in his pillow. This would enable me to record all sounds. I tucked him in, turned off the light, and sealed him in the chamber.

After about twenty minutes Ed settled down, and all the physiological monitors showed normal readings. Many minutes later Ed activated the intercom. "The shields are holding," he said with the cold, scientific detachment of Mr. Spock from "Star Trek."

"We're going to take the cage away for a few minutes to see what happens," I said. The technician and I bumped the chamber a few times but left the cage exactly where it had been.

Many minutes later I heard a mysterious noise from the pillow microphone! I refused to believe it was a buzzing and forced myself to hear it as a muffled clicking or crunching sound. It stopped as suddenly as it started. In a few moments Ed reported that he had heard the buzzing.

"Any pictures?" I asked. The monitors were picking up incipient stress.

"No." He sounded anxious.

"Let's wait a few more minutes," I said.

Five minutes elapsed.

"Put the cage back *now*," demanded Ed. His blood pressure and heart rate were higher. That meant he should be tingling.

"Do you see any pictures?" I asked.

"No. But I can feel them coming. I'm tingling all over." The tingling was not a hypochondriacal delusion.

"Let's wait to be sure." I tried to sound comforting, but it was hard because I was tingling, too.

A long pause.

"Yes. Those dwarfs again! *Dammit! Put the cage back,*" yelled Ed.

"Consider it done," I said with my own private humor.

According to the monitors, it took Ed another thirty minutes to calm down. Then he drifted asleep for a few minutes, snapped awake, pressed the intercom, and said he'd had enough. He had heard and seen nothing more and wanted to go home.

It was enough for me as well. The demonstration had convinced me that Ed's persecution by the satellite was all in his head and that he could stop it with the same trickery of suggestion I used to move the cage back and forth. In his mind, the shielding protected him, whether it was actually there or not. He heard the buzzing and saw the pictures only when he believed he was not shielded. The only problem preventing me from springing this revelation on Tolman was that both the technician and I had heard a noise as well! The buzzing was no more a delusion than the tingling. But until I could find the source of that noise as well as the reason for the specific pictures, Tolman would never accept my explanation.

The next day Mrs. Sonya Tolman called and asked to see me privately. Would I have to tell Ed? I explained that he would have to know, but I would delay mentioning it until she had time to tell him first. She accepted these conditions and arrived at my office two hours later.

Mrs. Tolman walked with assured, feminine movements, like the high-fashion model she had been in her youth. She was dressed in an elegant red suit and matching cap. Spiked heels added unnecessary inches to her tall frame. She was very attractive. Her large

doe eyes appeared red and teary. I suspected she had not slept well.
I pushed the box of Kleenex closer to her chair.

"What's wrong, Mrs. Tolman?" I asked.

"Please call me Cinnamon, Doctor. That's what Ed calls me, and
everyone else." She paused. "Because of my hair," she added. Her
hair was a lovely yellowish brown.

"Yes, it's a lovely name," I said. Does she know it's also the
name for a special breed of hamster? I wondered.

She came right to the point. "I don't know if my husband's crazy
or not. I don't know what to make of this satellite stuff. The jugs,
the tinfoil . . . it's all getting too much. And those coins. Did he tell
you?" I nodded. "Doctor, I don't know if I can continue to live
with him." She started to cry.

I told Cinnamon that I didn't have any answers yet, but Ed and
I were working on it. It was still a puzzle, and I tried to calm her by
saying that unsolved puzzles could often drive scientists a little bit
crazy. How long had Ed been acting this way?

"He's always been crazy about his work," she said. "That was
what attracted me to him. He's so dedicated. I never understood
his research, but he's so brilliant. I guess being peculiar goes with
the territory. Even our first date was strange." Cinnamon was rambling now, but I let her go on. It seemed to relax her.

"He took me to a movie and dinner," she continued. "I'll never
forget it. It was an awful foreign film, a horror film. He said he took
all his first dates to see it, but I was the only one who could eat a full
dinner afterward."

"Do you remember the name of the film?" I asked.

"*El Topo*. I'll never forget it." She puckered her cheeks in disgust.

I stared at Cinnamon in disbelief. I had seen the film in 1971
when it played in Los Angeles. Now images from the movie flashed
in my mind. I recognized them immediately as the same images Ed
saw when the satellite was zapping him. One showing was enough
for me to remember the haunting images, but Ed had watched it on
countless dates. The horrific scenes had been pounded into the core
of his memory, sleeping there until called forth by some unknown
trigger.

"Did Ed ever discuss any images that came from the satellite?" I
asked.

Now it was Cinnamon's turn to stare. She had no idea what I was talking about. "He complained about buzzing in his ears at night. That was all."

"Did you ever hear any buzzing?"

"No," she answered. "Does he see things, too?" She was fearing the worst.

"No, don't worry. He's not hallucinating. He just remembers things that are from the movie. Probably something reminds him, maybe the buzzing." I was trying to calm her, but inwardly I was excited about this revelation. "Is there anything in the bedroom that makes noise? A clock or fan?"

Cinnamon told me about his midnight experiments with electrical devices that caused the lights to flash, but she never heard any sounds.

"Do either of you snore?" I asked.

"Never . . . Wait. Ed grinds his teeth at night. Sometimes I wake up and hear it."

"Ed . . . Ed grinds his teeth at night?" I said. So that was the mysterious sound I'd heard from the chamber!

"Yes," she said. "He also does it sometimes when we make love."

"Does Ed have any sexual problems?" I was thinking about his concerns with microwave radiation.

"Oh, no, Doctor. He's so sexy. Thank God there are no problems in that department, otherwise I wouldn't have stayed with him. I wouldn't be here now . . . I love him." She started crying again.

Thank God indeed. Cinnamon's information was just what I had been looking for. The hearing tests had failed to find any evidence of tinnitus or other subjective noises that could be perceived as buzzing. But no one had asked Ed about bruxism, or teeth grinding. I knew that many people are unaware not only that they grind their teeth, but that such grinding can be misperceived as a sound from another source. It can even sound like buzzing.

There seemed to be two separate sources for Ed's buzzing, and both were linked to stress. The nighttime bruxism, probably from the tension and stress that Ed accumulated during the day, was one source. The other could be found in the hilly curves and tunnels of the Pasadena Freeway, where the radio static generated buzzing noises. Ed told me that driving through the tunnels in rush-hour traffic always frightened him. He clutched the wheel, clenched his teeth, and nearly choked with anxiety. Here, too, stress was the common denominator. The tingling was a combination of the high blood pressure I detected in the cage experiment coupled with a conditioned nervous reaction to the incipient horrific scenes Ed couldn't control.

It was the stress that was triggering memory images from the movie, a movie that had been viewed originally with a great deal of anxiety and stress. The buzzing had become a conditioned stimulus to the stress. The memories of the movie were encoded during a state of high arousal and stress. When similar levels of arousal or stress were induced, the statebound memories were evoked. In a sense, the images were just what Ed said they were: picture postcards. But they were postcards from a celluloid hell stored in a hidden vault in his memory. The buzzing rang the bells, which opened the vault and allowed the pictures to escape.

After Cinnamon left my office, I thought how easy it might be to stop the satellite without the need for conventional psychotherapy. Tranquilizers could stop much of the stress. Antihypertensive medication could reduce the tingling. Perhaps a mouth guard that would prevent the grinding might also stop the images. I didn't know if he would go for these suggestions, but it was all I could offer him.

The following week I met with Ed to present my findings and plead my case. I spoke of teeth grinding and tunnels, of stress and satellites. I even showed him stills from *El Topo* that were identical with the images he reported. He didn't seem too surprised and even confessed to his initial reactions to the film, but I could tell his mind was racing through revisions of his POSSE theories. I told him the images were only memories triggered by the stress. Many people experienced similar triggers without invoking paranoid explanations. Ed's images could be stopped now with some medication and a mouth guard.

"Don't be an asshole!" he yelled without a smirk. "POSSE is stimulating the memories. That's where the stress comes from. Asshole!"

I had no choice but to tell him about the cage experiment and confess my deception.

"The images started when you thought the cage had been removed. You stopped them yourself when you believed the cage was back in place, but it wasn't. Doesn't that prove anything to you?"

"Only that you run a piss-poor experiment," he said. "Maybe your cage didn't shield everything and POSSE started and stopped transmitting just at those times."

"Ed," I pleaded, "isn't that stretching it a bit? As a scientist, I find there are too many assumptions there. I like parsimony."

"Apparently you like Cinnamon, too," he snapped, and walked out the door.

In that single statement Ed had told me that he had progressed to a much more advanced stage of paranoia. His thought processes were now jumping around, and I had become part of his delusional system. In addition to everything else, he was showing the signs of paranoid delusional jealousy. He had probably been constantly watching and observing and thinking about his wife and me ever since he'd introduced us. Whatever trivial or inconsequential thing he saw or heard—such as an innocent remark I made that he had a lovely wife—was misinterpreted as confirmatory evidence for a relationship. It seemed hopeless. I was practically grinding my own teeth in frustration.

I gave Ed several weeks to calm down, then called him. Cinnamon answered the phone. Didn't I know? Ed had quit his job and moved out of the house. She didn't know where he was but was certain he would contact me. Why? She said I was his only friend. I promised to call her as soon as I heard anything.

I was downhearted. I thought Ed would be pleased with my discovery of the *El Topo* images and be receptive to my analysis. But he remained lost in an Oz where satellites ruled from over the rainbow. My offer of magic potions and mouth guards was the equivalent of asking him to click his heels in order to find his way home. Dr. Edwin Tolman was looking for a more technological remedy, one cloaked in the gadgetry of a mad scientist.

Months later I got a postcard from Ed. There was no return address, but the postmark was from Quebec. He didn't have to tell me why he was there. We had talked about it before. At the end of his life, Nikola Tesla had been conducting research in Canada. His last assistant, Arthur Matthews, was still living in Quebec. He was allegedly working on a beam weapon capable of knocking down aircraft. It could just as easily be turned against satellites. Tolman had gone to find him.

I picked up the phone to call Cinnamon. I told her that Ed had gone off to see the Wizard.

4

WHISPERS

The old woman unfolded a stained dish towel, revealing a collection of ancient dental instruments. She selected a small pick, rinsed it under the kitchen tap, then wiped it on the towel. She moved closer and opened her mouth. It was like a dark cave looming over me. I switched on a small flashlight. Her tongue was a quivering carpet on the cave floor. I played the light against the walls. Small deposits of silver and gold fillings sparkled like so many gems. Her pick came to rest on a filling that seemed no different from the others.

"This one," she said, tapping the tooth with the pick for my benefit. She was struggling to speak with the pick in her open mouth. "The whispers seem to come from this tooth." A drop of saliva drooled from her lip.

She closed her mouth and stood over the kitchen stool where I was perched. Her eyes were squinting behind reading glasses held together with a safety pin. She waved the pick in her raised hand. "Open wide," she ordered. Both the stool and I were shaking. I stretched my mouth open and flashed on the scene from *Marathon Man* in which the Nazi dentist played by Laurence Olivier created an unneeded cavity in Dustin Hoffman's front tooth. As Olivier prepared to examine Hoffman's teeth, he kept asking, "Is it safe?" Now I was asking myself the same question as the old woman began her inspection. My God! I thought. That pick was just in her mouth! I pushed aside my anxiety and tried to think about the events that had brought me to this witch's kitchen.

After Ed Tolman left town, I had gone to my dentist, Dr. Barry Rose, to find out if anyone had been asking questions. I saw Barry at the end of the day when he and his assistant were cleaning up.

"I recently went through a security clearance," I explained, "and I was told they might interview you, maybe even ask for my records. Did they?"

"Yeah," he said, deadpan. "There were some shady characters in trench coats. I told them you were always asking me for 'scripts, a real junkie."

"You're kidding?" He must be kidding!

"I told them you were always complaining about pain just to get drugs."

Tolman had said they would ask about pain. "You're kidding?" I repeated.

"I told them I thought you were injecting drugs. You're always wearing long-sleeved shirts, even on the hottest days in the summer. Hiding those needle tracks, I betcha."

His act was so spontaneous, so natural, I didn't know what to believe.

Dr. Rose ruined it by bursting into laughter. "Just fooling," he confessed. "Have a seat and tell me all about it." He was still laughing.

I told him about my encounter with Tolman and the satellite. The man had a good case of paranoia, and I confessed I was more than a little infected myself. I was intrigued by the discovery of this paranoid streak that we all seem to have. It was almost a hypnotic attraction. Something was stirring inside me. I wanted to study more paranoids. Suzie, the dental assistant, suggested that I meet Miss Lillian.

"Who's Miss Lillian?" I asked.

"Lillian Rush," said Dr. Rose. "Sweetest old paranoid you'd ever want to meet. She came to see me after I took over Doc Mulligan's practice. Lillian had been one of his oldest patients. She asked me for her records—the only patient I ever had who insisted on having a copy. Her teeth were in great shape for her age, but she wanted me to replace all her fillings. Now, some patients get concerned about the toxicity from mercury in the amalgam fillings. Lillian wanted *everything,* including the gold crowns, replaced with plastic. She said her teeth were 'whispering' to her."

"Whispering?" I asked.

"Crazy, huh? She figured Doc Mulligan put little transistors in her teeth. I gave her a complete examination, including a full X-ray series. The pictures showed nothing but old dental work. Some of it was done before transistors were invented! I explained all this and showed her the X-rays. She still wanted her work replaced. Instead I gave her the name of a shrink in the building."

Rose did the right thing. Some dentists might replace the work, assuring the patient that they are using restorations free of electronics. Other dentists might even extract the teeth. But patients who are so obviously delusional as Lillian should first be referred to a psychiatrist.

"Now, here's the part that really blew my mind," he continued. "A few months later she comes back with a clipping from a tabloid about nanotechnology. You know what that is, right?"

I nodded. Nanotechnology was a new science involving the development of ultraminiature robotic machines using submicroscopic computer chips, motors, and other components. Theoretically the machines could be made so small that they could be injected into the bloodstream and go to work repairing parts of the body directly. But nanotechnology was still in its infancy and certainly far younger than Lillian's dental work.

Dr. Rose continued. "So she tells me you can't see nanodevices on radiographs. She actually used the word *radiograph.* I tell her that nanodevices aren't available yet, and she starts arguing with me. She said the military perfected them years ago and kept it a secret. Mulligan learned about them when he was in the service. For Chrisakes! He served in World War Two! Back then everyone was still using vacuum tubes."

But Rose was no more capable of winning the argument with Lillian than I had been with Tolman. Lillian supported her theory with the same ambiguous references to secret and classified research. While Tolman had a job-related basis for his use of technical jargon, Lillian seemed to be getting her information from supermarket tabloids and God knew where. She spoke in the typical paranoid alphabet of agencies such as the CIA and FBI that were part of a conspiracy. The conspiracy enlisted dentists to implant these devices on people.

"She didn't trust me after that," Rose explained, "yet she still came in to have Suzie clean her teeth. She developed one nasty cavity and wanted me to extract the tooth rather than fix it. When I refused, she walked out and never came back."

Suzie went to the file room and pulled Lillian's chart for me. "We send her cards every six months," Suzie said, "but she hasn't been back for over two years."

"Will she talk to me?" I asked as I thumbed through the chart.

"Lillian will talk to anyone who will listen," said Suzie. "In fact, she set up an organization for victims like herself. She told me they had hundreds of members."

It was easy to find Miss Lillian's house with the detailed directions she had given me over the telephone. The long drive took me to one of the wooded canyons that snake through the outskirts of Los Angeles. I used the time to review the few facts that I had gleaned from her chart. She was eighty-three, a spinster, and worked in "business" until her retirement at sixty-five. The records did not list any relatives or friends to contact in case of an emergency. I suspected that she lived alone. There was no history of major medical problems, but I wondered about metabolic disorders like hypoglycemia or endocrine disorders like hypothyroidism, which have been known to precipitate paranoia.

Because of Lillian's age, I considered the possibility that she might be suffering from Alzheimer's disease or some other form of senility. Many elderly patients with Alzheimer's develop paranoid symptoms owing to their faltering memory. In the accompanying confusion, they often misperceive and distort information. They may come to believe that misplaced objects have been hidden deliberately or that their spouse is an imposter. However, Lillian's paranoia had a completely different ring to it. It seemed to be based on sounds that she heard, not objects or people she couldn't find. Her notion of whispering conspiracies was much more complex than the simple delusions of Alzheimer's patients. Besides, Dr. Rose had noted that she was as sharp as patients half her age.

Dr. Rose also noted that Lillian was different from other elderly patients. Most take huge amounts of medicines, which can produce adverse mental and physical side effects. When these side effects are either unexpected or unwanted, the elderly seem particularly prone to developing paranoid symptoms. Rose had given Lillian a checklist of the pharmaceuticals known to precipitate such reactions. The list included sedative hypnotics (sleeping pills), benzodiazepines (muscle relaxants), anti-inflammatory steroids, and antidepressants. He even asked her about over-the-counter medicines such as nasal decongestants containing phenylpropanolamine, which have been associated with paranoid reactions. Lillian denied use of any of these compounds.

The chart contained one entry that continued to puzzle me as I turned my car onto Lillian's street. She always got nitrous oxide. Nitrous oxide, or laughing gas, is an effective dental anesthetic, but it is also a hallucinogen. Under the influence, Lillian's mind could have been seeing and hearing almost anything. It was not surprising that nitrous oxide has been associated with some unusual paranoid reactions. I recalled one case involving a dentist who was taking too much of his own gas. He started to believe that his newly hired secretary was a spy who was trying to gather evidence against him. Then he believed that all the people with whom he had any kind of contact were part of a plot to get him. His conspiracy theory was similar to Lillian's, but it took the dentist six months of daily nitrous oxide inhalations in order to achieve this paranoid state. After a week without the nitrous, his symptoms disappeared.

Lillian went to the dentist only when absolutely necessary. There were fewer than a dozen visits over fifty years. While she may have had an unpleasant trip or two on the dental chair, there hadn't been enough exposures to the gas to keep it going. Somehow I didn't expect to find Lillian's house full of nitrous oxide cylinders. Something else had to be maintaining her delusion of whispering teeth and diabolic dentists. Since I had experienced more than my share of dental pain as a child because my dentist didn't offer local anesthetics, I was certain there was at least one diabolic dentist out there. But I was unwilling to believe that whispering teeth existed unless they told me so themselves.

I parked my car and walked up the brick path to Lillian's house. It was set behind deep woods, a tiny one-story cottage surrounded by a beautiful emerald-green lawn. A single, gigantic jacaranda tree was in full bloom, shedding its showy flowers across the grass like lavender snowflakes. Birds twittered around several feeders near the house. The sprinklers were spraying a fine mist, and a small rainbow was visible. It was like a fairy tale. Add a field of poppies and this could have been a cottage in the land of Oz.

Lillian answered the door. Her face reminded me of that of Whistler's mother, only with more wrinkles. She had the same chestnut hair and ankle-length black dress. But unlike the subject of that famous painting, Lillian was smiling. As I took her outstretched hand, I began my diagnosis. Her hands were warm and did not have the cool, dry feel that could be the telltale sign of endocrine disorders in the elderly. There were no obvious signs of osteoarthritis in the fingers. The fingernails were normal and pink—no signs of liver, kidney, or skin diseases. There were some yellow stains on two of her fingers, which I attributed to tobacco.

She led me through the house to a back room, which we entered through a screen door. I found myself on a porch that had been converted to an aviary. It was completely enclosed with screens and filled with a Technicolor assortment of finches fluttering about several potted trees. Lillian made a few birdcalls that sounded like "see see see," and the birds started twittering and whistling in reply. It was delightful. Since I had a pet parakeet as a child and had learned to imitate its call, I joined in with my own version of birdspeak. I managed to silence the aviary for several embarrassing seconds. Lillian recognized what I was doing.

"I don't have any parakeets or budgerigars, dear," she said, identifying my call correctly. "They could hurt the little finches." She gave another call, this one a loud, melodious whistle. Several canaries answered from a stack of cages I had not noticed before. "Even the canaries will fight with the finches if I let them out," she added.

We sat on comfortable wooden lawn furniture around a glass table in the center of the aviary. Miss Lillian, as she insisted on being called, told me about her years as an avid bird watcher and past president of a local chapter of the National Audubon Society. I confessed my past love of pigeons, deleting references to my laboratory experiments with them. We exchanged bird stories, and I found Lillian bright and highly educated. I thought she might be hard of hearing, but with all the singing and chirping I couldn't be certain. She seemed lonely, and I indulged her with small talk for over an hour before I popped *the* question about the whispering teeth. I told her that Dr. Rose was also my dentist, and I was concerned if he was involved in any conspiracy. It was the wrong approach to use because it identified me as a potential victim who had to be examined. Miss Lillian explained that she was planning a class action lawsuit against several dentists, including Rose. If I was his patient, I was in danger. That was when Lillian insisted on taking me into the kitchen to show me her teeth and look at mine. What was she going to do, I wondered, listen to them?

So here I was, teetering on a stool and letting this old woman explore the inside of my mouth. I could feel the pick against my teeth. Careful, lady, I thought. I can sue you for practicing without a license. As she worked her away around my teeth, she surprised me by identifying my fillings in terms of their precise location, using terms such as "lingual," "mesial," "distal," and "cervical line."

"You have very little work, so I guess you're not implanted," she said at the end. Actually I have considerable dental work, but it is camouflaged by porcelain crowns. But I wasn't going to correct Miss Lillian and initiate further violations. Instead I excused myself to use her bathroom.

Inside the bathroom, I checked my mouth for cuts—luckily for Miss Lillian, there were none—then checked out her medicine cabinet. I didn't see any prescription medicines, only aspirin, antacids, and a bottle of laxatives. The aspirins, which can cause ringing in the ears, reminded me of a recent case I had just read in the *New England Journal of Medicine*. A seventy-year-old woman who was taking twelve aspirins a day said the ringing sounded like the tune "When Irish Eyes Are Smiling." I, too, was smiling because if aspirins caused Miss Lillian's whispering, cutting her dose in half as recommended by the article should eliminate the problem. In a drawer next to the sink I found an assortment of gels and liquids for toothaches, antiseptic rinses, dental cements and wax, bleeding control sponges, cotton packs, and temporary filling material. She had everything necessary for taking care of her own teeth, which explained why she had not needed to see Dr. Rose again.

I rejoined Miss Lillian in the aviary. She was calling to a black-and-white zebra finch that had settled momentarily on the table. The call sounded like a child's toy trumpet. The bird cocked its head. I stood motionless. Miss Lillian embellished the trumpet with a flutelike whistle. The finch hopped to her chair, looked straight at her, then flew away. I took my seat again.

"I took one of your aspirins. I hope you don't mind," I said, baiting her.

"Of course not, dear. I hardly ever take them," she said. So much for my aspirin theory.

Miss Lillian was feeling comfortable enough to tell me more about the whispering. It began many years ago while Doc Mulligan was working on her teeth. She listened to the strange sounds with the same scrutiny she applied to bird songs. Each time she was on Mulligan's chair she heard them, and each time she got a little closer to identifying them. Eventually she realized the sounds were whispering voices. She even managed to catch a few words, but she couldn't remember them. But she did recall becoming very frightened.

"Do you think you were just hearing the dentist talking, maybe even whispering, to his assistant?" I asked. After all, she was under the influence of nitrous oxide and could have been confused.

"You see, dear, I heard it even when I was left alone in the room. He put something in my teeth to make them whisper." Miss Lillian explained that she never understood what the whispering was saying. But after corresponding with other people who'd had similar experiences with dentists, she became convinced that there was a conspiracy of dentists. They implanted devices in patients to harass them and spy on them.

Since she was so good at mimicking birdcalls, I asked Miss Lillian if she could imitate the whispering. She puckered her lips and produced a high-pitched rush of static. The static started to pulsate and whistle. I shuddered. It was an alien noise, yet it struck a chord deep inside my memory. I asked Miss Lillian if I could tape her and went to the car to get my recorder. When I returned she produced about three minutes of uninterrupted whispering. We both listened to the playback. This time it reminded me of a mechanical noise, but I still couldn't place it.

"Miss Lillian, does that remind you of anything?" I asked.

"Oh, dear. It's frightening to hear it like that. Don't play it anymore."

"I won't." But I was recording our conversation.

"I never liked whispering," she continued. "It's not polite. If people have something to say, they should say it without whispering." She never whispers, I thought. In fact, she almost yells—as if she's going deaf!

"Do you think they're whispering about you?" I asked, probing for the ideas of reference typical of paranoia.

"It's terrifying not knowing what they're saying," she said. "When I was a little girl, Mother took me to a stage show. A magician asked for a volunteer from the audience. He had a little midget come into the audience and grab me by the hand. I never saw a midget before. I didn't want to go, but Mother urged me to, so I went. When I got on stage the midget kept whispering in my ear. I didn't understand what he was saying. I got scared and ran back to my seat."

"Don't you think that the whispering midget is related to your whispering teeth?" It was the type of question the psychoanalyst Joel Morgan would have asked.

"No, dear," she said with a smile. "Not unless you know some midget dentists." Miss Lillian was obviously soberer and more concrete in her thinking than Joel would have been.

Suddenly a green parrot finch flew on the table. Miss Lillian said it was a female. She called to it in the long trill of the male. It answered with a shorter trill and stayed on the table.

"When exactly do you hear the whispering voices?" I asked.

"At the dentist."

"But you don't go anymore? Why does it still bother you?"

"Well, dear, they can still listen, can't they. So I stay in here as much as possible . . . the birds, you see."

Miss Lillian was using the aviary as a shield against the listening devices in the same way spies in the movies turned on the faucets whenever they suspected they were being bugged. Both the birds and the running water could produce enough masking noise to render listening devices useless.

The parrot finch hopped next to my tape recorder on the table. I realized the tape had stopped, and it was getting late. Miss Lillian *wanted* me to come back. She didn't get many visitors. But she had organized a group of other victims. Did any of them visit her? Yes, and she would arrange for me to meet Miss Louise next time. Miss Louise handled the correspondence with everyone.

At the door I asked her how many people there were in the group. Since we were no longer in the sanctuary of the aviary, she wrote a number on a piece of paper and handed it to me: 777.

"Holy shit!" I said loudly. I couldn't help myself.

"Watch your language, dear. Someone may be listening."

Lillian's whispering teeth were reminiscent of the apocryphal stories told about people who hear radio transmissions through the silver fillings in their teeth. Although this has never been proven, there is a theoretical basis for the alleged reception. Most silver fillings are an amalgam of silver, tin, copper, zinc, and mercury. Some contain other elements such as indium or palladium. In the strong signal field of a radio transmitter, such metals and their oxides can rectify the signal and permit reception. This is how radio broadcasts can sometimes be heard from faucets and other plumbing fixtures.

I recalled an amusing case involving a woman who heard fragments of a radio talk show coming from the toilet whenever she sat down. Amusement turned to terror when she distinctly heard "Move over." But other people also overheard words from the radio when they used the same toilet. Conspiracy theories aside, the ambiguous whispering Lillian heard didn't sound that crazy. It certainly wasn't like the detailed accusatory messages that Dennis Sweeney, a schizophrenic former political activist, heard from his teeth just before he killed Allard Lowenstein, a former congressman. I was certain there was a real physical stimulus in Miss Lillian's case. And I believed I had it on tape.

So I listened to the tape many times over the next few days. Something about it was bothering me. I Express-Mailed copies to an expert on bird songs and an electronic engineer. No one could identify the sounds. Then I played it for one of my classes at UCLA. I offered extra credit to anyone who could decipher the sounds.

The students made some wild guesses: a man with a lisp trying to whistle, a Swiss yodeler breaking wind, or an audience hissing the Swiss yodeler breaking wind. I felt like flunking the lot of them. Then it occurred to me to play it for Dr. Rose. Who should know better than one of the conspiring dentists?

He recognized it on the first playing. "Sounds like an aspirator," he said. He was right. It was the sound of an aspirator used to suction saliva from a patient's mouth. There were other sounds on the tape, but the aspirator was the basso continuo of Miss Lillian's song. I had an idea for identifying the other "voices" and persuaded Rose to let me use one of his empty rooms.

Suzie set me up in room five at the end of the hall. It had older equipment and was used only when necessary. Coincidentally, she said, this was the same room where she cleaned Miss Lillian's teeth. This is perfect, I thought.

As I sat on the chair, Suzie clipped a bib around my neck and put an aspirator in my mouth. Before she left me alone, I asked her to tilt the examining light on my face.

I did a quick scan of the audio environment. The aspirator made gurgling and sucking noises in my mouth. The water running around in the spittoon basin sounded like, well, running water. Dr. Rose was using a high-speed drill in the next room. I could even hear the clinking of metal instruments on the porcelain tray. Nothing else. I closed my eyes and tried to turn the noises into whispering teeth. Nothing happened. After thirty minutes I would have settled for any new sounds, even the Swiss yodeler. This is boring, I thought. At least Miss Lillian had nitrous. . . . Of course! That's it!

"Barry, Barry!" I shouted as I ran down the hall with my bib flapping. He was working on a patient and glared up at me.

"Um, sorry, Dr. Rose," I said. "Patient in room five needs nitrous."

"Be there in a minute," he said, holding back a laugh.

A few minutes later I was once again alone in the room. Just me, the aspirator, the spittoon basin, my trusty tape recorder, and two plastic tubes running into my nose. The tubes were connected to a Dentalgesic unit, which was pouring out a mixture of 70 percent nitrous oxide and 30 percent oxygen—just the way Miss Lillian liked it.

The gas rushing through the tubes was adding a new voice to the dental orchestra: a hissing. I closed my eyes and allowed myself to drift, hoping to turn it into a whisper. . . . It did sound a little like a whisper. I thought of Miss Lillian, her whispering teeth and her childhood scare with the whispering midget. . . . I was definitely drifting. . . . Maybe 70 percent was too much . . . yes . . . definitely . . . way too much. . . .

The whispered hissing of the aspirator and nitrous turns into the hissing of compressed air from a hose. A dwarf in a clown suit is holding the hose. It's Angelo Brienza!

Angelo was the dwarf clown at the Steeplechase amusement park on Coney Island. Every year my father took our family to Steeplechase. My favorite part was the famous horse ride. You sat on a metal horse that swept along a fourteen-hundred-foot elliptical track that rose and dipped like a mild roller coaster. The ride was controlled mechanically, but by leaning forward at the top of the small hills, you could increase your speed and edge out the other horses. It was both thrilling and frightening. My father sat behind me with his arms crossed around my body. I felt safe, but with the added weight I never won.

Crossed arms, however, offered no protection from the fate that awaited you after the ride. The single exit took you through a narrow corridor to the stage of the Insanitarium Theater. If you tried to turn around, you would wander through a maze before returning via another route to the same place. It was like a bad dream.

I am with my family on the stage of the Insanitarium Theater. Hundreds of old men pack the audience. They're all smiling, watching . . . and waiting. . . . Angelo waves us on, pointing to a big exit sign down stage. A large pink wooden elephant is standing next to the exit. We move forward over a grating on the floor. Suddenly a great blast of air pours up through the grating. It whisks my mother's and sister's skirts up around their ears. Angelo takes the compressed air hose and directs it to their panties, trying to whisk them off. He walks over to a fake tree on the stage and pulls a pair of

*panties off a limb, as if it had just blown there. Then he pulls down
a shade from the limb. On the shade is painted a full moon, symbolic of the exposure. The glass eyes of the elephant turn red. The
audience howls and weeps with laughter. My father and I are just
standing there, helpless.*

The scene fast-forwards to a later year.

*Now my mother and sister are wearing slacks. They walk across
the stage, smiling at Angelo. I hear the men in the crowd booing
and hissing.*

The hissing of the nitrous tubes seemed to change in pitch. Dr.
Rose had stopped the flow of gas and put me on pure oxygen for a
few moments in order to sober me up. I had been under the influence for over two hours, and he was ready to close the office.

It was not hard to imagine Joel Morgan's comments because my
trip was so rich with Freudian symbolism. The dwarf clown's hose
was obviously his penis. I had watched the clown humiliate my
mother and sister, and I hated him for that. Feelings of incest only
made it worse. Obviously I wanted to kill the dwarf, maybe my
father, too, for taking us there. I chuckled at such impossible
thoughts. They don't call it laughing gas for nothing.

There really was nothing Freudian about my nitrous oxide trip.
Rather, it was a faithful recall of a childhood experience. Sometimes a compressed air hose is just a hose and a clown is just a
clown. Indeed, I had several photographs of Angelo and me, side
by side. Over the years I got taller, while Angelo seemed to get
smaller. Eventually he shrank to the size of a distant childhood
memory. Still, I had to confess that I shared with Lillian a childhood apprehension of midgets and dwarfs. Why? Were they part of
the same paranoid streak that ran through Tolman's visions of
deformed dwarfs? The questions made me uncomfortable, and I
pushed them aside to return to Miss Lillian's teeth.

The experiment in room five had demonstrated that the noise

around the dental chair could be readily transformed into recognizable sounds. The evolution of hissing into an air hose or a whispering tooth were examples of the types of cognitive associations that occurred under the influence of nitrous oxide. I examined the medical literature for other reports of hissing or whispering noises. In a series of experiments conducted on students at the University College in London, a kettle of water was kept boiling to mask all extraneous sounds from the laboratory. However, the kettle itself influenced the auditory sensations reported by the students. One subject heard the kettle boiling and likened it to an orchestra playing a monotonous tune. Another heard the kettle as rhythmic drumming. Several subjects heard the kettle as the distinctive static of a radio. One even reported he could understand part of a radio program with someone cracking jokes and singing.

If Miss Lillian had misperceived the sounds of the dental chair, as I now believed based on my own experience, then the best way to eliminate the root cause of her whispering teeth was to help her perceive better. If only I could get her back into room five, I might be able to point out the sources of the sounds she heard. This would necessitate amplifying the room sounds to make sure she would hear them. I could do this with microphones and speakers or, better still, outfit her with hearing aids, which I suspected she might need anyway. Of course, I had failed with a similar approach to Tolman's misperceptions. However, my clinical instincts told me that Miss Lillian was not as rigid and inflexible as Tolman. My behavioral approach may not have been to the liking of a physical scientist like Tolman, but I thought it had a chance here. I decided to offer her a hearing aid when the time seemed right.

Meanwhile, however, there was another problem to solve. Miss Lillian had not been exposed to the sounds of the dental chair for over two years, yet she believed that the devices implanted in her teeth continued to listen even if they no longer whispered. What maintained this paranoid thinking when the original stimuli were no longer present? I suspected that her delusions were nourished and supported by stories from the other victims she recruited. Unless I could explain, devalue, or otherwise block such stories, Miss Lillian might never surrender her delusions. It was time to meet Miss Louise and the other victims of the conspiracy.

Miss Louise greeted me at the door to Miss Lillian's house. She was a thin, attractive woman who appeared to be in her middle sixties despite her dyed platinum-blond hair. Miss Lillian might be Whistler's mother, but Miss Louise looked like an Erté poster girl. Her pale skin was exaggerated by expertly applied fire-engine-red lipstick and matching fingernail polish. Pastel rings of eye shadow arced over her blue eyes, which kept blinking from bothersome contacts. She wore a colorful sweater with a checkerboard design and gold pants that matched the scarf draped around her neck. Her high-heeled mules revealed toenails polished with the same color as the lipstick. If Miss Lillian dressed in the drab colors of a zebra finch, Miss Louise resembled a gouldian, a finch known for its rainbow appearance.

She led me to the aviary, where Miss Lillian was tending her flock. Miss Lillian was holding a bird and dabbing its wings with a nicotine solution in order to get rid of mites. This accounted for the yellow stains on her fingers, which I had incorrectly deduced were caused by tobacco.

I offered to help Miss Lillian while Miss Louise went to get some cold drinks from the kitchen. She returned with tall glasses of lemonade and set one in front of me on the table. The glasses resembled Waterford crystal. I started drinking, only to discover that I had been given a trick "dribble glass" that dripped lemonade on me as I tipped it. Miss Louise hee-hawed so loudly that the finches scattered. Even the reserved Miss Lillian couldn't stifle a giggle. I entertained an impish thought to turn a set of wind-up yakking teeth loose on the floor as revenge. But I forced myself to laugh as I wiped my shirt with a napkin. Perhaps the joke had been an initiation rite into their group because now both women relaxed and talked freely.

They had been neighbors and friends for years. While Miss Louise never heard her teeth whisper, she shared Miss Lillian's belief about the conspiracy of dentists. For Miss Louise the paranoia arose from a basic phobia about dentists. While 90 percent of the population has some degree of fear or anxiety about visits to the dental office, only about 8 percent are truly phobic. Some are so emotional that they develop psychosomatic problems and become susceptible to periodontal disease, muscle spasms, and temporomandibular joint dysfunction. Miss Louise had suffered from all of these but attributed the cause to infections from the implanted devices.

"Louise never had those problems until they started putting crowns on her teeth a couple of years ago," explained Miss Lillian. "That's when they implanted her."

"A crowning achievement," Miss Louise quipped. She didn't sound upset at all.

"Can you tell me about the device you have?" I asked.

"She's got one of those new nanocontraptions," answered Miss Lillian.

"Nano nano," whined Miss Louise, imitating the line Robin Williams made famous in the "Mork and Mindy" TV series. She explained *her* device caused a clenching of her teeth and jaws, increased heart rate, and twitches. While this sounded like the typical anxiety or panic that might attack phobic patients, Miss Louise blamed it on the dental implant. She expressed an almost religious hysteria about avoiding the dentist at all costs.

"Have you been back to the dentist since your implant?" I asked.

"No," answered Miss Louise with a deep sigh. I sensed she wanted to go but was afraid. Just then a couple of finches buzzed Miss Louise's hairdo. "Fuckin' finches," she said softly as she swatted at them. Miss Lillian didn't seem to hear her!

"Why not?" I asked. "You said you still have problems."

Miss Lillian interrupted. "They'll put another device in her," she said. "Maybe a whispering one."

"Yes," agreed Miss Louise. "A voice of unknown extraction." Everyone laughed.

"That would really hit a nerve, wouldn't it?" I joked. Miss Louise's sense of humor was infectious, and we all continued to laugh.

When we recovered, Miss Louise explained that she had recently become a Christian Scientist. If she had any dental problems, she simply followed the Christian Science tradition of healing through prayer. "I prefer praying to paying," she quipped. We laughed some more.

Miss Louise was witty and intelligent and seemed open-minded. She could even laugh about her newfound religion. I decided to take advantage of the moment and plant a few ideas for her to think about. I was familiar with Mary Baker Eddy, the founder of Christian Science, because I had made a study of her lifelong morphine habit. My research suggested that Eddy's experiences with morphine played a key role in her religious thinking, and her efforts to keep it a secret probably influenced the development of her progressive paranoia. In her advanced years she began to believe that there were fifty thousand minds concentrating on trying to kill her by thoughts alone. But I was not eager to attack the founding mother of Miss Louise's religion. Rather, I discussed Eddy's relationship to dentists. Despite her claims that she could restore decaying bones to healthy conditions, Eddy sought the services of both dentists and dental surgeons throughout her life. In fact, her second husband was Daniel Patterson, a dentist who specialized in the use of nitrous oxide. According to the descriptions of Patterson, he resembled Dr. Rose in both looks and temperament. Miss Lillian and Miss Louise now seemed very interested. After Mary's divorce from Patterson, I continued, she went to numerous dentists to fill her teeth, extract them, and even make artificial dentures. For many years she kept a dentist on a yearly retainer so that he could attend to her at any time. While she went to great lengths to keep the visits unseen, she never avoided calling on a dentist when necessary.

Miss Louise seemed genuinely surprised by this information. I was hoping she would reconsider her religious opposition to dentists.

"Does Dr. Rose really look like Patterson?" she asked.

"Well, Patterson was tall, dark, and very handsome," I said. "What do you think, Miss Lillian?"

"I have to say that Dr. Rose is certainly handsome."

"Is he single?" asked Miss Louise.

"Louise!" Miss Lillian snapped.

"He's a very good dentist," I added. "Like Patterson, Rose is kind and caring. I don't think he would ever hurt a patient or implant a device in anyone." I looked directly at Miss Lillian. "And he only tried to help you by being honest with you. I'm certain he's not part of any conspiracy."

"Tsick tsick tsick tsreek," sang Miss Lillian. I noticed that whenever she became uncomfortable, she called to her birds.

I quickly turned the conversation back to the group of victims the women had organized. Were there really 777 members? Miss Louise hee-hawed again, then borrowed a piece of my note paper, wrote something, and passed it back to me. The number 777 was written on the note.

"Seven hundred seventy-seven," I read aloud.

"Turn it upside down," said Miss Louise. Both women were giggling.

"I don't get it," I said.

"L-L-L," explained Miss Louise. "Stands for Lillian, Louise, and Leroy . . . it's our little secret code."

"Leroy writes us from San Quentin," Miss Lillian said.

"Our token jailbird," added Miss Louise.

"Black jailbird, dear."

"We don't know, Lillian. We've never seen him."

"Well, dear. I think he's black."

"Wait, wait!" I shouted. "You mean to tell me there are only three of you?"

"We send information to many people, but Leroy is the only one who writes us back," said Miss Lillian.

Miss Louise produced two shoeboxes full of Leroy's letters. She also gave me a mailing list that included medical licensing boards, medical schools, government officials, and consumer advocates. The women had sent everyone a letter describing their experiences and asking for help investigating dentists. One of the organizations had responded with a thank-you note and enclosed a copy of a similar letter it had received from Leroy. Lillian and Louise had started corresponding with Leroy. The shoeboxes had begun to fill.

The women enjoyed corresponding with their jailhouse pen pal. They found his letters full of fascinating tidbits about prison life. I knew that prison was a breeding ground for paranoia. Because of the high incidence of criminal abuse and homosexual attack inside prisons, it's difficult to tell if the thoughts (and letters) of prisoners are based on reality or delusions. Leroy claimed to be an expert in the types of listening devices and transmitters used by dentists because he had been a victim for over twenty-five years. He provided almost all the information they had about the government conspiracy to implant and control people. They invited me to read the letters.

But it was late, and I could tell that everyone was tired. The women really didn't want me to leave. They wanted me to come back to visit and, as if to bribe me, insisted I read Leroy's last letter. There was really no need to bribe me. I was not going to abandon them. I was really tired. Reluctantly I took the letter and started reading.

Leroy had exciting news. He had just heard about Bob, a car mechanic in Colorado Springs, who was another victim of dental implants. The mechanic discovered that local dentists were implanting the devices in young children so that they could be controlled later in life. Bob decided to act. Posing as "Dr. Bob," the mechanic grabbed young boys in movie theaters, molested them, then pulled their teeth out! The letter contained graphic descriptions of both the molestations and the teeth pulling. Leroy had enclosed a newspaper clipping describing the bizarre case.

"Good stuff," said Miss Louise when I finished reading. She and Miss Lillian were watching me for my reaction. They obviously derived great entertainment from the letters.

"Yes," I said. "What's Leroy doing time for?"

"He's queer. Our little tooth fairy," said Miss Louise with a laugh.

"We don't know *that,* dear," said Miss Lillian. She gave a little "tshuree tshuree tshuree" call to the birds.

"But being gay is not a crime. What exactly did he do?" I asked.

"Tried to murder a dentist," said Miss Louise.

This was one tooth fairy I didn't want to find near my pillow.

I returned a few days later to read Leroy's letters. Leroy said that he had been implanted with an electronic device by a dentist while he was serving time in a California Youth Authority camp for "a crime I didn't do." When the device was activated, his tooth started to ache. The toothache jumped from one tooth to another, leapfrogging around his mouth. Then the pain radiated into his throat, where it became a tickle; into his ears, where it turned into a buzz; and around his eyes, where it became an excruciating headache. The attacks lasted only a few minutes, but his eyebrows would continue to itch for hours afterward. Sometimes a few hairs fell out.

Leroy blamed the CIA for orchestrating these implants in a campaign to control the population. Naturally they would experiment first on prisoners. They also recruited dentists in the community who had military backgrounds. After his release from the youth camp, Leroy broke into several dental offices, looking for evidence. He claimed that he had discovered definitive proof and even saw the devices wrapped in official government packages. A dentist surprised him one night, and Leroy had to fight for his life. The only reason he was now in prison was that they were afraid he would spread the truth about this conspiracy against the American people. He'd scrawled "Spread the News" across the bottom of every letter.

The women accepted Leroy's story, but I was skeptical. I decided to check on his criminal record with my friends in law enforcement. After getting a copy of Leroy's rap sheet of prior offenses, I contacted the district attorney and public defender who had worked on his last case. They provided me with copies of the police reports and trial transcripts. I also managed to get a copy of his medical records from prison and telephoned one of the prison doctors who had seen him. When I had all the information together, I paid another visit to Miss Lillian and Miss Louise.

I told the women what I had learned about Leroy. He had spent twenty-two of his forty-nine years behind bars for a variety of offenses ranging from auto theft to attempted murder. In recent years he specialized in burglarizing dental offices, not for devices, but for drugs. He was a cocaine addict and stole cocaine and narcotics, as well as computers, typewriters, and other office equipment, which he sold to support his habit. While I could imagine Leroy arguing that the drug thefts were only a cover-up to hide his true mission of finding evidence of the conspiracy, there was no mention of missing files or dental equipment. During one late-night burglary, he was surprised by the dentist. There was a struggle, and Leroy stabbed the dentist in the eye with a knife. At the scene the police found the knife, covered with Leroy's fingerprints, and arrested him a few days later. The dentist ended up losing the eye.

"Tsee tsee tshurrt," Miss Lillian sang nervously. Several canaries and finches twittered. Miss Louise squirmed on her chair. I sensed they were developing discomfort, if not dislike, for their prison pen pal. I decided to capitalize on this and sacrifice Leroy's reputation if I must in order to rescue them from his influence.

"You were right, Miss Louise," I continued, "Leroy's gay. But he had a series of arrests for assault and molestation of young boys. It wasn't just 'one crime,' like he said. There were over a dozen cases. And the evidence against him was overwhelming."

"He's still implanted, dear," protested Miss Lillian.

Perhaps. I reviewed his prison medical records. When Leroy developed an abscess in a tooth, the X-rays showed a small sliver embedded in his gum. The prison dentist removed both the tooth and the sliver. The sliver turned out to be the end of a lead pencil that had been deliberately jammed under the tooth. Leroy claimed it was a miniature electronic device that only resembled a pencil lead. The dentist suspected Leroy put it there himself to bolster his conspiratorial claims and referred him to the prison psychiatrist.

I told the women about my telephone consultation with the psychiatrist. I knew that they were afraid of mental patients. Mental illness was scary to them because they didn't understand it. A mentally disturbed patient was more unpredictable, hence more frightening, than someone who attempted to murder in the name of stopping a conspiracy. The psychiatrist made a preliminary diagnosis. The women looked at me expectantly.

"Now, ladies, I've got to use some bad words here." I paused to heighten the drama. "Leroy is a dangerous *psychotic* and *sociopath*. He threatened to attack the psychiatrist and his family."

Miss Lillian shook her head in disbelief. "He wrote us that all the prison doctors were part of the conspiracy," she said.

I explained to Miss Lillian that Leroy had a pathological tendency to twist the truth. I had checked with the authorities in Colorado Springs. The infamous "Dr. Bob" had pulled his victims' teeth, but he never mentioned dental devices or conspiracies. Leroy twisted the facts around the same way he twisted that pencil into his tooth. He was manufacturing both the conspiracy and the evidence.

"Dentalgate," ejaculated Miss Louise.

"Dentalgate," I agreed.

Miss Lillian muttered a "see see see" call.

It was enough for one day. I would let the women digest what I had said. I hoped I had weakened Leroy's hold enough so that the women might allow me to help them deal with their own dental complaints without the burden of fighting Leroy and his conspiracy.

Miss Louise walked me to the door. "I'll talk to her, Doctor Ron," she said with a wink. Then she kissed me on the cheek.

Over the next few weeks I had several private meetings with Miss Louise. She had been "working" on Miss Lillian and finally told her that she would no longer correspond with Leroy. If Lillian wanted to write to him, fine, but she wanted no part of it. Louise confirmed my suspicion that Miss Lillian was losing her hearing, and together we convinced her to get a hearing test, which I arranged at UCLA. Two weeks later Miss Lillian was wearing the bilateral hearing aids I had purchased for her. There was an immediate improvement in her mood and spirit. She had never called me before, but now she telephoned me several times a week to tell me about all the new birdcalls she was hearing. It was time to find out if she could still hear the whispering teeth. After much persuasion, Miss Louise and I escorted Miss Lillian into Dr. Rose's office for a long overdue check-up.

Dr. Rose was wonderful with Miss Lillian. He and Suzie welcomed her back with half a dozen long-stemmed roses, which I had supplied. Then he held her hand and took her into room five while Miss Louise sat in the waiting room, marveling at how handsome and unmarried he was. As Rose examined Miss Lillian's teeth, I stood to the side of the room. He found only one cavity and complimented Miss Lillian on the expert way in which she had applied the temporary filling that was now washing away. Rose suggested that he simply patch it properly with a composite resin, which he guaranteed was free of electronics. To our collective relief, Miss Lillian agreed. In a few minutes she was breathing nitrous oxide and sucking playfully on the aspirator in her mouth. In a few more minutes the tooth was repaired. Miss Lillian stood up to leave.

"Did you hear anything, Miss Lillian?" I asked as Rose and I walked her down the hall. I was so anxious, I must have been yelling in her ear.

"Don't shout," she said with a wince. "I can hear a whisper, and I didn't."

Rose said good-bye at the door and gave a single rose to Miss Louise, who batted her gouldian eyes excitedly. As I drove the women home, it became apparent from their conversation that Dr. Rose now had *two* new patients.

A few weeks later I visited Miss Lillian. As I approached the house, I noticed that the outdoor bird feeders had been dismantled. It took a few moments for Miss Lillian to unlock the new dead bolt and chain on her front door. We went to the aviary. Many of the finches were inside cages. Miss Lillian was frantic.

"What's wrong?" I asked, feeling very protective of my new friend.

Miss Lillian explained that she had written Leroy and told him what I had said about him. She didn't want him to write anymore. It was a good-bye letter. She handed me his reply. I read it. The letter was filled with a tirade of four-letter words. He said he was coming down to Los Angeles soon and would get even. He was going to bring a bunch of butcher birds over to her house.

"What's a butcher bird?" I asked.

Miss Lillian could not compose herself enough to tell me. Instead she handed me an encyclopedia with a page already marked. Butcher birds, I read, were large gray birds the size of crows but with ugly hooked beaks. They not only looked like witches' birds, they behaved like them as well. Butcher birds were cantankerous meat eaters. They killed small birds and impaled them on twigs in order to eat them later.

"Holy shit!" I said under my breath after reading the entry. I was certain that Miss Lillian heard me. The good news was that she no longer believed anyone else was listening. The bad news was that Leroy and his butcher birds were coming to town.

I told Miss Lillian that I would check on Leroy's release from prison and alert the proper authorities to a potential threat. If necessary, I would request protection for her. I promised to call her as soon as I had any information.

A frantic call to the district attorney told me that Leroy had been transported to Los Angeles County Jail in order to testify as a witness in a murder trial. He would be there for about a week, then return to San Quentin. I decided to pay Leroy a visit at the jail. Since I knew Leroy would refuse the visit if he knew I was connected with psychiatry, I put down on the request form that I was a member of Lillian Rush's group.

Leroy came into the glass interview room at the jail but refused to sit down. I was glad the guards were watching. He seemed ready to walk out any second if the vibes weren't right. I asked him simply to listen to me. I told him he was scaring Miss Lillian. She was old and frail. It wasn't a kind thing to do. I cared about her and wanted to know that she was safe.

"What you mean, old?" he asked.

"Well, she's eighty-three. And Louise, who wrote you many of the letters, is turning seventy soon."

Leroy didn't know. He thought they were much younger.

"Tell those dyke bitches I don't want nothing to do with them. If they get money from the lawsuit, I want what's coming to me."

He started to leave. But I still didn't know if he was a con man or a true believer. I quickly threw out a question about dental devices. Lots of us have them, I lied. Did his still bother him? Leroy said that when he had his tooth extracted in prison, they'd removed the device. But while he was asleep in the chair, they'd implanted another device in his frontal sinus. This one made a clicking sound.

"It's a radio system that communicates with a satellite," he said.

"Holy shit."

"Shit happens," he snarled as he turned and walked back to his cage.

5

SHADOW DANCING

1

"We're now on the edge of the black forest," exclaimed Joel Morgan.

Joel and I were driving to a restaurant near a dangerous section of Los Angeles where black gangs shoot it out with each other on a nightly basis. This was the same neighborhood where Leroy grew up, a world where feelings of family came from fellow gang members. It was an unlikely setting for a good Italian restaurant, but Joel said they had the best homemade tortoni in town. And I grew up with tortoni the way Leroy grew up with crack. It was my favorite treat. I always ordered it whenever my father took our family to the local Italian restaurant in our small town. It had been years since I'd tasted it. I told Joel I'd die for a good tortoni.

As we approached the restaurant, a dark figure jumped in front of the car and flagged us down with a flashlight. He said he would park the car for us. He wasn't wearing a valet uniform. Joel hesitated just long enough for the legitimate valet to appear and chase away the would-be carjacker. I was shaking a little. Joel treated the incident with the same detached calm he employed when listening to patients confess the gruesome details of their darkest nightmares. I was still nervous as we opened the door to the restaurant.

The muted strains of Vivaldi's "The Four Seasons" calmed me as soon as I entered the restaurant. I could never explain my response to this piece, which Vivaldi composed to accompany a series of explanatory sonnets. It wasn't rational. Perhaps it had something to do with the theme of Nature imposing her will over man. The music went straight to my heart, quieting its beat and erasing any anxiety left over from the encounter with the carjacker. The soft lighting from candles on the tables helped my mood. Too bad I had to waste such a lovely setting on Joel, but I could almost hear the tortoni calling my name. Besides, I wanted to brag about my success with Miss Lillian. Although I hadn't needed to use psychoanalysis to help her, I was eager to learn any verbal tricks of Joel's trade that would assist me in future encounters with more dangerous paranoids like Leroy.

We were both at a loss for words when the hostess greeted us. She stunned us with her sensual beauty. Hers was the face of youth, with clear pale skin, delicate cheekbones, and full lips. She wore her thick black hair up in the back with tiny wisps falling seductively on her forehead and cheeks. A pair of white ballet slippers were barely visible beneath her elegant long white slip dress. She seemed to glide on a cushion of air as she led us through the crowded restaurant; she reminded me of Cinderella entering the ball, not in the fairy tale, but in the Prokofiev ballet, where her radiance dazzled the entire assembly. Here and there in the restaurant heads turned, both male and female, as she wove the way to our table. She pointed to our chairs with a dancer's exaggerated turn of an outstretched hand. I kept staring at her dark eyes. They were like wishing wells. How many men must have fallen into those eyes? Who would have dreamed that this beauty was the one who was drowning?

"Lei è molto bella," said Joel to her back as she was gliding away. He was not only saying she was very beautiful, but showing off the perfect accent he'd acquired during several years of study in Rome. "What a knockout," he said to me. I agreed. We watched her for several minutes as she guided other guests to their tables. No one failed to notice her as she moved by their table. I could imagine the women chattering like jealous stepsisters about this mysterious beauty who was commanding everyone's attention.

"I'd like to get her on my couch," Joel said unabashedly.

"As therapy for you or for her?" I teased. But, God, my own fantasies were running wild.

"For me, of course," he admitted, never taking his eyes off her.

"There are already too many psychiatrists screwing their patients, Joel," I said.

"But I haven't done my share yet. Remember, the dick is more powerful than the brain."

"Spoken like a true Freudian."

The waiter brought a giant bottle of chianti, and Joel finally turned away from the hostess. *"Alla salute!"* he said, and raised his glass.

"Salute!"

Joel downed two glasses in rapid succession. I sipped mine, and we both nibbled on wonderful crusty bread, dipping it in a tiny saucer of olive oil and herbs. At Joel's request I turned off the tape recorder that I had placed earlier on the table. I knew him well enough to know what was coming. He immediately launched into a discourse on his fantasies about the hostess, inventing anatomical positions that even Leonardo da Vinci would have found impossible to draw. I glanced at her. She was studying the reservation list at her podium near the front entrance. The light on the podium bathed her face in mysterious shadows. She was truly lovely.

By the time the salads were served, Joel was finishing his third glass of wine. His fantasies had moved from the couch to the gutter, and I was getting tired of listening to them. I turned on the tape recorder, knowing that it would elevate the conversation to a more tax-deductible level.

I told Joel about a recent dream. In the dream, my nose and sinuses felt totally clogged. It was worse than my worst cold. I couldn't breathe. Something hard and solid was blocking my passages. I stood up and shook my head back and forth, then up and down. The plug started moving. I bent forward over a table. A large globe, about the size of a golf ball, fell from my nose. It was pulsating with a greenish glow. I woke up.

"Do you really want me to analyze that?" asked Joel. He was smiling.

"Well, if a patient told you such a dream, what would you say?"

"Would you call it a nightmare?" he asked.

"Yes," I muttered as I stuffed my mouth with my not-so-warm spinach salad with goat cheese. The dream was frightening. When I woke up I was sweating, and I had a hard time getting back to sleep.

"Then I would consider the possibility that your nightmare was a projection of an unconscious fear. You felt weak, helpless, totally vulnerable to attack by this alien booger."

"It wasn't a booger ... more like a ball," I corrected him. I pushed the goat cheese to the side of my plate and continued eating the spinach.

"Booger, ball, whatever," he continued. "It symbolizes some unconscious terror. It might be related to an early childhood trauma, perhaps something that happened to you when you were sick."

"Why couldn't my dreaming brain be elaborating on something more immediate, such as a real stuffy nose?" I asked, then went on to answer the question. I believed this was the case because I had to blow my nose when I woke up. But I also recognized the general structure of the dream triggered by the stuffy nose. It came from my recent meeting with Leroy, who had told me about such a device that had been implanted in his frontal sinus. Years later I would be uncannily reminded of this when I saw the science fiction movie *Total Recall*. In the film, Arnold Schwarzenegger plays a secret agent who has been implanted with a homing device in his frontal sinus. He inserts a special tool in his nose and pulls out a large glowing ball, just like the one in my dream.

Joel accepted my explanation but insisted that without such clear-cut determinants, nightmares such as mine are a sign of paranoia. "The feelings of persecution in a nightmare," he said, "are identical to feelings of persecution in acute paranoid states. The delusions are the same."

"I like the notion that paranoia is like a waking nightmare," I said.

"Like your first marriage," said Joel.

I laughed, but Joel was right. My wife admitted cheating on me once, and after that I was always paranoid about her activities. It became a nightmare for both of us, ending in divorce. I told Joel my theory that a paranoid state resulted from a separation of the rational from the emotional brain. A paranoid's feelings are so persistent, so intense, so vivid, they make the thoughts, however deluded, seem real. Just as our normal affective feelings assure us of the reality of ourselves and the environment around us, the feelings of the paranoid assure them of their reality. When such strong feelings are unbridled by the rational brain, the inner paranoid world becomes as believable as the real external world. Like a child who believes in monsters under the bed because he keeps seeing them in vivid night terrors, the paranoid inhabits a nightmarish world where the persistent vividness of feelings substitutes for truthfulness.

"It's not always scary," said Joel as the waiter brought our main courses. He refilled Joel's glass, but I held my hand over mine, a move that insured at least one of us would be able to drive home. I started on my angel-hair pasta while Joel reminded me that sometimes the delusions are of lovers, not monsters. He recounted a textbook case of paranoid eroticism, also known as erotomania, a state of pathological preoccupation with erotic fantasies or activities. In this case, a woman went to several performances of a famous opera singer. Since she was a sensitive woman—actually a writer—she *knew* the singer was really in love with her. He signaled this in a thousand subtle ways that only she could perceive. She wrote him a series of letters accepting his love and admitting her own. Then she started stalking his performances, hoping to see him alone. Finally she broke into his dressing room. He treated her like just another opera groupie and asked if she wanted to fuck. She panicked, accused him of being a beast, and ran away crying.

"Probably a very lonely woman," I said.

"Lonely and homely," said Joel. "Not at all like our *molto bella* hostess." He started to look around for her.

"Joel, you'll never get her to sing opera on your couch with pieces of linguini in your beard." He couldn't find the specks, and I reached over and helped him.

The waiter cleared the table and came back to take our dessert order. I couldn't believe it. The restaurant didn't have tortoni tonight. I sulked with my coffee while Joel gobbled up a cannoli. I didn't tell him about his beard this time.

On the way out I stared at the hostess again. She smiled, but her eyes seemed glazed over. It was as if she were far away, in another world. Months later I learned that she never noticed the man with the cannoli beard who spoke to her in perfect Italian and handed her a business card that night. She was preoccupied with her own erotic fantasies, not Joel's. Like a character caught in the descending octaves of the winter movement from Vivaldi's concerto, which was playing again, she was descending into a dreadful storm. It would leave her frozen in a waking nightmare. Her name was Victoria Torto. It was perfect. In Italian, *torto* can mean either gloomy or twisted or wrong. And Vicki, as I would learn when I finally talked with her many months later in jail, was an all-Italian girl.

2

Vicki was a happy child growing up in Riverside, California. Her parents, Frank and Maggie, ran a small hardware store that gave them a comfortable life and a weekend cabin in the San Bernardino Mountains near Lake Arrowhead. It was there that Vicki discovered the seasons. The hot, smoggy air around the city always obscured them. But a mile above the freeways and orange fields of Riverside, Vicki saw a new world, the promised land of her storybooks. There were tall trees, thick woods, little cabins, even a bear or two. In the spring she would hand-feed the squirrels, watch birds build their nests, and skip through the wildflowers. Summer nights were a time to listen to the crickets and wonder at the stars. In the fall, when the leaves started turning, Vicki collected a bag full of the prettiest ones and brought them home. She asked her mother, who was a skilled dressmaker, to make a Halloween costume. Before the costume was completed, the entire family developed a painful allergic dermatitis. Some of those pretty leaves were poison ivy. But rather than get angry, her mother collected another batch of leaves and made Vicki a terrific costume. And in the winter Vicki built a whole family of "snowpeople" with faces as happy as those of her own family.

When Vicki was eight she started ballet classes. At ten she was taking pointe class and by twelve was accomplished enough to help the teacher demonstrate steps for the younger pupils. She seemed to have a natural, almost uncanny ability for ballet, bending her tiny body into the torturous positions with ease. Her turns from a "turned-out" position were exceptionally advanced for her age and physical development. (In this position the legs and feet are turned out and close together. One foot is crossed exactly in front of the other and parallel to it. The toes of one are next to the heel of the other. The dancer now springs up in the air, feet crossed, and executes one or two complete turns, coming down into any number of poses. The turn itself is really a spiral, a circular movement involving the torso, arms, and legs.) Vicki turned out like the pro she would become, demonstrating both grace and strength. At the same time, she was turning inward to a mental ballet of fantasy and romance.

At an age when her high school friends were gossiping about boys, Vicki was imagining herself dancing in the world's greatest romantic ballets. She was the seductive creature in Stravinsky's *The Firebird* who mesmerizes everyone with spellbinding leaps, hops, and spins. She was Odette dancing tenderly with Siegfried in *Swan Lake,* surrendering herself to his love. She was Juliet dancing a rapturous pas de deux with Romeo.

Vicki shared these dreams with her parents, who supported her decision to pursue a professional career, but only with the promise that she would finish high school along the way. She did both and joined the corps of a small professional company. It was a constant financial struggle, but her parents gave her enough money to keep her in shoes and her own apartment. Mr. Torto joked that the least Vicki could do to repay the debt was dance in public with the sweatshirt her mother had made. The embroidered script on the back read "Frank's Hardware." Vicki wore it proudly in class.

Endless hours of barre exercises in front of the mirror gave her a mastery of all the basic moves. She studied videotapes of other dancers, dissecting their steps frame by frame, then duplicating them in rehearsal after rehearsal. Vicki could copy the steps and movements of any role, but they remained mechanical. That made her a perfect choice for the part of the life-size mechanical doll who comes to life in *Coppelia,* but the role was denied to her. Vicki thought the girl who got the part was a slut.

Vicki's technical brilliance was never questioned. In the words of her critics, she lacked a certain emotional maturity to play the romantic roles of her dreams. She had trouble expressing herself. Ballet dancers don't actually need to speak or write very well, and Vicki was certainly poorly educated in this respect. But dancers employ a range of voice and lines of expression to their dance by being good actors. And like all good actors, they must draw on a reservoir of inner emotions and memories. Sure, she could dance the empty, childish pantomimes of *The Nutcracker* or any number of minor roles in other ballets. But her attempts at the big romantic leads lacked something her director called "believability." Vicki didn't believe her own performances, either. She had never had a romantic love.

Her social life had been severely restricted by her dedication to ballet. When she wasn't taking class or rehearsing, Vicki filled her time watching other dancers, visiting exercise therapists and gyms to help with the constant physical pains, and even studying mime as a complement to her dance. Dates were rare. She was so beautiful that most men assumed she was unattainable and didn't even approach her. The only ones who did were fellow dancers, and most of them were gay. In her twenty-eight years, Vicki had had only two sexual partners.

Part of the problem may have been the mirror. Vicki spent inordinate amounts of time in the front of mirrors. She'd even had a barre and mirror installed in the giant living room of her apartment, courtesy of Frank's Hardware. A little rosin on the hardwood floor turned the room into a workable studio. In class she stared at the mirror and concentrated on her positions. In the apartment, without the restraints of formal classes, she could concentrate on her fantasies.

She usually began by standing before the mirror in the nude and admiring her body. Her small breasts, delicate hands, and shapely legs were perfectly suited to her profession. She shaved her pubic hairs to give her an extra-clean line that helped balance her muscular thighs. Vicki was sensual yet bony in all the right places for a ballerina. She kept it that way with a diet of Coca-Cola, popcorn, and apples. After weighing herself—something she did several times a day—Vicki selected an exercise costume from the vast collection made by her mother. Many of the costumes were modeled after those worn by the prima ballerinas in the romantic ballets. After dressing, Vicki took a few moments to admire her selection. It wasn't so much that the costume was perfect for the part, it was that Vicki managed to convince herself she was the perfect choice to wear it. It was an attitude full of grandiosity and narcissism that she sometimes projected to others outside the apartment. It was another reason she didn't get asked out too often. Like Narcissus, who rejected all lovers and finally fell in love with his own image in a mountain pool, Vicki was destined to fall in love with the fantasies she saw in the mirror.

With the flip of a switch on the tape recorder, Vicki would fling herself onto the hardwood floor. No matter what dance she was practicing, it always turned into a melancholy solo. It wasn't true that there was no expression in her dancing. There was very definite expression. It was always the same, a yearning for romantic love. She was like a wistful theme, alone in the apartment, searching for accompaniment. Her fantasy dancing excited her to the point that many times she would end the session with frenzied masturbation in front of the mirror. A little saliva to moisten her fingers was all she needed. Vicki always prided herself on great hand movements. She studied her face after orgasm. Men always seemed to have a moronic expression when they came. Vicki was flushed and radiant. Dancing was good for the complexion. Then she would fall asleep, utterly exhausted and alone.

While Vicki felt neither guilt nor shame about her "dancing" at home, she was becoming embarrassed by continually having to ask her parents for money. Corps dancers were paid poorly, and Vicki still needed financial help. So she got a hostess job in a restaurant during the ballet off season. She worked four nights a week, ate in the kitchen anytime she wanted, and tripled her income.

Several weeks after Vicki started working in the restaurant, a new waiter was hired. She noticed him right away. His smile was dazzling, his teeth perfect. He reminded her of a young Mikhail Baryshnikov, only with darker hair and more muscular. He must work out, she thought. Physical fitness was important to Vicki. He came over to where she was standing. She took a tiny step backward. It was a habit she always had when meeting men. She didn't even know she did it. But the men could tell, especially if they moved a bit closer. Then Vicki would take another tiny step back. It wasn't even a graceful step but executed more like a stutter. The movement established a space, a gulf that could not be crossed.

The new waiter reached over and grabbed her hand with both of his.

"Io sono Michael. Capisce?" ("I'm Michael. Do you understand?")

"Mi chiamo Victoria," replied Vicki. His grip was preventing her from stepping back again.

"Piacere." ("Delighted.") He squeezed her hand, smiled again, then turned and went to his station.

Vicki was stunned. No one ever touched her like that before.

Vicki watched Michael at a distance for several nights after that first encounter. A passing glance or a flash of his luminous eyes told her that he was watching her, too. Sometimes he smiled at her, a big white, happy smile. Like a snowman, thought Vicki. The smile was just for her. He was trying to tell her something. The smile was melting her heart.

She began dissecting his movements in the same way she went about analyzing another dancer's steps. Nothing he did escaped her notice. From the way he set the table to the little bow he gave customers after the meal, the camera of her mind's eye recorded everything. She made it a point to walk past his tables as often as possible. He set the tables with fastidious attention to detail. The handles of all the silverware were always lined up exactly one inch from the edge of the table. The knives and forks were as evenly spaced and parallel as if they were bar lines on a musical staff. The butter plate, always on the left, was at a precise level with the water glass on the right. Michael always placed the butter knife horizontally across the butter plate. She thought he showed good sense to move the flowers in the center vase slightly to one side. There was nothing more distracting than dodging a floral centerpiece while trying to establish an intimate relationship.

Once, while she was leaning over and scrutinizing one of his tables, Michael approached.

"Is everything okay?" he asked, then looked at the table for an answer. He moved the silverware a bit, straightened the starched white tablecloth, then rushed to another table. Vicki looked down at one of the settings. The salad fork and dinner fork were tilted toward each other, the tines almost touching.

"Oh, my," she said under her breath, then quickly straightened the mess.

The next night a knife on one of Michael's tables was tilted ever so slightly, pointing directly to her podium. Vicki knew that Michael had done this deliberately. It was his little way of saying "hello." She caught his eye later in the evening, and they smiled at each other. Michael probably found it as difficult as she did to talk in the hustle and bustle of the restaurant.

There were other signs that started to appear in the following weeks: a spoon too close to the edge of the table, a tilted fork, a misplaced butter knife. Vicki was enjoying this secret game Michael was playing with her. She especially enjoyed the fact that he always moved the flowers from the center of the table to the side closest to her podium. He was such a darling.

One night Michael came up behind her while she was leaning over the podium and working on the reservation list. She turned around quickly, took a step back, and nearly stumbled over the podium. He caught her and then apologized immediately. He had a present for her and pressed it into her hand. It was a beautiful silver Cartier cigarette lighter. Someone had left it on one of his tables and hadn't claimed it for two weeks. Since she was the only one he knew in the restaurant who smoked, he wanted her to have it.

"È favoloso," Vicki said. ("It's great.") *"Mille grazie."* She gave a little curtsy. Michael bowed and went back to work.

Vicki skipped home like a schoolgirl in love, clutching the lighter in her hand. When she got back to the apartment she lay down on her bed—actually a queen-size mattress on the floor—and lit a cigarette. She was excited as the menthol smoke filled her lungs. It reminded her of her first cigarette. She and a girlfriend were spending the weekend at the Torto cabin. Vicki stole a pack of cigarettes from her parents, and the two girls ran outside to a field of high grass behind the cabin. Lying on their backs, surrounded by the grass and smells from the nearby woods, they puffed on several cigarettes. Vicki inhaled and felt the menthol smoke blow like a fresh wind through her body. She was sexually aroused for the first time in her life. The girls giggled and told each other how great it was. And it was.

Now, smoking on her bed, Vicki closed her eyes and was sexually excited again. This time images of Michael filled her vision. She leaned back, slipped off her panties, and began to masturbate. *I love the way you come, Vicki. I love the way you make me come, Michael.*

Vicki had the following night off but decided to grab a free dinner in the restaurant kitchen. She dressed carefully for the occasion. First she put on a pair of crotchless panties—just in case. Next came the strapless bra with push-up underwire cups to make her small breasts stand out. Then she slipped on the Giselle costume, a peasant dress with a sweeping skirt and low-cut fitted bodice.

The head chef fixed her a plate of pasta and a small salad. He knew she would eat anything as long as it didn't contain garlic (dancers didn't like the smell that saturated their sweat afterward). Vicki sat down at a table in the kitchen, purposely positioning herself with a view of the swinging doors used by the waiters. The first time Michael came in he didn't even see her until she called to him. She was the model of flirtation, with a seductive glance over her shoulder and a coquettish smile. Michael flashed his snowman smile, yelled at one of the assistant chefs, and ran out with some hot plates. Vicki picked at her food and waited. Michael came back several more times that night. They exchanged some shop talk and smiled a lot. Before Vicki left for the evening, she went over to the stack of plates Michael had just cleared from a table. The jumble of knives and forks spoke to her in a silent language. The silverware said that he loved her.

When she got home that night she did a little stretching at the barre without changing her clothes. Her thoughts were of Michael. For weeks Vicki had been caught in the country dance of Vivaldi's spring movement. Round and round she danced with a shadow from her fantasies. The lone violin heard earlier in the movement was now joined by another on ascending scales of ecstasy. The words of the silverware were still ringing in her ears: *Ti amo. Ti amo.* Vicki's body rose on full pointe and turned slowly, her eyes searching the room. Gracefully, like a flower opening, her arms started to beckon to the elusive dream, her fingers groping. Then came a series of rapid fouettés, in which she rose on one foot and whipped the other, extended leg around for each turn. *To wrap around you, my darling.* Finally a jeté across the living room and into the bedroom. Orgasm shattered the dream, tearing it from her wet fingers.

As the following days and weeks passed, Vicki got better at deciphering Michael's secret communications. Her natural instincts to step back from men meant that she could not be the aggressive one in the relationship. She would have to wait for him. He was not quite ready. The spoon said so. One night it was concave side up on the table.

Several people at the restaurant thought she was gaining weight. No, Vicki said honestly. She was still weighing herself several times a day and had not put on an ounce despite her access to the free gourmet meals. As a technically trained dancer, Vicki had learned to create the illusion of weight by changing the placement and dynamics of her movements. Unconsciously she was now creating the appearance of added pounds. She was unaware of this new dynamic that was governing her body. The dynamic was depression, and she clothed it with fuller, less flattering outfits.

The new ballet season was approaching, and Vicki increased her workouts. This year she would be touring in Europe for several months. She didn't know how Michael would react. It was certainly going to put pressure on their relationship. Practice finally forced her to cut back to just two nights a week at the restaurant. She was reluctant to let go of those nights. It would hurt Michael too much.

Vicki went through the motions of dancing and hostessing in a style that was more mechanical and detached than ever. Her movements were slow and deliberate, as if she were caught in the languor of Vivaldi's summer movement. Rehearsals seemed more tiring and her need for sleep greater. Even masturbation seemed harder and less satisfying.

One day Vicki and the company were rehearsing a scene from the Oriental ballet *La Bayadère*. The scene, known as the "Kingdom of the Shades," takes place inside an opium dream. Vicki was dancing in the corps as one of the Shades, the beautiful but emotionless hallucinatory figures who appear in the dream. Her hypnotic pacing was appropriate to the role, but she kept stumbling over the simple positions and steps. The director yelled at her over and over again. During a break, one of her friends in the corps gave her a couple of hits from a small vial of cocaine. It was Vicki's first time. She resumed the rehearsal with newfound energy, effortlessly performing simple steps as well as the difficult *arabesques penchées*. In this movement the dancer balances on one leg with the other leg raised and extended behind. Then, leaning forward, the dancer raises the extended leg high while lowering the head and forward arm. Vicki was brilliant in her execution of the countless repetitions of sustained *arabesques penchées* called for in the scene.

Cocaine became a staple in Vicki's ballet diet. The drug not only energized her, it seemed to go straight to her genital area, exciting her already hyperexcitable sexual appetite. Masturbation became violent to the point that several times she cut herself with a sharp fingernail. Her gynecologist prescribed an antibiotic ointment and recommended a vaginal lubricant. Vicki ignored his advice to refrain from further stimulation for a while. She discovered that the pain of her fiery masturbations could be soothed by first mixing a little cocaine in the lubricant.

Her increased energy was noticeable at the restaurant. She started to radiate a more confident spirit, and customers began tipping her more or even, as in Joel Morgan's case, slipping her their business cards. She ignored these overtures, focusing with increased acuity on the hidden signals from Michael. One night she watched as Michael sorted some silverware from a supply drawer in the kitchen. After he took what he needed and left, she ran over and looked in the drawer. The seemingly random pile of dessert forks actually spelled out her initials! Vicki's heart skipped a beat. She stepped into the alley behind the kitchen and snorted enough cocaine to freeze over the gulf she created by her backward steps. After cornering Michael, she coaxed him into the alley and offered him some cocaine. He sniffed it like a pro, flashed a smile, and went back to work. Later that night Michael gave Vicki a rose from one of the floral arrangements. He came up close behind her. She turned without stepping back, accepted his gift, then lowered her head and gave a lingering curtsy. When she looked up, he was already back at the tables. He's not ready yet, she thought.

A few weeks later Vicki found two spoons from the restaurant in the bottom of her ballet bag. They were nested together. The spoons told her Michael wanted to make love. *Oh, yes, my darling, yes.* That night Vicki improvised a little dance back at the apartment. She selected a tape of a fandango, a lively Spanish dance performed in triple time. Using the spoons as castanets, she began stamping her feet, clapping the spoons, jumping and turning in

place. Out of the corner of her eye she saw Michael's shadow dart
behind the French doors leading to the garden. His luminous eyes
shone like those of a beast caught in the glare of headlights. She
swung open the doors and let the gentle wind carry the dream to
her. Her dancing was more sensuous now, hips and thighs moving
rhythmically to the beat of the music. The shadow carried her into
the bedroom and onto the mattress. Hips and thighs continued to
move with the music as she wiggled out of her clothes. She arched
her back, and Michael curved seamlessly within her arch and entered her from behind. The spoon didn't hurt at all as she moved it
in triple time. Hips and thighs. Beads of sweat formed on the extended muscles of her neck. One hand on the spoon, the other with
flattened palm pushing heavenward. Her eyes squeezed shut, then
popped open. *"Olé!"* she screamed.

Her thoughts about sex with Michael repeated throughout the
following days with maddening insistence. Cocaine kept the
thoughts racing through her sleep time as well. Her nights were full
of pain. She tossed about restlessly, her pale skin becoming paler,
her frail body thinner and covered with sweat. Her eyes started to
glaze over permanently, and she moaned throughout the night. She
had a dream in which she saw Michael. He was naked and preparing to mount someone for anal intercourse. She didn't recognize
the other person, but it certainly wasn't her. Could it be a man?
"Wait," she gasped, holding out her limp hand as she woke up.
Vicki rushed to the bathroom and retched and vomited. This was
followed by dry heaves, then mucus streaked with bright red blood.
She flushed away the signs of cocaine poisoning.

Vicki spent many days and nights watching the clock in her bedroom, waiting for Michael to call. She had been playing his game
patiently. But time was running out. Soon she would have to quit
the restaurant job and devote herself to the upcoming tour. And
her escalating cocaine habit was making her more impatient than
ever.

The clock Vicki watched was a brass alarm clock with a battery-
powered quartz movement. She had bought it at Tiffany for $235.
It represented a lot of coke, but she had purchased it as a present
for Michael. Eventually she would give it to him. He'd once said he
didn't have a decent alarm clock in his house. House? She didn't

know if he lived in a house or apartment. Or where. Or with whom. The questions plagued her. Then she began to think about how little she actually knew about him.

She lit a cigarette and paced around her living room. The talk among the staff at the restaurant was that Michael was gay. She clutched the lighter. Impossible. She knew gay guys when she saw them. After all, she danced with them every day. Michael didn't have "the look." He was too big, too muscular. Of course he was attractive enough to have been approached by men in the past. He may have even experimented once or twice. But that wasn't unusual and didn't mean that he was gay. Vicki recalled her own experimentation as a teenager with a girl in her ballet class. They'd engaged in mutual fondling and masturbation. Afterward the girl had told Vicki she had great hand movements. Vicki knew they were better than anyone else's and never felt the desire to experiment again.

Now time was running out. Vicki was at the age when she realized that her professional ballet career had only a few more good years before she would be replaced by a younger dancer. Then she would go into teaching, maybe even open up her own school. But she also wanted a family—a daughter, especially—before she was thirty. Michael would make a wonderful father. She *knew* he wanted a daughter, too. Little girls who came to the restaurant with their parents always got extra-special attention from him.

So Vicki watched the clock. The quartz movement caused the second hand to skip from one second to the next with no continuous flow. Sometimes she would stare at it between skips, and for what seemed like a period longer than a second, time would stop. But, of course, it always started again. It reminded her of watching that giant electric clock in grade school, literally counting the seconds to the end of the day when she could dash off to ballet.

She was watching the clock one day when it seemed to stop again. Funny how it can do that, she thought. It'll start now. This very next second.

But it didn't. Not then, not later, not ever. That was when things got very strange. Rather than check the clock for dead batteries, Vicki rushed around her apartment, looking for other signs. A picture frame near the front door was tilted at an unusual angle. She didn't remember doing that. There were strange shapes in the rosin on the living room floor. They resembled a man's shoeprint, about Michael's size. She ran into the kitchen and opened the silverware drawer. Yes, it had been rearranged. She picked up a sugar spoon from the drawer. It was from the restaurant. *Michael is ready,* it told her. The dirty dishes were stacked next to the sink in a restaurant-neat arrangement, with all the utensils on the top plate. *Don't waste any more time! Do it now!* they said in unison.

Yes, time *was* running out. It was a Vivaldi autumn now when the dancing and singing was over, when "the hunt" section of the movement begins with relentless double stops in allegro. Vicki was ready to go after Michael with the same bold and expressive force.

First came the bait. Vicki withdrew $2,000 from her savings and scored an ounce of the best cocaine she could find in the city. Next she carefully prepared a bindle, a type of paper envelope for holding small amounts of the drug. She started with a bridal magazine. Selecting a glossy page showing a formally attired bride and groom, she cut out a five-inch-square piece and folded it in half diagonally. She folded in the sides of the resulting triangle, then folded the lower portion upward. Next she reopened the package and placed a pile of cocaine directly onto the happy couple. It was at least two grams. Then she refolded the packet and carefully tucked in the top flap to make the rectangular bindle. Vicki had to laugh when she looked at the finished product. Quite by accident, part of an advertisement for sterling-silver flatware was visible on the outside of the bindle.

Vicki slipped the bindle into Michael's hand at the restaurant. He was surprised.

"Quanto?" he asked. He didn't know if he could afford it.

"È rigalo, cameriere," she explained—a gift for her favorite waiter. Then it was her turn to leave abruptly and return to work.

The next several days were filled with preparations for the rest of the plan. Vicki started practicing new dance steps. She had been trained not to turn out from the hips and thighs, as that movement placed too much emphasis on her genital area. Now she forced her body to break with its years of discipline. She practiced turning out from the hips with a not-too-subtle pelvic thrust. The movement turned her out and into a dazzling striptease artist. She used the

movement in a new dance she choreographed and rehearsed. As
part of her plan, Vicki refrained from masturbating in order to
build the appropriate emotional force for her performance.

She shopped for a new outfit since there was no way she could
ask her mother to make what she had in mind. After a single dress
rehearsal, during which she worked herself into such a state of
sexual arousal that she almost broke down and masturbated, Vicki
was ready.

The following night was one of her off nights at the restaurant.
After a long bath, Vicki dressed, snorted some cocaine, and went to
the restaurant under the pretense of grabbing a late snack. She was
wearing a baggy sweatshirt, blue jeans, and running shoes. It was
near closing time and she asked Michael if he'd like to stop by her
place after work. She had some extra coke for him. It would only
take a few minutes, and she didn't live far. He agreed, and Vicki
waited for him, then drove back to her apartment with Michael
following in his car. She lived in a crowded neighborhood, and
Michael couldn't find a parking space. He settled for an illegal
space on the corner—it was only going to take a few minutes.

Inside, Vicki directed Michael to a cushioned bench that she had
pushed against a wall in the living room. She brought out an ashtray overflowing with a small mountain of cocaine, and they both
snorted several piles scooped up with a nail file. The cocaine fueled
their conversation, and they chatted and snorted for more than a
few minutes. Michael did most of the snorting while Vicki did most
of the talking. It was frustrating for her because, despite the drug,
she had a limited high school vocabulary full of empty slang expressions. Michael, who told her he had been to college, was years
ahead of her both chronologically and intellectually. *You could
teach me so much, my darling.* Vicki tried talking about ballet, but
she knew she was not expressing herself well with words.

"Let me dance for you, Michael," she finally said.

Michael was getting nervous. The cocaine was making him jit-
tery, and he kept looking out the window to check on his car. It
was getting late.

"Please," she pleaded.

"Okay," he agreed. After all, she had given him two bindles of
cocaine and a plastic bag full of what was left in the ashtray to take
home.

Vicki went over to the tape recorder, inserted a cassette, and turned up the volume. Everything had to be timed perfectly now. In full view of Michael she slipped out of her jeans and put on her toe shoes. The oversize sweatshirt was still hiding most of her body except for her bare legs. She took a moment to stretch and caress them, letting her hands linger where the sweatshirt met her thighs. Standing with her back to Michael, Vicki started to move with the music.

The dance began with a lone flute and the sensuous swaying of arms, head, and legs, like a single blade of grass bending in the breeze. She rose to full pointe, her legs seemed to shudder as the flute trilled, then she relaxed on demipointe and continued to sway. The movement was repeated several times, and each time the convulsive shuddering seemed to travel farther up her body. When the shuddering arrived at her fingers, they fluttered and provocatively reached down for the sweatshirt and slowly lifted it off. Vicki was wearing a sheer black body suit. Her nipples were visible under the transparent stretch fabric. Michael could still see only her back, but he couldn't miss the hint of sheen on the fabric. It was as dazzling as her dancing.

Vicki stretched into a sustained arabesque, with her hyperextended leg revealing to Michael the crotch of the body suit. Then came a series of slow fouettés, Vicki flashing her sexiest smile while coming to rest with her back to him. She started to turn around, stopped and started, each time turning out more and more from the hips and thighs. This tease continued until she finally turned and faced her audience on pointe. Vicki executed an erotic grande batterie, springing into the air with her legs beating against each other. The music exploded into pounding rhythms as she launched into forward and backward pelvic thrusts and contrapuntal jabbing of her feet. Then a few quick steps brought her directly in front of Michael. Her erect nipples were clearly visible to him.

In a series of spectacular and sensuous leg reaches, Vicki stood on pointe and alternately moved one outstretched leg after the other slowly up the inside of Michael's thighs, each time lightly brushing his groin with her foot. It was a move good enough, she knew, to make Romeo, Siegfried, even Apollo himself come in their codpieces. But Michael seemed uncomfortable. He started glancing toward the window again. She was forced to improvise. After slinking up to him, she threw one leg up on his shoulder and pressed her body close to his. Her mouth was slightly open. They were both breathing hard and sweating.

"Vicki, no. I never wanted this."

She pressed harder, her lips touching his, her tongue searching, until he pushed her firmly but slowly away.

"I want you, Michael," she whispered.

"Vicki, please. I didn't want this to happen." He let her rest her head on his chest.

"I love you," she whispered.

He held her away from him again. "Jesus, Vicki. I'm gay. I live with a man . . . Lawrence. . . . He expects me home now."

You wanted to fuck me, said the spoon.

You loved me, said the knife.

"Don't you want me? . . ." She started to say something else but began crying.

"Vicki, I don't cheat on Lawrence. I'm not bi. Jesus, I'm sorry, Vicki. I'm sorry." He was trying to explain.

Vickie ran from the living room, tears streaming down her face. She rushed into the kitchen and opened a drawer. Inside were dozens of Michael's love notes.

"Liars!" she screamed at the pile of silverware she had taken from the restaurant over the past months. *"Liars!"*

She ran into the bathroom, closed the door, and began sobbing uncontrollably. After a few minutes Michael knocked on the bathroom door. She didn't answer. He opened the door. She was standing at the sink. Something was in her hand. He approached, ready to comfort her. Vicki saw his face in the mirror. She turned around and with a lunge drove a knife through his heart, forever closing the gulf between them. He made a sound like a man screaming underwater, then collapsed on the tile floor. Vicki stared at the knife in her hand. It was dripping blood.

"Oh God, oh God . . . What am I going to do?"

Call the police, said the knife.

3

I stared at her from across a table in an interview room at the Sybil
Brand Institute, where she was awaiting trial for murder. There was
something almost otherworldly about her. Her ghostly paleness and
emaciated frame gave her a fragile appearance. She was wearing a
baggy jail dress that hung like a tent. Her eyes were red and swollen.
She looked as if she might burst into tears. At one time she must have
been stunning in her beauty, I thought. Then the shock of recogni-
tion hit me. I knew from reading the police reports that she worked
at a restaurant with the victim. But I did not recognize the name as
the restaurant where Joel Morgan and I had dined. Suddenly I remembered this pale face in front of me. She was the Cinderella hostess who had dazzled us that night. Now, through the magic of her
own fairy tale, she had been turned into a lonely, frightened little
girl, a prisoner in a castle dungeon of her own making.

Her defense attorney had hired me as an expert witness to investigate the role of cocaine in the murder. A large amount of the drug
had been found at the scene. The autopsy showed high levels of
cocaine in the victim's blood. Lower levels were found in the defendant's blood. The attorney sent me a copy of the murder book,
which included the police and evidence reports, photographs of the
crime scene, interviews with neighbors and other witnesses, and
the coroner's report.

Vicki made a 911 emergency call to the police after the murder.
I listened to the tape. "There's been a terrible accident," she said.
"He's dead." Her voice was calm, but she was whispering, as if
afraid to wake someone. She gave the street address, then dropped
the telephone. On the tape I listened to several minutes of muffled
sobbing until the police broke down the apartment door.

They found Vicki draped over the body on the bathroom floor.
The report said she was wearing underwear and a pair of ballet
slippers. She went limp in their arms as they lifted her off the body.
The police asked questions, but Vicki could only stare and sob. She
appeared remote, trancelike, with dead eyes.

Michael's body was cold when they discovered it. A knife with
Vicki's fingerprints was found next to the body. It matched similar

knives in the kitchen and corresponded to the size and nature of the wound. The knife had entered through the skin and soft tissue of the chest wall. It had passed through the left lung and through the left ventricle of the heart, ending in the right ventricle. The coroner said it was a rapidly fatal injury. Curiously, the victim had ejaculated just prior to death, either from the stabbing or something else.

The police searched for clues. Inside Michael's pants pockets they found two bindles of cocaine, along with a Ziploc bag containing more than a half ounce. There was some cocaine residue in an ashtray found in the living room. A nail file resting in the ashtray also had traces of the drug. There were dozens of ballet costumes inside a hall closet. The police took two that appeared to have bloodstains on them. Analysis of the blood was pending.

Michael's car was eventually discovered on the corner after several parking tickets accumulated on the windshield. The police found a bindle with a small amount of cocaine inside the glove compartment. The glossy paper with bridal pictures matched the bindles found in the victim's pockets.

The police thought they had the case wrapped up. The victim was a coke dealer who came over to the defendant's apartment to exchange coke for sex. They partied in the living room, where the defendant removed her clothes. They had an argument, and she killed him. Coke whore versus coke dealer. Another L.A. story, open and shut. The defense attorney was hoping that it might be a case of self-defense. But thus far Vicki had refused to discuss what happened. All she would say was that she'd killed him and wanted to die. The jail had her under a "suicide watch."

There were many unanswered questions. The police said the victim was a dealer, but the papers he used for the bindles appeared to come from a stack of bridal magazines found in Vicki's apartment. If there was a fight, where was the evidence? Vicki didn't have a mark on her body. Whose blood was on the costumes? That Vicki had killed the victim was apparent, but her motive was not. I had my own wild theory. The victim came over with cocaine to have sex with the defendant. They snorted cocaine in the living room, then she changed into some sexy costumes. They fooled around, and he ejaculated prematurely. He went into the bathroom to clean himself, and she killed him in a cocaine-induced rage of frustration.

But what happened next? The coroner said death occurred twelve hours before Vicki made the 911 call in the early afternoon. Why did she wait so long? What was she doing alone in the apartment with the body?

The questions were spinning in my head as I sat across from Vicki. She wasn't ready to answer them, so I did most of the talking as I tried to get her to relax. I complained about my wobbly chair, the dirty interview room, and the bossy female guards who gave my briefcase and me an unnecessary inspection. When I suggested that the guard uniforms were not nearly as feminine as the inmate dresses, Vicki came to life. She sat up, straightened her dress, and brushed the hair away from her face with her hands. It was a good sign. I told her I was a dancer. She looked at me with a quizzical expression. I recited my classical repertoire: box step, do-si-do, and the bunny hop. I did the hora at my Bar Mitzvah, and everyone gave me lots of money, so I guess I was good at that dance, too. Vicki laughed.

Despite her ability to relax with me, I limited my first visit to obtaining hair samples for later drug analysis. As hair grows, it is nourished by the blood vessels in the skin. Drugs in the blood are deposited in each day's hair growth, locked inside, then pushed outward by the next day's growth. The drugs or their metabolites stay in the hair until the hair is cut off or falls out. Head hair grows relatively quickly—about a half inch each month. Long head hair like Vicki's promised to give me a history of her drug use for the past several years. I told her it would not be necessary to take slower-growing pubic hair, which normally provides such long history. That was lucky because Vicki explained that she used to shave her pubic hair. Samples taken now would only show drug use over the past few months while she was in jail. The root ends of her head hair also contained the recent history that Vicki told me would show no use of drugs, although they were readily available in the jail.

I stood behind her and started combing her hair, trying to isolate the longest strands I could find. Her hair was beautiful, and I complimented her on it. I was particulary excited about its thickness, perfect for the chemical analysis. But Vicki was embarrassed about the slightly wild and frizzy look it had because of the lack of appropriate hair care products.

"I could play the mad scene from *Giselle* without a wig," she said cryptically. After collecting the samples, I left, promising to return as soon as I had the results.

Vicki seemed happy to see me on the following weekend. I launched into a recitation of her drug history as revealed by the hair analysis. The hair doesn't lie, I told her, but correct me if I've made any mistakes. There was no evidence of any drug use until last year. About four months before the incident she'd started using small amounts of cocaine, probably snorting it just a couple of times a week. Her use escalated dramatically in the month prior to the incident, then quadrupled in the last week. It looked as if she had been bingeing and had probably done cocaine round-the-clock some nights.

"Only one night, really," she said. "The last night."

"Looks like you smoked a little marijuana here in jail over Christmas," I told her.

"Oh, my. I forgot about that. . . . Did you do this with Michael's hair?" she asked.

I explained that the coroner had not taken hair samples. Sometimes we can exhume the body to take them, but Michael had been cremated and his ashes scattered over the ocean.

"Who told you this?" she asked, very interested.

"His roommate," I said. "He told me many of Michael's friends were there. It was a moving ceremony."

"Was . . . was he really gay?"

"Yes."

Vicki started sobbing. "Giselle would have killed herself," she said softly. That was the second cryptic reference to *Giselle*.

"Vicki, did you try to kill yourself?" I asked.

"No," she whispered.

"The police found blood on two of your dresses in the closet. It was your blood. Did Michael hurt you?" She started sobbing again. I reached across the table and held her hands in mine. "Tell me, Vicki, did he try to hurt you?"

She stared at our clasped hands, sobbing. Then she started rubbing my fingers compulsively, manipulating them like worry beads. "No," she whispered. "He never hurt me." More sobbing.

"How, then?" It was difficult watching her pain.

"I hurt myself . . . masturbating too hard, I guess."

"Did you use some object?"

She shook her head. "My finger." Her tears were falling on my hands, melting my clinical detachment.

"Tell me, Vicki. Tell me about that last night." I was whispering. She shook her head.

"Okay. Tell me a story. Once upon a time there was a little girl who wanted to be a ballet dancer. Finish it for me, Vicki."

She did. Not right away, but gradually, in a dozen more sessions over the next few weeks. I listened and didn't start asking probing questions until she got to the part where she met Michael. She described her initial attraction to him, the snowman smile, those promising luminous eyes, the secret messages with the silverware, and, throughout it all, the poetic love. Vicki was certain of these things. My interviews with Michael's roommate, other employees at the restaurant, and dancers in her company told me otherwise. But I did not confront Vicki with any of this. She was still in the grips of a massive delusion. Her condition was fragile, and the possibility of suicide remained. Already her weight was dropping at an alarming rate. I would not ring down the curtain on her fantasy. Time might do that. And Vicki was likely to have a lot of it.

Time stood still for Vicki on that fateful night when her alarm clock stopped ticking. She was alone on a stage with Michael, her elusive dream of poetic perfection. The rest of the world ceased to exist, fading into the darkness beyond the footlights. Psychiatrists might call this a nihilistic delusion. But romantic love, even one driven by paranoid eroticism, still catapults its victims, involuntarily and helplessly, into a place where nothing else exists.

Vicki literally and figuratively held my hand and took me into her private world. In my mind's eye I watched her dance with a shadow from her own mind. She shared every intimate detail, as if the telling made it all the more real. While her paranoia began without cocaine, I was convinced the drug had hastened its development. It was both food for dance and food for thought. The coke increased her sensitivity to the subtle signs of Michael's love, then excited and stimulated her own erotic drives. It made her wishes and fantasies more vivid, more vivacious, more valid.

Her stories of the subsequent erotomania always came to an

abrupt stop on the night of the murder. Vicki still refused to discuss it. I remembered her cryptic references to *Giselle* and reread the story of that most famous of all romantic ballets. Giselle is an innocent peasant girl who falls in love with Albrecht, a count. Albrecht has disguised himself as a peasant by hiding his nobleman's cloak and sword. They romp and dance together in bliss and ecstasy. Giselle is so happy that she performs a solo dance famous for its electrifying virtuosity. But she discovers that Albrecht is not only a count, he is engaged to be married. In the famous "mad scene," Giselle does a disjointed and deranged dance, then plunges the tip of Albrecht's sword into her breast. The curtain rises on Act II as Giselle rises from the grave as a ghost. Guided by evil spirits, she leads Albrecht into the forest, where her dance of death causes him to fall to the ground in deathly exhaustion. But Giselle is still under the influence of her earthly love, and she lingers over her fallen beloved. This last gesture awakens the spirit of everlasting love in Albrecht, and he rises to watch, with broken heart, as Giselle returns to her grave.

In our next meeting I asked Vicki if she was playing Giselle to Michael's Albrecht. Did she linger over the body for twelve hours hoping to resurrect it? Apparently the question hit directly on one of the fantasies she was protecting, and it was enough for her to raise the curtain on the rest.

Vicki told me of the carefully choreographed night of seduction, a night of cocaine and erotic dancing. She was proud of her dance and seemed eager to describe every step and position. Vicki explained that her choreography was based on animal courtship displays and the erotic moves of the Greek satyrs. I felt that the real choreographer was none other than Circe, the mythic Greek enchantress who lulled men to tragic ends.

When Michael rejected her, she ran into the kitchen. She remembered grabbing a knife from the drawer and running into the bathroom. The world had stopped, but her head was spinning. She didn't know if she was going to kill herself or Michael. His sudden appearance settled the question. Her lunge was reflexive, full of rage and frustration.

After he fell, a dirgelike atmosphere enveloped the apartment. It filled with ghosts of ballets past and yearnings for lost love. For hours Vicki snorted cocaine, paced from room to room, and watched the images swirl through her mind. She felt—indeed, lived—the pathos and tragedy of her ballet heroines. Emotions previously mimicked in dance were now vibrant, alive, surging through her body.

She knew this was turning her into the brilliantly expressive dancer she was destined to be. In her mind, she began dancing with Giselle. She saw herself suddenly demure, plucking the petals from a daisy to test Albrecht's love. When they tell her "he loves me not," Albrecht throws her an extra petal and joins her in a blissful dance. She saw herself soar in the famous solo dance celebrating her happiness. She saw herself in the mad scene, desperate to hang on to Albrecht's love with halting, disjointed movements from their former blissful dances.

When the sun came up in the morning, Vicki could almost hear the eerie theme played by a harp and strings that sets the mood in Act II. By this time she was not a ghost, but a cocaine zombie. She walked back and forth across the stage of her living room. Finally she forced herself to look at the body, then the knife. In the early afternoon she called the police, then lingered like Giselle over the body.

Now Vicki was utterly exhausted after telling me about her final act. She had performed a remarkable dance for Michael that night. It was the most important dance of her life and, in many ways, her best. As it turned out, it would also be her last for eight years. I knew she longed for someone to appreciate it. She didn't think Michael liked it. As I stood to leave, I gave her the only applause I could. I told her that Michael had ejaculated when he saw it.

She mouthed, "Thank you," then curtsied. Her birdlike body seemed to keep moving slowly to the concrete floor, the arms drooping pitifully to her sides. Cinderella had turned into a dying swan.

6

INVASION OF BUGS

1

The invasion began over Christmas vacation. I was staying at home, looking forward to three weeks without students, criminal defendants to interview, or court appearances. It was going to be an ideal time to master my new chess computer, which I had given myself as a present. During that first week, I was absorbed in losing one electronic battle after another, often turning off the computer in frustration. Meanwhile four people, whose cases I would be called to investigate many months later, were engaged in their own battles after indulging in a special Christmas shipment of cocaine from Bolivia. For Johnny Comstock, Albert Martinez, Jennifer Long, and Bill Carpenter, there was no way to turn off the enemy.

December 18. Rodeo Drive, Beverly Hills. Santa Claus, a.k.a. Johnny Comstock, was standing outside a store window on Rodeo Drive in Beverly Hills, the most expensive shopping area in the country. The sign next to his collection pot read "Feed the Homeless." This was no place for a nickel-and-dime Santa. People cheerfully dropped fives and tens into his pot. It worked according to some perverted Pavlovian principle. Johnny salivated, rang his little bell, then people gave him money. "Merry Christmas. God bless," he would say with a noticeable sniffle. Johnny's hunger was for cocaine, and he needed hundreds of dollars a day just to feed his habit. No problem for a Rodeo Santa. He had been out here ring-ing his bell for over a week and had taken in enough money to continue his compulsive whiffs of the white stuff. This was no small feat considering that Johnny was using cocaine every hour, twenty hours a day. Nobody paid any attention to the faux nasal inhaler filled with cocaine he kept inside one of his gloves. Many people in Beverly Hills used nasal inhalers. A few of them probably had colds.

High noon, the busiest and hottest part of the day. Santa rang in the hour with winks and smiles at the mob of lunchtime shoppers. Then, out of the corner of his winking eye, he caught a fleeting glimpse of a snowflake. Well, not exactly a snowflake. It was shaped like one—a symmetrical geometric design—but it was black. There were several others scooting across the corners of his visual field. But they disappeared before he could get a good look. Then Santa got an itch under his heavy jacket. He unbuttoned his jacket, reached inside with an ungloved hand, and scratched furiously.

A few minutes later the itch started to crawl up his back. He took off his jacket and shook it. Then he removed his T-shirt. Johnny couldn't see anything, but he *knew* that something was crawling in his skin. He brushed at his body, twisting and turning like a break dancer. Then he used the edge of the bell to scrape at his skin. Small rivulets of blood ran down his arms and chest. The itching spread to his legs. He hopped around like a Santa on a hot tin roof. A little girl watched for a moment, then dropped a coin in the pot. Johnny ran down the street, screaming and ringing for help.

December 19. Euclid Avenue, Los Angeles. It was early morning when Albert Martinez came home after working the night shift. He tiptoed through the house, trying not to wake up his wife. After taking off his clothes, he jumped into a hot shower. He stood under the fine spray for several minutes, allowing his pores to open. Some-thing came up through the shower drain and latched on to his legs. He looked down. Little black specks, like snowflakes, danced on his legs. They were alive, crawling upward. They started sucking on his skin. He could feel it! In seconds his legs were covered with tiny ringlike welts where they had bitten holes and crawled inside.

They moved quickly now, traveling under his skin, upward. He felt them moving in his chest, then into his throat. His lips tingled as they crawled around under his face. He saw one dart across his visual field. My God! he realized. They're in my eyes! And still they moved upward. When they entered his brain they stopped. Then came the most horrible sucking sounds. My brain! he thought, frantic now. They're eating my brain! A vision flashed in his mind. He saw his body completely dehydrated, a sagging sack of skin hanging on some skinny bones. He bolted from the shower and ran out of the house.

"They're all over me. They're all over me!" he screamed as he streaked down the street. A meter maid, who was writing a ticket for a car parked illegally on the corner, looked up at the naked man running toward her. There were scratch marks on his legs. He seemed agitated. He kept screaming about something.

"Do you have any identification?" she asked the naked man.

"They're all over me!" he screamed.

"You should always carry identification with you. Even if you're jogging," she said.

"They're all over me!" he screamed again.

"Is that your van?" she asked, pointing to a vehicle in front of his house.

He nodded. "Help me," he cried.

She opened the van, hoping to find some identification in the glove compartment. Inside the van there were several hundred pounds of cocaine.

She called for backup. The police arrived and took Albert into custody. He begged for help.

"They're all over me!" he screamed.

The police laughed it off. After all, they had just caught a big-time coke dealer naked with the goods.

December 19. Latigo Shore Drive, Malibu. It was the middle of the afternoon and David's date was still sleeping. He was anxious to get her up and out of his beachfront house. After all, it was just a one-night stand—he wasn't planning on inviting her to move in with him. David opened the curtains and the sliding doors in the bedroom, hoping that the sun and ocean breeze might revive her.

He sat on the bed and studied the outline of her figure under the sheets. She had a sexy body and certainly knew how to use it. But it was pitch dark when they tore off their clothes and hopped into bed. He never got a good look at her. Now he was seized with a mischievous desire to look at her while she was still sleeping. She was lying on her stomach with her face turned away from him. He took the corner of the bedsheet and slowly pulled it off the backs of her feet and legs. Her legs were long and slender. The thighs were firm and smelled of sex. David was getting excited. He pulled the sheet back a little more, exposing her cute little ass, just the kind he loved. He touched it ever so lightly.

Jennifer Long moaned. She started to reach back with her hand, then fell limp again. David noticed she was still wearing her watch, a Cartier tank. It must have irritated her because there were red marks on her wrist near the band. His eyes traveled up her arm, where he saw more red marks and small black blemishes underneath the skin. There were drops of dried blood around some of the blemishes. He pulled the rest of the sheet off her. Her back was smooth and clean—not a mark on it. Her golden hair cascaded around her face, which was still buried in the pillow. David gently moved the hair away from her cheek.

Jennifer moaned again and turned over. "Hi," she said sleepily.

David was speechless. Some of her heavy makeup had rubbed off on the pillow. On the middle of her left cheek was a group of four round sores, each about the size of a pencil eraser. They were arranged in an arc that was so linear, they resembled a series of animal bites. Each sore was actually a ring. The center of each ring was filled with a wad of pancake makeup, but David could see they were very deep depressions, like wells. Words flashed through his mind: Cancer? Herpes? Syphilis? The correct word had only four letters: bugs!

December 20. Beachwood Drive, Hollywood. Bill Carpenter picked up a Christmas tree for his apartment. He invited his girlfriend, Carol, to come by that night and help trim the tree. When she arrived they sniffed a little cocaine and had a couple of mixed drinks while they decorated the tree. Bill excused himself and went to the bedroom to get some more cocaine. Suddenly he came bursting out of the bedroom, screaming.

"I got bugs on me!" he yelled, brushing his arms frantically.

"Calm down, Bill. There are no bugs on you," Carol said.

"Yes. They're on me. Some type of spiders. Crawling on me!" Bill screamed as he ran around the living room in a frenzy, knocking over lamps and furniture. He bumped into Pinocchio, his pet parrot, and the bird jumped to his shoulder just as the perch went tumbling to the floor. "The bugs are biting me!" he shouted with renewed panic. Pinocchio squawked. "They're on the bird!" Pinocchio made a "kuckkuck" sound and jumped to a bookshelf.

Bill ran over to the drinks and studied his glass carefully. He thought he saw little specks—like black snowflakes—floating on the surface.

"You bitch!" he yelled at Carol. "You put bugs in my drink." He ran over to her and shook her hard. "Why did you put the bugs on me?"

"No, no!" cried Carol as she broke loose and ran.

Bill grabbed her again and threw her on the couch. Then he began kicking and hitting her. She ran into the bathroom and locked the door. He broke down the door, grabbed Carol by the throat, and dragged her back into the living room, where he continued kicking and punching her. Blood was splattering everywhere.

He's going to kill me, thought Carol. It's over. I'm dead.

The bugs continued their attack on Bill, biting him. He kept jumping up in the air to get away from them. Each time he came down with both feet on Carol's body. "Why did you plant bugs in my apartment?" he cried.

Carol couldn't answer. It's over, she thought. I'm going to die.

But the bugs saved Carol's life. They were getting the better of Bill. They were under his skin now, biting everywhere. He couldn't get to them. He ran to the telephone and called the police. Carol managed to crawl into a closet and hide.

Bill was outside screaming and yelling when the police arrived. He waved at them with both arms, then charged toward them. They saw a large parrot sitting on his shoulder. They drew their guns and ordered him to stop. He kept coming. They wrestled him to the ground and handcuffed him.

"Be quiet, Pinocchio," he whispered to the bird. "Don't say anything."

Bill told the officers not to handle the expensive bird because it had been injected with bugs. The bugs could change it into a monster at any moment. "Stay away from my bird," he warned them. "I've been injected with the bugs, too!" he screamed. "They're inside my body. Look at the welts on my body. There's an injection site on my back."

The police looked at his back. They saw no welts, only a large pimple that had been picked recently. But after finding Carol's crippled body inside the closet, they were convinced that something had changed Bill into a monster.

2

December 23. Midvale Avenue, Westwood. It was the second week of my vacation. The telephone rang and rescued me from another losing game with my chess computer. The caller introduced himself as a friend of a technician in my lab. He apologized for disturbing me at home but quickly explained he was a cocaine researcher with an important finding to show me. I was always willing to talk to fellow researchers. And it was, after all, Christmas vacation. I invited the caller to my home, forgetting for the moment that Ed Tolman had entered my life under the similar pretense of being a fellow researcher.

Matthew Nichols kept knocking on the back door. I was in the bathroom, and it took me several minutes to get to the door. He didn't stop knocking until I opened it and extended my hand. His hand felt ice cold. We went through the kitchen, where I offered him a cup of coffee. I started to dislike him right away. My coffee was Jamaican Blue Mountain—the finest money could buy—but Matt was ruining it with heaps of sugar and creamer. We took the cups into the den.

I studied him from across the coffee table. He didn't seem to have a sense of taste for coffee or clothes. His red-checked wool jacket, worn open over a Hawaiian shirt with floral designs, seemed to violate even California's loose standards of taste, not to mention the seventy-degree winter temperatures we were enjoying. On top of that, he had a full beard and shoulder-length curly brown hair. His leather boots were scruffy and caked with mud. The combined effect made him seem more like a lumberjack than the "researcher" he claimed to be.

Matt got right to the point. He put his canvas shoulder bag on the table and pulled out a dozen small clear glass vials with black plastic screw caps. The vials were identical with the type used for cocaine. Each vial was filled with a white substance.

"Here," he said, pushing the vials across the table like a rack of pool balls. "These are for you."

"I'm sorry, Matt. I can't accept any gifts of cocaine," I said. Although I routinely analyzed samples submitted by my research subjects and patients, Matt was neither. Judging from the amount of cocaine in these vials, Matt might have been a dealer as well as a user. I didn't want to be used as a quality-control laboratory for street sales. And if he really was a researcher, there were government forms that had to be filled out for any exchange of controlled substances. He should have known that unless he was setting me up for a bust. Well, they wouldn't find Siegel's fingerprints on these vials. No sirree.

"They're not cocaine," he protested. "They're bugs . . . coke bugs. . . . I've been researching them."

I grabbed a vial and held it up to the light as I studied the contents. The white substance appeared to be a mixture of flakes of dried skin, some darker spongy material, and a sprinkling of black debris. The contents of the other vials appeared similar. The letters *H* or *P* were printed on the caps with a wax pencil. As I put my fingerprints all over the vials, Matt began to explain his "research" project.

He had recently purchased a large quantity of cocaine for the holidays. It was from a new shipment of Bolivian rock that had just hit the streets of Los Angeles. I was familiar with this alleged shipment because several of my subjects had submitted samples of it for analysis. They'd told me there were tons of the stuff on the street. Matt was correct when he claimed it was strong: our analysis indicated it was close to 100 percent pure.

Matt decided to have a party with Sherry, his live-in girlfriend. First he prepared the cocaine for smoking by dissolving it in water, adding some baking soda, then boiling the mixture until only chunks of white cocaine freebase (crack) remained. After drying,

he placed the chunks in a glass pipe and smoked. Three days and
five ounces later Matt was scratching and picking at his hands. He
wasn't even aware of this until Sherry pointed it out to him. Matt
saw that his hands were getting red, especially around the knuckles. The picking had produced tiny excoriations. They looked suspicious. He placed his hands under a stereo microscope he had
once used in a biology class for dissections. At ten power magnifi-
cation he saw something moving inside the excoriations. At thirty
power, long white threads, like translucent snakes, were visible. He
used a pair of tweezers to peel the skin away in order to get a better
look. At sixty power he saw the snakes burrowing into deeper tissue. Inside the deep tissue were tiny black specks. Matt figured
these were the antibodies rushing to his body's defense. But he was
horrified to see that the snakes had been eating the antibodies. The
black specks were clearly visible inside the translucent snakes. His
own body needed help. Matt grabbed his old high school dissecting
kit and went to work.

After another three days without sleep, Matt finished excavating
the burrows. This necessitated cutting deep into his skin and carefully removing globs of fat and muscle tissue. He purposely allowed the excavations to bleed so that there would be plenty of
white blood cells to fight any infection. The burrows, and their
inhabitants, were now sealed in the vials. Matt felt he'd got them
all. He was smiling with pride.

I asked about the markings on the caps.

"The 'H' is for hands," Matt explained as he held his hands
out for me to see. Despite the telltale signs of cocaine intoxication
in his dilated pupils and agitated speech, his hands were as steady
as a surgeon's. I grabbed his fingertips and inspected them. The
skin around the nails had been pulled off. Scabs and scars covered the back of his hands. His knuckles were raw, and there
were signs of recent bleeding. I turned the hands over. The skin
on the palms was dry and flaking. I pushed up one of the sleeves
of his jacket, exposing a very hairy wrist and forearm. There were
no lesions here, but I wondered why there was no hair on his
hands.

"I think they enter through the hair follicles first and lay their
eggs there. So I removed all the entry points," he explained. "There

are some hairs in the 'H' vials. Maybe you'll find some egg sacs, too."

"And the 'P' vials?" I asked. There were only two of these.

"Penis," Matt said, practically spitting the word.

Somehow I felt uncomfortable asking to see it. After all, we'd just met. I waited for Matt to say more. He didn't. Instead he started telling me his theory about cocaine bugs. Matt believed that the snakes were the larval form of the bugs. They came from eggs deposited on the coca plants in South America. I ignored the paranoid nature of his thinking and began arguing with him. The coca plant is relatively pest free, I explained, and most animals ignore it. The cocaine alkaloid in the leaf tastes bitter and keeps away browsing herbivores. The coca leaf also contains substances that repel most insects. A few caterpillars and leaf-cutting ants have evolved mechanisms for handling the plant, but neither they nor their eggs could survive the chemical processes used to extract and purify the cocaine.

Matt insisted that the bugs were a special breed developed by genetic engineers working under contract for the CIA and the DEA (Drug Enforcement Administration). He said the DEA sprayed the coca crops with the eggs of these bugs. It was true that scientists once experimented with using weevils to eat opium poppies, but I'd never heard of any effort to eradicate coca crops with insects. Besides, I was a consultant to the DEA and accompanied agents on coca eradication missions as an observer. Although I thought it best not to mention this to Matt, I told him that the only things sprayed on the plants by the DEA were chemical herbicides. Not so, said Matt. These eggs were designed to eradicate users, not plants. They were especially developed to survive the chemical extraction processes and infest anyone who touched the drug.

"Look," he said as he put a hand flat on the coffee table between us. "What do you think these are?" He was pointing to the array of lesions and scars he had made with his dissecting kit. I stared at them, not knowing what else I was supposed to be seeing.

"Look," he said again, this time handing me a magnifying glass he pulled from his bag. "Look at these burrows. Just like scabies, only deeper."

He was right. Scabies is a skin infestation by a mite, *Sarcoptes scabiei.* The threadlike burrows of this mite are linear or wavy ridges on the skin, but the burrows on Matt's hand were very deep below the skin. His burrows were on the knuckles and back of the hand, unlike scabies, which favor the finger webs and palms.

"I think you're right, but a dermatologist should really look at this," I said as I peered through the glass. "Scabies attack the penis just like your coke bugs. Maybe they're a special form of scabies or some other skin parasite." I thought it best to be sure.

Matt was already sure. And now he was getting angry. He stood up, unzipped his fly, and pulled out his penis.

"Look," he said as he exposed the shaft. "You think some ordinary parasite did this?"

I noticed the ulcerated areas where Matt had collected the tissue he put in the vials. Next to the ulcers were a series of thin snakelike lesions that resembled the cutaneous lesions caused by hookworms as the larvae migrate beneath the skin. But hookworms don't attack penises, and they can't spell! The lesions of Matt's penis clearly spelled out the letters *D* and *I* in blood red script.

"I stopped them before they could finish it."

"Finish what?" I had never seen tattooing on a penis before.

"Add the *E*. The word is *DIE*. The fuckin' DEA wants to kill us all," he said loudly. "What the fuck do you think DEA means? It's the first three letters of DEATH."

Silently I began to see how this conspiracy had flourished in his mind. Matt had started scratching himself with the same neurotic energy that caused other cocaine users to talk incessantly, grind their teeth, tap their feet, or engage in any number of repetitive behaviors. The scratching became neurotic excoriations as he picked, dug, and squeezed his skin. His suspicious cocaine brain, looking with the microscope for hidden details and meanings below the surface, turned the self-produced lesions into the architecture of a conspiracy to invade his body. Matt's mental calligraphy guided the macabre penmanship on his penis. The message was all too clear and true. He was doomed unless he stopped using cocaine.

I told Matt that the idea of poisoning users was as farfetched and paranoid as the notion that the AIDS virus was developed by some secret agency to kill homosexuals and intravenous drug addicts. "The coke has made you paranoid," I said. "I think the whole

problem will disappear as soon as we get you detoxified." I assumed he wanted help.

It was the wrong thing to say. Matt now realized that the DEA
was attacking coke users not only with bugs, but with AIDS as
well. He jumped to his feet and prepared to leave. Before he left, I
gave him back the vials, although I kept two for analysis. I told
Matt that I didn't know how long the analysis might take because
of the holidays. Then I walked him outside to his car. When I returned to my apartment I saw blood on the outside of the door
where he had been knocking. While the holiday was Christmas and
not Passover, I amused myself with the thought that the blood on
the door might keep the infestation from invading my home just as
lamb's blood kept the angel of death from entering the Hebrew
homes in ancient Egypt. I was still laughing at this silly thought as
I washed the blood from the door.

The lab informed me that it would take several days to analyze
the vials. Even without the analysis report in my hands, I was certain Matt was suffering from a paranoid condition that has afflicted humankind since long before the biblical plagues descended
on ancient Egypt. The condition, once called Ekbom's syndrome or
acarophobia (fear of scabies), is known today as delusion of infestation or delusion of parasitosis. It is a persistent condition in which
a person believes that small animals such as insects, lice, vermin, or
maggots are living and thriving on or in the skin. Despite any and
all evidence to the contrary, the person remains firmly convinced
that he or she is infested. The belief is unshakable.

No one knows how widespread this delusion is since most patients refuse to seek psychiatric attention—they are more likely to
treat themselves or consult with dermatologists, entomologists,
public health officials, and pest control specialists. It is interesting
to note that psychiatrists themselves are among the most frequent
sufferers. The condition also occurs among drug addicts, who account for many of the cases.

The delusion usually begins with an actual physical sensation
such as paresthesia: a tingling, pricking, or creeping feeling in the
skin. Alternatively, the sensation may be one of burning, flushing,
or numbing. These sensations can be triggered by a variety of physical illnesses. Hypertension, arteriosclerosis, cardiovascular disor-

ders, diabetes, endocrine disorders, renal dysfunction, and vitamin deficiencies can all cause itching and paresthesias. Many patients with delusions of infestation suffer from these illnesses. In many cases the delusions disappear when the patients recover from the physical problems. Perhaps the most common causes of skin sensations are the side effects from medicines and drugs. For example, alcohol warms and flushes the skin, caffeine cools and tingles, and opiates turn it into gooseflesh.

The false belief that such sensations are parasites crawling in the skin can develop in several psychiatric conditions, including schizophrenia, but you don't have to be crazy to be infested. Indeed, the delusion of parasitosis is known as a monosymptomatic disorder: all else is normal, and there need be no other symptoms. All you need is fear to literally and figuratively tingle down the paranoid streak and awaken the demon.

In the healthy, sober individual fear can change the temperature and electrical properties of the skin. Smooth muscles at the base of body hairs contract, thus causing surface hairs to become erect and gooseflesh to appear. When such physical sensations are experienced, higher cortical centers go to work interpreting them. Errors in this system of information processing generate the delusion of parasitosis. The sensation "*as if* something were crawling in my skin" becomes "something *is* crawling in my skin." In this sense, the parasites are tactile illusions that turn into tactile hallucinations that fool the person. Some people develop accompanying visual hallucinations of the bugs themselves.

People with histories of real skin problems caused by lice or other parasites are particularly prone to the delusion. The original infestation may be gone, but some patients fear that they will become reinfested. The fear leads to itching, which starts the patients scratching . . . and thinking. Social isolation and imprisonment can speed the development. James Harrington, a personal attendant to Charles I, was imprisoned in the Tower of London in 1660. The stress of his confinement caused him to believe that his sweat turned into flies, bees, and other insects, which continued to plague him long after his release. The delusion was coupled with visual hallucinations. "Don't you see that these flies come from me?" he would cry to visitors.

In a sense Harrington was correct, in that the insects, parasites, and other bugs that inhabit this delusion do come from the individual. They are imaginary creations of the brain, cognitive elaborations of actual sensations caused by physical or psychological triggers. The precise mechanisms are unknown, but current research suggests that the delusions are linked to overactivity of the neurotransmitter dopamine. This occurs deep inside the limbic system, the home of the demon. Not surprisingly, the delusion of parasitosis often accompanies various forms of paranoia.

Perhaps the best way to awaken these imaginary parasites is to pump stimulants such as amphetamine or cocaine into the body. These drugs further prolong the action of dopamine, thus speeding the onset of the delusion and intensifying its severity. Matt was not the first sufferer I had seen. I was familiar with the syndrome in monkeys I studied many years before. In only four or five days of round-the-clock amphetamine or cocaine use, the monkeys started acting just like their uncle Matt. They scratched, picked, and dug at their skin with their fingernails. Then they started biting it. I saw this same behavior when the monkeys were infested with real skin mites. However, the monkeys could always catch the skin mites. Coke bugs were another matter. The drugged monkeys bit and picked until the skin was raw. Clenching their teeth in fear grimaces, they started excavating deep wounds. Some researchers allowed their monkeys to rip the flesh away from their bones, even amputate their own fingers. I always stopped the drug treatments before my monkeys did such terrible self-mutilation. But no one stopped a young Bolivian cocaine addict who chewed off two fingers on his left hand in search of the bugs.

What makes these drug-induced delusions all the more believable are the actual changes produced in the skin. When people inject drugs, the injection sites may show vascular congestion, tissue edema, and necrosis. Small blood vessels may tear and hemorrhage. Repeated injections at the same sites cause inflammation and abscesses. Hyperpigmented needle tracks and scars can form. Keloid formations can make the tracks look like long white snakes or worms under the skin. Injection of nonsterile and contaminated drugs can result in actual infections with a variety of microorganisms. Desperate addicts who grind up tablets intended for oral use and inject them are also injecting a variety of fillers such as talc and cornstarch used to hold the tablets together. These substances can cause violent inflammations and scars deep inside the skin.

Users who administer drugs such as cocaine by sniffing or smoking are not immune to skin problems. Chronic use of cocaine by any route of administration can constrict blood flow to the skin and cause a thickening and sclerosis of the dermal collagen. This can result in gross deformities. Fingers resemble swollen sausages, and hands turn into red, white, and blue–mottled claws. Dermatologists see high levels of antibodies in the blood, deposits of immunoglobulin in the outer layers of the skin, and other indicators of connective tissue disease. Users like Matt see only snakes and bugs. When Matt discovered he was infested, his reaction was reminiscent of an anxiety attack. He had trouble breathing. He thought he might faint. Fear, dread, and horror overwhelmed him. Something had to be done, right away. He had to get rid of them. He grabbed his dissecting instruments and went to work.

While I continued to wait for the lab report on Matt's vials, I turned to the medical literature, only to learn that the prognosis for him was not good. Even when drug users are detoxified and the skin heals, the delusion can persist. Plastic surgeons are sometimes called upon to repair any remaining damage, but they can't erase the thoughts. I read one case of a cocaine user with a facial excoriation that exposed her chinbone. Following reconstructive surgery, she showed up with similar excoriations and ulcerations covering the entire lower half of her body. She insisted that the bugs had left eggs in the old wound.

The more cases I read, the more I found myself hoping that Matt was right when he'd said that he had picked out all the snakes. If they returned, he might be forced to seek out even more drastic treatments, either medical or self-help. In earlier times physicians used bleeding, boiling hot baths, electroshock, and prefrontal lobotomies. But the bugs survived. Today, turbocharged antipsychotic medicines like pimozide, which block the action of dopamine, are prescribed. These drugs have a list of side effects and adverse reactions that make even lobotomies look mild. Some patients develop potentially irreversible neurological problems, yet the little bugs remain unscathed in at least half the cases.

The self-help treatments used by patients are equally drastic and equally ineffective. One woman soaked her head in kerosene every day, scraped her skin with a knife, then covered her body with adhesive tape to prevent further infestations. It didn't help. Another patient regularly slashed her body with a razor to allow the bugs a chance to escape. They didn't. After much experimentation, many sufferers resign themselves to sharing their bodies with the invaders.

Finally I got back the pathology reports on Matt's vials. It was good news. There were no bugs or eggs, just dried deep skin tissue, dirt, and hair. I called to tell him.

"No, no. When the snakes are dry, they look like dry skin tissue. When they're wet, you can see they're snakes!" he yelled. I had to hold the phone away from my ear. "Did you use an electron microscope? You should look under an electron microscope for the eggs." I heard him making angry, growling noises in his throat.

"They did," I lied. "There was nothing there." I was certain the lab only used a light microscope. But skin samples submitted in other published cases have been studied with scanning electron microscopes. These instruments are capable of scanning objects as small as eight-billionths of an inch in diameter. The imaginary parasites have never been seen.

"Matt, how about coming in and talking about this?" I asked. "I've got an idea for helping you." My idea was to get him into detox.

"No. I'll get it together. I'll handle it." He hung up.

3

December 30. UCLA, Westwood. The telephone rang, and I immediately knew it had been a mistake to sneak into the office before my Christmas vacation was over. A criminal attorney was calling to ask me to run down to the jail ward at the county hospital to see his client, Cliff Hill, who had just been busted for driving under the influence and possession of a large amount of cocaine for sale. The attorney wanted me to determine if Cliff had a big enough habit to justify possession of the coke for personal use. He also wanted me to design a treatment program for Cliff as an alternative to jail.

"It's Christmas," I grumbled. The first thing I wanted to do was get back to my chess computer, the last thing was to drive across town to the county hospital.

"He freaked out when the police arrested him," said the attorney. "Something about bugs."

Jesus! What's going on in this town? I thought as I raced to the hospital. Then I realized that cocaine use always went up at Christmastime. That new multiton shipment from Bolivia, now being sold at bargain-basement prices throughout the Los Angeles area, was irresistible. Put an infinite number of monkeys in front of an infinite amount of cocaine, and eventually all of them will start itching and scratching. And, as I would soon discover, one of them would end up quoting Shakespeare.

When I arrived on the jail ward I found Cliff Hill on a gurney in the hall. There was a shortage of rooms, and gurneys were lined up against the hall walls with an assortment of gunshot victims, spaced-out drivers, and a screaming man with heavy makeup and a knife wound in his shoulder. He pursed his lips and threw me a kiss as I walked past. I was glad he was chained to the gurney.

Cliff was finishing his dinner tray when I found him. He was literally licking the plates. "Can you get me some more food?" he asked. "I'm still hungry, but they won't give me any more." He stared down the hall at a sheriff's deputy still passing out trays to other gurneys. Cliff had tears in his dark eyes as he looked back at me. "Please."

I stole some pudding from a nearby patient who was too sedated to notice. As Cliff lapped it up, I studied him. He looked like a young mustached Charles Bronson, but with a nose that suggested he had been in more than one barroom fight without a stunt double. His skin looked as rough as his well-developed chest and biceps. The chart on the gurney indicated he was still waiting for a physician to check him out.

Cliff had been arrested just after buying a large amount of cocaine. As he was driving away from the dealer, four police cars converged on him.

"Why did they bring you here?" I asked. He seemed all right

except for the ravenous appetite that usually accompanied cocaine withdrawal.

"They thought I was shot," Cliff said as he pulled the sheet down from his naked chest.

I took a deep breath and fought to suppress the acid taste that was filling the back of my throat. On Cliff's chest, just above the right nipple, was a large round ulcer about the size of a silver dollar. It had a sharply demarcated, punched-out appearance. The outer rim was raised and inflamed, almost crusty. The inside dropped down a good half inch and was filled with a glistening mass of creamy yellow fluid and red necrotic tissue. The whole thing resembled a piece of pizza that had been pushed into his chest. Cliff poked the pizza with his finger, picked out a glob, rolled it between his thumb and finger as he smelled it, then flicked it away.

"I probably shouldn't pick at them, huh?" he said sheepishly. "I thought I had bugs in my skin—wormy little things."

"Them?" I asked. "Where else have you been picking?"

"They have made worms' meat of me," said Cliff. "That's Shakespeare, from *Romeo and Juliet*, our favorite." His eyes started tearing again. "But I'm so ashamed of my body, I don't let Mary see it. We don't make love anymore."

He took off the sheet and showed me. His legs, arms, and testicles were spotted with multiple ulcers. They were much smaller than the one on his chest, but they had the same raised borders, some with a dirty yellow-gray crust. Several appeared burned. Cliff told me they were. Despite his incessant picking, he had been unable to catch any bugs. So he'd scorched the areas with a propane torch. Now, picking is one thing. But toasting your testicles must have been painful, even for a chronic cocaine smoker like Cliff, who was going through an ounce of the drug every week. But he didn't care about the pain. He was willing to try anything to save his family. I assumed Cliff was referring to the destructive effects a cocaine addict had on family relations.

"That's not it," said Cliff. He was crying now. "They all have bugs. I was trying to figure out how to help them."

"Who in your family has bugs?"

"My wife, Mary, and my daughter. Also my mother. She lives with us."

"Does everybody use cocaine?"

"No." He sounded surprised by my question. "What does coke have to do with it?"

I told him.

"That's not it," he said. "Chico's got them, too. I always thought we got them from him."

"Who's Chico?"

"Our Chihuahua. Smart little dog. Does the most incredible tricks."

Cliff told me that when he first discovered he was itching and scratching, he thought the dog had brought fleas into the house. They had the house sprayed and tried every type of powder and shampoo known to man and dog, but Cliff's problem only got worse. Finally they took Chico to the veterinarian, but no fleas, ticks, or parasites were found. The vet could offer no explanation for the dog's alleged scratching. Then the itching and scratching spread to the rest of the family.

I considered two alternative explanations. First, there could be a real infestation in the household. Neither Cliff nor his family had sought any professional help except for the visit to the vet. Instead they relied on elaborate daily purification rituals involving baths, powders, and sprays. A significant part of the family budget was dedicated to disinfectants, cleaning bills, and linen, which they replaced periodically. Since Cliff was now in a hospital, I made arrangements for an examination by a dermatologist. I knew it would be desirable to examine the other family members, but that would have to wait.

While we waited for the dermatologist, I took a detailed history from Cliff with the idea of exploring a second possible explanation. If no bugs were found, this might be a case of a shared delusional disorder, a condition that psychiatrists generally label with French terms. When two closely related persons, usually in the same family, share the same delusion, it is known as *folie à deux*. When the condition involves three people, it is *folie à trois*. When an entire family shares the same delusion, it is known as folie à famille. There are cases on record of *folie à famille*, but none involve family pets. If Chico was also suffering, as Cliff insisted, then the Hill family might be a unique case in medical history. I was excited with the possibility of receiving credit for the discovery. Of course, I needed to have a name for the disorder. Since it involved two parents, a child, a grandmother, a dog that did tricks, and imaginary fleas that jumped from one member to another, I called it *folie à cirque*, for "mad circus."

I suspected that Cliff was the original victim of the delusion, which was induced by his use of cocaine. His chronic itching and scratching behavior awakened in others their ancestral fear of infestation. Many anthropologists consider scratching, along with yawning, one of the most highly contagious behaviors in the primate repertoire. The behaviors are readily mimicked, either consciously or unconsciously, by close and frequent observers. Not surprisingly, fully 12 percent of patients with delusions of infestation "catch" it from others, usually close family members, relatives, or co-workers.

Cliff was forty-four and had been a "baser" (smoking cocaine freebase) for approximately one year. He experienced the typical symptoms of chronic intoxication, including anxiety, hypervigilance, and "snow lights," seen as flashes of light and geometric forms in the visual periphery. Some of these geometric forms resemble black snowflakes. The snow lights and other effects are the result of a storm of electrical and chemical excitation unleashed by cocaine in the brain.

Meanwhile, in the periphery of his body, cocaine was constricting blood vessels, drying out the skin, and causing paresthesias. Cliff itched and scratched. His superalert brain noticed the dog doing the same thing. That's when he suspected fleas and took the dog to the vet. The vet gave the dog a clean bill of health and told Cliff that the marks on his body did not resemble the clusters of small domed lesions caused by flea bites.

Cliff went home and continued smoking, itching, and picking. Sores opened on his body. Once or twice he caught a fleeting glimpse of a bug moving inside the sores. When the rest of his family began itching and scratching, Cliff knew there was a real problem in the house. He stayed up for days at a time, trying to figure out how to get rid of the bugs. The cocaine gave him lots of ideas. He tried them all but discovered only minor relief. For example, he found that drinking Pepsi seemed to reduce the itching a little. "Small things make base men proud," said Cliff. *"King Henry the Sixth,"* he added for my benefit. I was sure Shakespeare was turning over in his grave with this twisted comparison to cocaine freebasers.

Why didn't Cliff ever try abstinence? After all, the bug problem started at the same time his cocaine problem started. The answer, of course, was that he was so blinded by his addiction that he couldn't see a connection. Then what was his explanation for the bugs?

"They're trying to eat me alive."

"Why?"

"They like the taste."

Cliff should know. Throughout our brief conversation he kept picking pieces from his chest wound and smelling them. Now he was bringing small globs to his mouth, where he proceeded to nip them with his front teeth before tossing the fragments over the side of the gurney. He finally stopped when the dermatologist arrived. The examination revealed that most of the "bug" and "worm" holes were ulcerative impetigo, a confusing term that refers to sores caused by bacterial infection. Antibiotics were prescribed for these. The chest wound was another matter. The dermatologist had never seen anything like it. The gummy appearance resembled advanced syphilis, which was one of the reasons earlier reports of delusions of parasitosis were often reported in medical journals devoted to syphilis and allied diseases. But Cliff had no other symptoms of such diseases. The dermatologist decided that the antibiotics would handle this, too, as long as Cliff could keep his own hands out of the wound. Cliff promised to be good. He knew that his wife had already arranged bail, and he didn't want to stay on the jail ward any longer than necessary. I knew that monkeys on cocaine would promise anything to get their next hit of the drug.

The next week I met Mary, the show girl of the Hill family circus, who came to my office. Mary had pretty features, but her skin was a mess. In addition to a few minor lesions on her hands and forearms, the result of scratching and picking the bugs that Cliff said were there, she had multiple bruises. The bruises were caused by Cliff's periodic cocaine rages.

"I tried smoking cocaine a few times," Mary confessed. "It felt like heaven." She batted her fake eyelashes. "Cliff didn't have the strength to stay away from it; I did."

Mary also had the good sense to stay away from Cliff, but not because of the unprovoked beatings. She believed that the bugs jumped from one body to another. The entire family avoided all bodily contact with each other. Cliff was the most isolated. He stayed in the master bedroom by himself. Meals and Pepsis were brought to him on trays. He was afraid to let anyone near him, but at times he would stick his head out into the hall and, with tears in his eyes, say, "I love you," to whoever was there.

"Cliff wanted to die for hurting us," Mary said as she wiped away a tear. An eyelash came loose, and she started adjusting it as she continued talking. "He tried to kill himself several times. One time he tried hanging himself from the roof. He tried to drive off a canyon in his car. He tried to get a gun."

One night there was an explosion in the kitchen. Mary thought it was a gunshot and rushed from her bedroom. So did Ashley, her teenage daughter. Even seventy-six-year-old Granny Hill hobbled down the hall from the guest bedroom. They found Cliff hunched over the kitchen floor, cleaning. He had been boiling a glass bottle on the stove when it exploded. He told everyone he wasn't feeling well and was making his "medicine." Granny Hill believed him. Mary and Ashley knew all about Cliff's midnight cooking of cocaine freebase.

"Why do you put up with this?" I asked.

"I am not happy about it," said Mary. "He treats me like a whore, beats me, and makes me do things to him. But I'm afraid he'll hurt himself more if I leave."

"And the bugs?" I asked. Mary had not scratched once during the entire interview.

"They only bother me when I'm around Cliff. But I have to stay and help him. How do I do that?"

I didn't answer her question. The purpose of the interview was to further understand Cliff's condition so the court could consider a treatment program as an alternative to jail time for his offense. Actually, jail time was beginning to look like a promising way to force him to detoxify. After getting out of the hospital jail ward, Cliff was arrested again for possession of cocaine. The amounts he was buying, possessing, and smoking were so great, the police thought he was a dealer. He was now back in jail. I took advantage of his absence to visit the Hill house.

Chico started yapping as soon as I knocked on the front door. Mary was at work, but Granny Hill opened the door and ushered me into the living room. Actually Chico led the way, yapping constantly, turning in tight circles, and jumping in the air. He was the most hyperactive dog I had ever seen. When Granny and I started talking, Chico went ballistic. He ran around the perimeter of the living room, ricocheting off the walls at impossible angles. Eventually he stopped and stared at us with glassy, doleful eyes, his large ears searching for approval.

"Chico! Fuck off!" said Granny Hill. The remark shocked me more than the dog, who calmly went over to an empty chair and curled up in a sleeping position.

"My son taught him that," explained Granny. "It's the only command that will quiet him down."

I looked over at the dog. He was quiet now. He wasn't even scratching. I asked Granny about the bugs.

"Cliff says we all have them. I looked all over. Never saw them. Cliff is always crying about them, always frightened and scared. I told him he had to go to a doctor. I tried to make Mary make him go. It never happened."

"Do the bugs ever bother you?" She didn't appear to have a mark on her.

"Sometimes they itch, but I drink Pepsi and that helps. Cliff gives us all kinds of soaps to use. That helps."

Granny Hill described the typical signs of cocaine intoxication and dependency in Cliff, although she had no idea what she was describing. Her maternal eyes saw only a sick son who didn't sleep and eat enough. To her the problem was simple: the bugs were keeping him up and ruining his appetite.

I took a tour of the house—it was clean and orderly—but Cliff's bedroom remained locked and off limits to everyone. I collected dust and fiber samples from the vacuum cleaner bag, air-conditioning filter, clothes dryer filter, and carpets. I also took samples of the tap water and some indoor plants, and I checked the food in the pantry for signs of weevils or other insects. Chico allowed me to check him for fleas and ticks, but I found none. I swabbed his ears for mites and took a stool sample from the backyard. I suspected that there were no unusual parasites present, and subsequent analysis proved me correct.

Granny Hill was showing me the family picture album when Ashley came home from school. Chico got up and started his little circus act. "Chico! Fuck off!" said Ashley, and the dog quieted down immediately. "I have to shower," she announced, and disappeared into her room. Granny Hill explained that it might be a long wait. Like everyone else in the family, Ashley spent hours showering and shampooing. One hour later she emerged, ready to talk.

Ashley was a lovely, slightly plump girl with long black hair and several jeweled studs in each ear. She was wearing shorts and a T-shirt that revealed perfect skin without a scratch or blemish. Yet she was constantly rubbing lotion on her face and running her fingers through her hair. I asked about the bugs.

"Daddy had them first," she explained, twisting her face into an expression of disgust. "He scratched until he was bleeding, then burned them. I wanted to earl," she said, using a slang term for vomit.

"Did you ever see them?" I asked.

"No, but his skin got pasty. Yueech."

"What about you?"

"They don't bother me as long I keep showering and rubbing lotion. Then they can't jump me."

"Do they ever get to you?"

"Sometimes at night I'll start itching. Then I'll really sketch out," said Ashley. She was using the slang expression for having a paranoid reaction. "I get afraid that I'll get like Daddy, or turn into a pizza face or a total grossola."

Ashley, like her mother and grandmother, itched and scratched mostly when they saw Cliff doing the same. They failed to recognize the contagious aspects of either this behavior or the accompanying delusion that Cliff screamed and yelled about. Instead they accepted it as evidence that there were bugs capable of jumping from one person to another. Now that Cliff was safely tucked away in jail with his imaginary bugs, they appeared less bothered but remained distrustful of any suggestion that the bugs were gone.

"Do you have any clues as to what to do?" asked Ashley.

I answered her in her own slang. "Yeah. I think your father was psyched"—fooled—"by the coke. When he freaked, you all started freaking. We got to stop him from doing coke." It was a long shot, like nailing Jell-O to a tree, as Ashley might say. Most cases of *folie à famille* last for years or until psychiatrists get tired of trying unsuccessful treatments. Only one ever claimed a total cure. In 1950 a psychiatrist boasted that he had cured three people afflicted with delusions of infestation with a single operation: a prefrontal lobotomy on the one individual who was the infector. The delusions cleared in the infector, then in the two others. I saw the possibility of the long prison sentence Cliff was facing as functionally equivalent to such an operation. There had to be another way.

Several weeks later I thought I had found it. I convinced the court that Cliff was a user, not a dealer. Furthermore, he needed immediate inpatient care. Cliff was ordered to spend several months in an inpatient facility. Pending successful completion of the program, he would be placed on supervised probation and urine testing. I wished him luck. "Take care of yourself," I said.

"Our bodies are our gardens," he said, quoting from *Othello*. I didn't like the quotation. It left too much room for the bugs.

4

April 10. Midvale Avenue, Westwood. Matt Nichols called me late at night. It was my first contact with him since Christmas, and he still sounded high. He had the rapid speech and labored breathing of someone with a toxic dose of cocaine in his system.

"I can see in the dark," he proclaimed.

"And, pray tell, what do you see?" I heard my sarcasm, but I was annoyed at getting disturbed so late at home.

"The snakes," he said. "They flash in the dark." I knew he was probably seeing the "snow lights" induced by cocaine.

"And you've been smoking coke again, right?"

"Nope. Injecting—"

I tried to interrupt.

"Listen, listen," he continued, "I caught some of the snakes and put them in a dish. Then I added ten units of my blood. The snakes ate the blood. It took them three and a half minutes. Then I injected some cocaine, waited several minutes, and withdrew another ten units of blood. This time it took the snakes five and a half minutes." He paused for emphasis, then went on. "Coke is good for you. Slows them down—"

I tried to interrupt again.

"Listen, listen, something better," he said excitedly. What could be better than a cocaine addict discovering proof positive that cocaine is good for you? I wondered. "When the blood is gone . . . the snakes eat each other."

Omigod! He's going to bleed himself to death, I thought. "Matt, Matt," I started to say. But the line was already dead.

October 2. UCLA, Westwood. Matt called me just as I was getting ready to leave my office for lunch.

"My hands are swollen twice their size, my skin is cracked, and I'm bleeding from my fingertips," he said. He sounded out of breath.

"And you've been picking at the snakes again, right?"

"I don't know if there are any snakes. My hands are swollen twice their size, my skin is cracked, and I'm bleeding from my fingertips." He sounded like a broken record.

Matt told me he had been up all night smoking cocaine freebase. This morning he'd noticed that his hands were swollen and bleeding. I went through a symptom checklist and determined that he was experiencing chest pains as well as numbness in his left arm and leg. This suggested an incipient cardiac problem, and I advised him that I could have the paramedics at his house in five minutes. He preferred to have Sherry, his girlfriend, drive him. We agreed to meet at the UCLA Hospital emergency room.

I found Matt in the waiting room. The first thing I noticed were his hands. They were swollen twice their size, the skin was cracked, and he was bleeding from the fingertips. I had never seen anything like it and grabbed my camera to photograph his hand from every conceivable angle. As I focused on the lesions with a close-up lens, I couldn't see the strange twitchings of his face.

Matt thought something was wrong with his cocaine and produced a large Ziploc bag full of the suspect drug. I took a small sample for later analysis. Since we were still waiting for an examination room to become available, I asked Matt to go into the restroom and give me a urine specimen. As soon as he left, Sherry came up to me.

"He's crazy," she whispered in my ear as she stood on tiptoes.

"What are you talking about?" I asked as I continued to marvel at the skin reaction. "Look at his hands. They're swollen twice their size and he's bleeding from his fingertips." I couldn't get over it. I was already thinking about writing a clinical note for a medical journal.

"He's crazy," she repeated. "He held a gun in my ear during the drive over here. He thinks I'm a secret agent working for the DEA. He thinks you're one, too."

I looked at her. Her pupils were gigantic, and she was shaking. She's as loaded as he is, I thought.

"He's armed and ready to pop at any moment," Sherry said.

"You mean he has a gun on him? Where?"

"In his bag," she said, referring to the canvas shoulder bag he always carried.

Matt emerged from the restroom with an empty urine container. He was so busy doing more cocaine that he had forgotten to take a leak. It didn't matter. I was more anxious to find out about his hands than the amount of cocaine he had used. An examination room became available, and I had Matt and Sherry wait inside while I waited outside for one of the emergency room physicians to appear.

It seemed like a long wait. You can die waiting for a doctor in this place, I thought. I used the time by mentally outlining the journal article I would prepare on this case. Finally a young intern appeared. I briefed him in the hall.

"Patient has an extreme skin reaction. His hands are swollen twice their size, his skin is cracked, and he's bleeding from his fingertips," I said excitedly. "He's been up all night basing."

"Basing? What's that?"

"Smoking cocaine," I explained.

"You can smoke it?" His eyes widened with interest. "How do you do that?"

"That's not important. You've got to see his hands. They're really swollen. But I should tell you before you go in that he's armed."

"He's got a gun?"

"Yeah."

"I can't go in there if he's got a gun." The intern's eyes got even bigger. "I'll have to tell security."

The intern started down the hall. I persuaded him to stop outside Matt's room. Matt came to the door and held his hands out across the doorway.

"Look," I said. Even an intern who didn't appear old enough to shave should be able to see that Matt's hands were swollen twice their size, the skin was cracked, and the fingertips were bleeding. They were also steady compared with this young doctor's hands: they were now shaking noticeably.

"We'll be right back," the intern said as he closed the examination room door on Matt. Then he made a beeline to the nearest telephone.

University police arrived faster than the doctor. A large burly officer, whose hand seemed frozen in air just inches over his service revolver, took a position outside Matt's room while his sergeant stood at the end of the hall. Between officer and sergeant was a mass of nurses and orderlies. There was a brief discussion about evacuating the rooms adjoining Matt's. The hall started to empty. I approached the sergeant.

"Look," I said, "this patient's high and paranoid. He's got a big bag of cocaine. He's going to think this is a bust. I'll go in and talk to him."

"You can't go in there," he said as his eyes remained riveted on Matt's door.

"But he's going to freak out if he sees police and guns." I noticed hospital security arriving on the scene. Someone mentioned a SWAT team. "I can go in there and talk to him."

The sergeant turned to me. "You can't go in there. This is not a medical matter. This is a police matter. We got a suspect who may be armed and dangerous. We're going to disarm him and save lives."

"You shouldn't go in there showing all this force," I argued as several more badges started appearing down the hall. "He'll freak. At least put on a white lab coat and I'll—"

Matt opened the door to see what all the fuss was about. He was looking very simian and very scared. His face was twisted into an expression of fear and rage. His eyes darted up and down the hall, checking out every detail.

"Stay right where you are!" barked the officer standing near the door.

Matt's paranoid-guided eyes zoomed in on the officer's hand hovering over his holster.

"Oh, no! No!" said Matt, his voice cracking with fright. He pulled out his own gun and fired a shot. The officer started to return fire.

The sergeant next to me ran toward the gunfight. I ran the other way, thankful that I was wearing my Nikes. I ducked into an empty room, closed the door, and huddled on the floor next to a file cabinet.

I was breathing far too hard for the short sprint into this office. It was fear that stole my breath. The fear transported me. For a moment, just for a moment, I was back in the dungeon in Quebec. More shots rang out, hitting my paranoid streak and overwhelming me with uncertainty and panic. I stared at the door and thought the gunfire outside was meant for me. A voice yelled my name over and over. Someone was running down the hall. Did Matt get away from the police? Was he coming after me, the secret agent who started it all?

The door flew open and a nurse ran into the room, slammed the door behind her, and took a position next to me on the floor. Her lips were slightly parted. She was breathing audibly. Wisps of blond hair, shaken loose from her perm, dribbled seductively across her face. Her uniform was pushed up to her thighs, revealing a garter belt holding up white stockings. A secret agent's dream.

More gunfire.

"Oh, shit!" she gasped. Secret agents love it when they talk dirty.

I heard doors opening around me. More yelling. It was getting closer. A garbled voice came over the public address system. It sounded like someone croaking to death. The nurse stood, straightened her uniform, opened the door, and left. Silently I thanked her.

By the time I emerged from hiding, Matt was safely cuffed and being led away. There were bullet holes in the door and hall walls, but luckily no one had been hit, even though the police had been shooting at him from a distant of only four feet. Inside Matt's shoulder bag the police found a second handgun, ammunition, a cherry bomb, and other assorted fireworks. This was nothing compared to the pyrotechnics I discovered going on inside Matt's brain. His cocaine, which was not from the Bolivian shipment, contained a significant amount of procaine, a cheaper drug sometimes used to cut cocaine. Procaine can be smoked, but large amounts cause paresthesia and swelling of the hands, giving Matt something real to pick at to the point of bleeding from his fingertips. But procaine is also more potent than cocaine in activating the limbic system with seizurelike intensity. The drug spreads abnormal electrical discharges throughout the system, thereby evoking tension, anxiety, confusion, and fear. These emotions can become strong enough to twist the face into displays of animal fear and rage. If the body feels like a frightened or cornered animal, and looks like an animal, it often acts like one.

Matt's face and brain remained twisted even when he was booked at the police station a few hours later. He gave the police an alias and false identification to prove it. They didn't know that he was an ex-convict on probation for armed robbery. Possession of a handgun violated the conditions of his probation, and he should not have been given bail. Yet police computers were no better than police marksmanship. Matt was released that night. His attorney immediately called me at home.

"Better get out of there," warned the attorney. "He's looking for you. Thinks you're a secret agent who turned him in to the police."

"Do you think he's really going to hurt me?" My paranoid streak was still tingling.

"I don't know. He sounds crazy. He has a forty-four Magnum. Says you gave him some bugs. What's that all about?"

I didn't have time to explain. Matt knew where I lived. It was only minutes away from where he was last seen by the attorney. I hung up the phone, packed a bag, and moved in with a friend for a few days until the police were able to track Matt down and place him in jail. After a brief trial, during which I testified on his behalf about cocaine paranoia and delusions of infestation, Matt and his imaginary parasites were returned to state prison. I hoped when he was released it would be without them.

5

November 14. Grand Canyon, Arizona. Sunrise at the Grand Canyon bathes the rocks with a blood red glow. The slanting light marching across the canyon is an awesome sight that inspired poet Carl Sandburg to think of God. Cliff Hill was also thinking of God . . . and peace. He and his family had driven all night to get to this deserted spot on the rim.

The Grand Canyon takes one's breath away. A common reaction is a sudden loss of words. But Cliff did not need to tell his family why they were there. He didn't need to articulate the reasons why they would have to leap to their death. He had discussed it with them many times. It was the only way to get rid of the bugs. He was certain they understood.

They stood on the edge, stark silhouettes ready to swim in the cleansing rays of God's early morning light.

It's beautiful, thought Ashley as she cradled Chico in her arms.

Beautiful, echoed the thoughts of Mary and Granny.

Cliff jumped first. His body fell through time. Falling past the top layers of dirt and lava, it bounced and rolled into the Paleozoic era. It fell past the limestone and sandstone fossil deposits, past the shale, coming to rest on a rust-colored ledge in the Pennsylvanian period. It was an appropriate resting place for the body that Cliff Hill had shared with his bugs. The ledge marked a time known as the age of insects.

The family got back in their station wagon and went for help. After the body was recovered, they returned with it for burial in Los Angeles. The bugs never bothered them again.

7

RICHIE IN WHACKYLAND

Porky Pig lost his voice today. I was on an airplane bound for Boston to interview another criminal defendant who claimed to have been attacked by bugs when I read the news. Mel Blanc, who provided the voices of Porky, Bugs Bunny, Daffy Duck, and other delightful cartoon characters, had died. I was saddened at the passing of such an incredible talent. In my mind's ear I could hear Porky give an appropriate eulogy with his immortal stuttering of "B'dee, b'dee, th-th-that's all, folks!" I put down the obituary page of the paper, gazed out the plane window, and began reminiscing about the cartoon heroes of my childhood.

Of all the Blanc characters, I liked Porky Pig the best. His childlike innocence and wide-eyed, apple-cheeked appearance made him especially appealing. Blanc's voice made every line sound funny. And the animators at Warner Brothers gave Porky some of the most inventive stories ever done in cartoons. He was always playing the role of an intrepid explorer or detective, but underneath he was really timid. My favorite was the 1938 classic *Porky in Wackyland* (remade in 1949 as *Dough for the Do-Do*), which I had seen many times on videotape as an adult.

The cartoon opens with Porky piloting an airplane into "Darkest Africa" in search of the last dodo bird, worth a fortune in reward money. He lands at the border of Wackyland. A sign reads

"It Can Happen Here." Porky tiptoes across the border and immediately finds himself in a surreal landscape reminiscent of a Dali painting, with eerie trees, melting watches, and disembodied eyes. He's greeted by a menagerie of monsters, odd-shaped midgets with strange pets, and a wormlike rubber band that creeps and twangs across the landscape. All this frightens Porky, who tries to hide, only to run into more impossible creatures. Finally Porky sees the dodo and gives chase. But the dodo is a wily prankster who has the ability to appear and disappear into another dimension. The bird produces a pencil from thin air, draws a door, then ducks into it just as the pursuing pig pounces against it. In another chase scene, the fleeing dodo simply lifts the Daliesque scenery off the ground in order to escape. After much taunting and teasing, Porky finally handcuffs the bird. As he leaves Wackyland to claim his reward for capturing the last dodo, a crowd of identical dodos appear to hoot their good-byes.

I was saying my own good-byes to these childhood memories as the American Airlines pilot announced we were on our final approach to Boston. After landing, I took a taxi to my hotel. I never saw a sign on the side of the highway that read "It Can Happen Here."

I checked into the hotel, then took a short walk to the Charles Street Jail. After clearing several security areas, I entered a central rotunda with a high Gothic ceiling. The room was alive with the murmur of hundreds of inmates, iron doors clanging open or closed, and the occasional scream, all mixing together in echoes so deafening, I had to mouth my words to the guard. He directed me to an empty office where I would conduct my interviews over the next few days. The office was a mess, but at least it had a door that shut out some of the noise.

Richie D. came into the office. At first glance I thought the guards had sent the wrong man to see me. I had studied the mug shots of the suspect they'd arrested eleven months earlier. That man had a wild look, from his overgrown Afro with unkempt dreadlocks, to his bushy beard and mustache, down to the zebra-striped shirt and shredded jeans. In the glare of the camera's flash, his slightly crossed eyes reflected an unseen horror. But the man sitting on the chair next to my desk had short hair and a clean-shaven face. He was actually quite handsome. His body movements were slow and hesitant, giving the appearance of mild, not wild, manners. But the eyes gave him away: they were still filled with a look of horror.

As I took out my pen and legal pad, those eyes seemed to criss-cross even more, their lines of sight following my every movement. They tracked my hands as I opened my gray metallic Haliburton briefcase. They scanned the interior, then locked on to the piece of paper I had removed and placed on the desk. It was a letter from Richie's attorney authorizing my visit. I started to introduce myself, but Richie was not listening to me. He wanted to know what else was in my briefcase. So I showed him. For good measure I even let him browse through my appointment book, wallet, and other personal items. When he was satisfied, he nodded once and forced a grin. I continued to expose things he'd missed: eyeglass case, airline tickets, and breath spray. Then I stood up and started emptying my pockets.

"Okay, okay. It's okay." He spoke softly, almost in a whisper.

"Hey, I understand," I said. "Gotta be careful." Then I began to take a medical and drug history. As I wrote, Richie's eyes followed the movements of my pen. His answers were as clipped and mechanical as his eye movements. He appeared spellbound with fear.

After the history taking, I tried to break the spell. "I know something about the bugs," I said, imitating his whisper. The police and investigative reports had told me that Richie appeared delusional and talked about bugs infesting his home. What I didn't know at the time was that his case would prove to be the most elaborate, most bizarre, and best-documented invasion of bugs in medical history.

Richie lifted his eyes from the desk and looked straight at me for the first time. The pupils seemed to cross in a question mark.

"I've talked to many people who have seen the bugs," I continued. "Most of them were coke users just like you."

"They've seen them, too?" he asked.

I nodded.

"Do you know how lonely it is?" he asked, then went on to answer the question. "It's a lonely life being aware of things that exist and nobody believes it. They seemed so real . . . so real." He was fighting tears.

"The bugs are real, Richie. We have bottles full of them in the lab." I needed to tell this half lie to break the spell and get him talking more. His reaction eliminated my guilt about the deception.

"Thank God," he said, then broke down and cried. I gave him some Kleenex from my case. He was sobbing and gasping for breath so hard that his sentences broke down to two words. "Thank God. . . . Thank God. . . . Thank God." After a few moments he inched his chair closer to mine.

"Not only bugs," he whispered.

"What else?" I was prepared for him to mention worms, snakes, or any number of parasites.

"Mites . . . worms . . . snakes . . ."

I was nodding and writing.

"Small midgets with thin heads, about a foot high. They run around and peek up my shirt."

"Holy shit." I dropped my pen.

Richie started tapping his fingers rhythmically on the metal desk. *Da Dum. Da Dum.* "Sometimes I hear their footsteps. They're very fast." *DaDum DaDum DaDum DaDum.*

"What do they look like?" I was almost afraid to ask.

"They're always blurred. It's like seeing something out of focus. I see them over and over again, but never in focus. They run and hide in the corners or under the furniture." *DaDum DaDum Da-Dum.* "Sometimes I see something like a small animal, like a cat. They're very quiet. I think the midgets keep them as pets . . . I saw them when I first came to jail."

It was unnecessary to prod Richie with more questions. After eleven months of silence, the dam was breaking. He continued describing the creatures in the present tense, underlying his belief in their existence even though he no longer saw them.

"The worms are different," he continued, tears streaming over his apple cheeks. "They're almost invisible to the naked eye. Donna pulled a worm out of my finger. It jumped. They're capable of shaping—changing themselves into different kinds. Some float in the air and attack. I saw a whole pile of black ones on the couch. Robin never admitted she saw them. So I threw them on her, and she started brushing them away and jumped back. I saw them on Melvin. He played with them."

My face must have registered disbelief.

"I know it sounds unbelievable," he said. "My father believed in UFOs. I saw them once. I grew up prepared to believe the unbelievable."

"Richie, I saw a UFO once. I saw it when I was going to Brandeis in Waltham. It was hovering near some marshes. I didn't know what to make of it. Maybe it was burning marsh gas. I don't know. But I do know that extraordinary claims require extraordinary proof." It was the standard line of a skeptic, but I was hoping to slow down his story and get him to present the evidence to me in the same chronological development it was presented to him. I appealed to his training as an engineer. Lay it out for me, step by step, I pleaded. Take me through the evidence as it happened to you, step by step. Slowly. *Da . . . Dum.*

He did. In a series of interviews over the following months, Richie told his story. The other people he mentioned told their side as well. The case was uniquely documented with the most extraordinary records: Richie had captured his war against the bugs and midgets on videotape recorded from five different cameras and numerous microphones located throughout his house. The library of tapes spanned a wartime period of three years. It was the most covered war in the entire history of infestation. Although I was still itching and scratching from my previous adventures ("Invasion of Bugs"), I couldn't resist diving into this case and seeing the invasion from start to finish through the same camera "eyes" as its victim.

Richie was born in Florida during the fireworks of a Fourth of July some forty years before. He was a good kid. He had to be. His father was a policeman who never took off his badge at home. The old man ruled the family with an iron fist, beating Richie as well as his mother. Eventually Mrs. D. took Richie and his brothers and sisters to live in Boston. Richie finished school, then married his high school sweetheart, Donna. Friends described the marriage as idyllic. The couple had five daughters, and Richie worked hard to support them, holding down a day job as an outfitter and carpenter in the local shipyard, and free-lancing as both a carpenter and auto mechanic at night.

One day a gigantic staging collapsed at the shipyard. A steel beam came crashing down on Richie's head. Richie saw stars, the kind cartoon characters see when they're bopped on the head. Then he passed out. But, unlike cartoon characters who bounce right back into action, Richie remained immobilized for several minutes. He regained consciousness but was forever plagued by severe headaches. And he never regained complete control of his hands; they were weakened permanently, preventing him from holding a firm grip. Unfit for heavy work, Richie lost his jobs and joined the ranks of the unemployed. It was then that he started to lose his grip on reality.

It happened slowly. After the accident Richie returned to school and studied engineering. Things seemed to be going well for a couple of years until the robbery. Richie was mistakenly identified as a suspect in a local bank robbery. He was arrested as he emerged from school, right in front of his startled classmates. The case lingered for months until the actual suspect was caught and the charges against Richie were dismissed. But the episode left him humiliated and depressed. Then he discovered cocaine. The drug lifted the depression, making his studies easier and family life more enjoyable.

New Year's Eve. Time to celebrate. The criminal case against Richie was history, and he was now working hard to make up for lost class time. He deserved a big hit of cocaine. "Much too big," he whispered to the paramedics as they transported him to the hospital. He was experiencing chest pains and difficulty breathing. Donna thought he might be having a heart attack. By the time he got to the emergency room, he was feeling better and skipped out a side door.

Richie dropped out of school and stayed home, where he spent much of his time doing coke and staring out the rear window. He had a spacious backyard surrounded by a natural fence of tall spruce trees. He admired the trees for their strength. Even the winter snows couldn't make the branches droop more than a fraction of an inch. Richie knew this because he watched the seasons pass as he studied the trees. During one spring thunderstorm, he saw something moving along the branches, causing the blue-green needles to quiver ever so slightly. At the same time a quiver ran through his skin. It started to itch. His mind searched for explanations to connect the two events. Like the opening witches' scene in *Macbeth,* Richie sensed a conspiracy was at hand. Perhaps his brain recognized a remote connection because he immediately reached for a bottle of witch hazel and rubbed it on his skin. The refreshing smell and astringent action helped him to maintain his vigil, and he started using the lotion on a regular basis.

In the summer Richie put an inflatable wading pool in the backyard for his daughters. Donna asked him to take videos of them playing. The girls performed a little dance for the camera, hopping around the tiny pool, then jumping in and splashing each other. When they lined up to show off their swimsuits, Richie zoomed in on their smiling faces. He continued zooming over their shoulders, right into the quivering needles of a spruce tree. The camera followed the movement, then panned across the other trees. The light was bad and the focus was blurred, but something was definitely moving in the trees.

Richie set up a video camera on a tripod in the rear window overlooking the yard and began to monitor the trees. Each day he reviewed the tapes, scrutinizing every branch and needle. Finally he discovered the reason for the quivering: snakes. He showed the tapes to friends, but no one would admit to seeing snakes. Why are they trying to cover up? Richie wondered. He had caught enough snakes as a boy in Florida to know what they looked like. Hiding in the spruce trees were brown coachwhips, among the fastest snakes in the world. Richie believed the old legend that this snake preyed on humans. It supposedly chased people, then hypnotized them before striking. Actually, real coachwhips were harmless, but Richie's imaginary ones prompted him to declare the pool and backyard off limits. It was lucky for the girls. Richie sat in the rear window and fired his crossbow at the snakes. Arrows rained down on the empty pool.

The snakes didn't prevent Richie from leaving the house. He enjoyed going out in the evenings to visit friends. Before leaving, however, he would peep through the holes he'd drilled in the front walls of the house. After surveying the street from each hole—a routine that could take an hour or more—he ran to his car. When he returned, he used a spotlight in his car to check out the front yard and sidewalk before racing back inside.

Richie was afraid that the snakes, or something worse, might enter the house. Fear turned him into a constant fidget. He tossed and turned so much at night that Donna worried he might fall out of bed. Eventually Richie decided not to take it lying down. He spent his nights patroling the house, checking out every sound. He placed sensitive wireless microphones in the basement as well as in the rooms on the first and second floor. The microphones fed into a master tape recorder in his study. One night they picked up a strange noise. He played it back again and again through sophisticated amplifiers and filters until the sound was clear. Richie was now listening to the growling and snarling of an unknown animal. It reminded him of a mad dog. Now he had definite proof that something was in the house. He told Donna. That night he fell out of bed.

One day a few friends came to visit. While they were sitting in the living room, Richie heard muffled footsteps.

Da Dum. Da Dum.

He didn't say a word but watched his friends carefully. One turned and looked around.

"Why are you looking like that?" Richie snapped. "What are you looking at?"

"I was just looking around," said the friend. He couldn't understand why Richie was so uptight.

Why is he covering up? Richie wondered.

Richie still didn't know what was causing the footsteps. Coachwhips didn't have feet. And they didn't growl. He searched the house from top to bottom. In the basement he found a sack of powdered chalk and used it to dust the halls, stairs, and windowsills. The next day he saw little wiggly tracks in the chalk. The same shapes were appearing everywhere he dusted, even in the bedroom. He suspected that baby snakes or worms were making the tracks.

"I became obsessed with trying to catch them," explained Richie during one of our many interviews. "But I was afraid of what they would do." Although he couldn't see them—yet—he tried to kill them with a propane torch. He blasted away at the floors, under furniture, and in the cupboards. The hunt was not in vain, as Richie discovered a family of house mice living in the wall.

"Crazy mice," said Richie. "They were all hopped up from eating my cocaine. They spun around on the floor like whirling dervishes. One would try to hypnotize me by spinning while the others went after my stash." This was undoubtedly a delusion, but Richie managed to trap the entire family of mice and burn them to a crisp.

He was less successful in finding the baby snakes or worms. In case people were bringing in the creatures on their shoes, Richie torched everyone's shoes when they visited the house. More than one guest left with singed socks. But telltale tracks were still appearing in the chalk. Richie tried following the tracks, but they didn't seem to lead anywhere. It was almost as if they disappeared into some invisible hiding place. A secret dimension, he thought.

One day the door to this dimension opened right in front of Richie's eyes. He was staring at the wall, ruminating about the government's secret ways, when it happened. A flash of light in the corner of his eye told him it was opening. Then a worm popped out of thin air and landed on his finger. It was barely visible, sliding in and out of focus. It looked like a tiny earthworm, maroon and rubbery. He touched it. It felt electric. Then it dove into his skin. Richie watched in horror as it burrowed straight down and disappeared, just like the earthworms he used to toss overboard in the lake when he went fishing.

"Donna, Donna!" he screamed as he ran into the kitchen. "Pull it out."

"What's the matter, babe?" she asked. Richie was holding his finger.

"Pull it out. Pull it out." If she couldn't pull it out, he would have to cut his finger off. He looked around for the meat cleaver.

Donna saw something that looked like a splinter. She pulled it out with her fingernails and flicked it away. "Got it, babe," she said.

Richie watched the worm jump right back into the secret dimension. She didn't get it, he thought. He ran to the bathroom and swabbed witch hazel over his finger. In the mirror he saw another worm pop out of thin air and drop onto his hair. Now his hair was quivering like needles on a spruce tree. He emptied the bottle of witch hazel on his head. The quivering stopped.

The worm hunt started in earnest that night. Richie knew that nightcrawlers, even those from a secret dimension, were more likely to come out after dark. He chased them all over the house with a spray can of Lysol. In the morning he checked the carpet and furniture for dead ones, collecting them in a plastic sandwich bag. When the bag was full, he tied a knot in the top and ran to get Donna. He'd been telling her about the worms, but she didn't believe him. Now she'd see.

"But, babe," she said, "the bag is empty."

Richie was dumbfounded. The bag *was* empty. The worms weren't dead after all. They'd only been stunned. Someone has opened the bag and let them escape, Richie thought.

The worms launched a massive counterattack. They started jumping and crawling all over Richie's body. The worms were joined by tiny mites, which caused his skin to flake, although chronic cocaine users often have dry, flaking skin from peripheral vasoconstriction and poor nutrition. He brushed them away with his hands or ran the propane torch lightly over his clothes and skin.

The way Richie figured it, there was a doorway to the secret dimension located directly above his head, just beyond his vision. He began installing mirrors around the house: on doors, bookcases, walls, and tables. They were arranged in such a way that he could always glance in the mirrors and watch the dimensional doorway.

The worms came out in the shower—just like nightcrawlers in a rainstorm—and Richie had to be very careful. He only showered once a month and learned to hold a mirror in one hand as he soaped himself with the other. When the worms attacked, he would jump up and down, hooting and hollering like an Indian performing a rain dance. When he began dancing next to his bed in the middle of the night, Donna moved out with the kids. Richie didn't notice they were gone until a week later.

Now that everyone was gone, Richie decided to clean the house—really clean it. First he gave everything a good torching. Then he dusted DDT into all the cracks in the floor boards. He set off several flea bombs in the basement, then used a flea spray on the furniture for good measure. He sprinkled pesticide powder around the outside perimeter of the house. After another spraying with Lysol, the place was ready. He invited his former lover, Robin, and her three-year-old son, Melvin, to move in.

It was January and a new year. Things are really going well now, thought Richie as he sat on the toilet. It had been nice having Robin around for the past few weeks. The worms and mites seemed to be gone. He felt confident that there was no way for them to get into the house without crossing the line of pesticides he'd sprinkled around every entrance. Now he could relax and enjoy himself. And there was nothing more relaxing and enjoyable than a good shit. He started off each morning with a gigantic hit of cocaine. It went directly to his bowels. He could almost imagine it working its way down the labyrinth of his intestines. Today's bowel movement was particularly large. He could feel it coming out like one long, curving snake. Richie sat for a moment, enjoying the feeling. Suddenly he stiffened. Something just went up my butt! he thought, and leapt off the seat. He waddled across the bathroom with his pants around his knees until he found the Lysol can, which he emptied on his buttocks. Did I kill it? Richie thought. The question kept him awake all night. By morning his skin was itching again, especially around his groin. There was a strange mucus discharge in the seat of his underpants. And there were new tracks in the chalk. They looked like tiny footprints.

He installed four more video cameras in addition to the one constantly monitoring the backyard. One camera was focused on the trees and sidewalk in front of the house, while the others were in the basement, living room, and kitchen. They stayed on all the time. Robin and Melvin were never told that the cameras were watching their every word and movement.

Richie stared at one of the monitors in his den. He could see Robin in the living room, playing with something on her lap, like a pet or something. Her body blocked a clear view, so Richie tiptoed down the hall. Just as he turned the corner into the living room, Robin made a quick movement as if she were hiding something. What was it? Tell me. Robin denied hiding anything. Wasn't she playing with something? Worms? Snakes? Robin didn't know what Richie was talking about. He pleaded with her to tell him. If she loved him, she would tell him. No secrets. Please, he begged, tell me.

"I can't tell you anything," said Robin. "There's nothing to tell."

"What's in your hand, then?" asked Richie. Her hand was clenched in a fist.

She extended her hand and opened it. "See! There's nothing."

Richie saw a red worm jump from her opening hand. It landed in his hair. When he reached for it, the worm went down the back of his neck, under his shirt. Quickly he tied the shirt at the waist to prevent the worm from escaping. Then he stood in front of a mirror and started beating his body with a stick, hoping to drive the worm up to his open collar where he could catch it. After several minutes of frantic beating, Richie was sure the worm was as tired as he was. He looked at Robin. She had a worried expression. But just as he looked up at her, the worm slipped out of his collar, jumped to the floor, and wiggled under the couch. Robin put down the book she had been reading in her lap and left the room. Richie noticed that she placed the book on the floor near the couch. So she could hide him, he thought. He decided that she didn't have a worried expression after all. It was really a sadistic grin.

The next day Richie confronted Robin again. He cried. He pleaded. "Why are you torturing me like this? Why?"

"I can't tell you anything," she said.

Richie could tell she was extremely nervous. Her responses were measured, almost calculating. What was she hiding? Now her eyes were looking past him into the darkness of the dining room.

Da Dum. Da Dum. Da Dum. Da Dum.

Footsteps. And a faint voice! He decided it was a male voice, but it stopped before he could understand what it was saying. As he turned back to Robin, she had a look of fright. She was obviously afraid to say anything.

Richie leaned over and whispered into her ear, "I know someone is watching and you'll get in trouble if you tell me. But you can tell me. I won't hate you or be angry or let on that I know."

"I can't tell you anything," she said.

Richie was frustrated, but he knew that pressuring Robin to talk might only put her in danger from the creatures. He went to his study and continued watching her on the monitor. Robin sat on the living couch and started talking to someone. In the corner of the screen Richie saw a midget rush out of the living room in a blur. It was headed for the dining room. When Richie got to the dining room, the blur zipped into the kitchen, then into the bedroom. He could hear the bedroom window opening and closing. The midget got away. Richie went back to the living room and told Robin what he had seen.

"What?" she said, then laughed.

"Why, baby? Why are you doing this to me?"

Robin was still laughing. Richie went back to the study, put his head on the desk, and cried.

February. Richie was on the couch watching a television special about assassination theories and government cover-ups. Robin came in and cuddled next to him. She said she loved him. It was a good time for Richie to pop the question.

"Tell me about the worms. What's going on?" he asked.

She turned to him and mouthed, "No." Her open mouth was full of worms. They wiggled out and started crawling all over her face. Richie started beating them off her with his open hand. Hard.

"Stop!" she pleaded. "Stop before you get them upset." She didn't know what else to say.

Richie stopped hitting her. "You can trust me, baby," he said. "Just tell me what's going on, and we can deal with this together," he whined.

"Please, Richie. Don't make me say things." She was already sorry she had played into his worm theory.

Richie now knew that there was some sort of government conspiracy to hush up evidence of the secret dimension. Somehow Robin was involved. She was pretending to watch the movie again, but he knew she was actually listening to the staticlike whispering that was coming from behind the television set. Suddenly an army of worms marched from behind the television. They jumped on his feet, then crawled up his legs. A midget came from under the couch, ran over to Richie, and picked up his shirt. The worms slithered under the shirt and onto his chest. They burned and stung. Richie dove into his rain dance. He grabbed a steel rod and started swinging it in the air.

"Help me, Robin!"

She backed away in shock. Now Richie knew he was in deep trouble because she was distancing herself from the creatures. He looked at her in disbelief. Then a dull thumping, like a hammer wrapped in cotton. Footsteps? No! Richie was listening to the thumping of his own heart. In the background he could hear Robin.

"No, no, no, no," she cried as she ran over to hold him.

"Stop!" barked Richie as he swung the rod at her. "Stay back." He knew she was trying to get closer in order to throw worms on him.

"I'm not doing anything!" she screamed.

Richie continued to flail at the imaginary creatures. The cotton came off the hammer and banged away at his head. His vision started to dim. The worms were filling up his nostrils and throat, suffocating him. Then they closed his eyes.

Richie woke up on the floor. The house was dark and quiet. He ran to the study. Someone had turned off the cameras and monitors. But the microphones were still working. He heard the faint sound of Robin's crying. It was coming from the front hall. He chased after the sound, following it from the front hall to the living room, then upstairs. When he got to the bedroom, he saw Robin and a midget dash into the bathroom. The crying turned to the moans and cries of lovemaking. What kind of freak is she? he wondered. How can she fuck a midget? He banged on the bathroom door.

DaDum DaDum. Something was coming up the stairs. He could hear growling and snarling. Whatever it was had him cornered. His back was against the bedroom window.

February 29. Leap Day. Cambridge Hospital. Patient Richie D. was admitted today with moderately deep lacerations over his neck, back, and head. It appeared that he had fallen or been pushed through a window. Patient refused to say what happened. Sutures were used to close the wounds.

The emergency room physician kept up a steady patter to distract Richie from the tedious process.

"How high was that window, anyway?" asked the doctor.

He knows I'm high. Christ, now I'm gonna be busted, thought Richie.

"Good thing you came here right away. A stitch in time saves nine, you know."

A cat's got nine lives, thought Richie. Then he realized that he had been attacked by a catlike creature. It had rushed to the defense of the midget. Must have been some sort of pet, like a guard dog. That's why it was growling and snarling, thought Richie. He made a mental note to pick up some cat repellent at a pet store.

A few days later Robin invited Willie, one of Richie's close friends, to come over and talk some sense into him. Richie was in the basement work area, converting one of his propane torches to a flame thrower. When he heard Willie arrive, he scrambled up the stairs. Robin and Willie were sitting in the living room, whispering. They stopped as soon as Richie burst in the room. Robin left the two men alone and went to the kitchen.

There were muffled voices coming from elsewhere in the house. "Willie, did you hear that talking?" asked Richie.

"I don't know," answered Willie with a sneaky look on his face.

"Hey, man, don't bullshit me. You know if you heard something or not."

Richie went into the kitchen to find Robin. She made a quick movement to hide something. "What have you just done?" he asked.

"Nothing." She had a sneaky smile.

Richie returned to the living room. Willie reached in his pocket and threw something on the floor. It landed near Richie's chair. Richie jumped up, went for a broom, and started sweeping the floor. There were dozens of worms, barely visible to the naked eye. Richie swept them over toward Willie's chair. Willie had a sneaky smile like Robin's.

"I didn't think you'd do this to me. We've been friends for a long time. I thought I could trust you, Willie."

A four-inch-long worm jumped at Richie from the pile of dust he was sweeping.

"You dirty mother-fucker!" screamed Richie. He reached for a propane torch and started burning the floor in a complete circle around where he was standing. The worms were closing in fast. He turned up the torch full blast. They started crossing the line he'd burned in the floor. He grabbed another torch, one of many he kept stationed around the house, and ignited it. Now, with torches blazing in each hand, he attacked the closing circle of worms.

Willie had been frozen in disbelief. Now he erupted with uncontrollable laughter. Richie looked at him. The fucker. He's throwing

more at me, he thought. Robin came into the room and exchanged
looks with Willie. She burst out laughing. So, they're in on this
together, Richie realized. I knew it!

Robin walked over to Richie and attempted to put a reassuring
hand on his shoulder. Richie panicked. She's throwing something
at me! he thought. She's throwing something at me! It was raining
bugs. Richie waved his torches like a madman. Robin backed away.
She's looking at something behind me, Richie thought, and turned
around just in time to see a midget and a guard cat run under the
table. If I stay on the floor, they'll kill me, he told himself. He
jumped up on a chair in the center of the room. His heart was
beating audibly again. Sweat was soaking through his shirt. Everything seemed blurry. He could no longer see Robin or Willie, but he
could hear their sadistic laughter echoing in his head.

"I just want to let you know that I don't think this is one goddamn bit funny," he yelled to them. "Fuck you," he yelled to the
midget. "Fuck you all." Richie fought to keep his balance on the
chair as he juggled the torches. Now the laughter seemed to drift
into the distance as the floor rushed toward him.

When Richie came to, he found himself sitting on the chair nursing a beer and a twisted ankle. The two flickering torches were
resting on the charred floor. Robin and Willie were sitting across
from him, whispering again. They're up to something, thought
Richie. Playing with me. Using me for their sick amusement. He
was thinking of asking Willie to leave.

"You have to leave now, Willie," said Robin.

She read my mind! That woman is a cold-blooded witch, Richie
thought.

Richie returned to the basement to work on the flame thrower.
He knew the midgets were watching him from under the stairs.
"Fuck you," he yelled at them. "You don't belong here. Get out."
He put a machete on the workbench for emphasis. "You heard me,
get out." Richie held the machete high in the air. "Get out or I'll
call the police." The guard cats started growling. Richie quickly
changed his tune. "Look," he whined, "whatever you want—the
coke or whatever—come get it. I'm not gonna bother you." The
midgets and their pets dashed upstairs. Later Richie discovered
that they had taken all his cocaine.

Many days and nights were spent working on the flame thrower. Richie named it "Mr. Discipline," as in "Don't fuck with me or I'll send in Mr. Discipline to roast your midget ass." Richie's father had yelled these words at him, and they still made him tremble. But it was a hollow threat to the midgets, because he never managed to get the flame thrower to work. One day a midget rushed out from under the workbench and lifted up Richie's T-shirt. Richie looked down through the neck opening. He saw a thin head and a body less than a foot high standing on a box. The midget was peeking up at Richie. For the first time he saw that the midget had lips. Then it bit him.

April 23. Cambridge Hospital. Richie D. was admitted to the emergency ward with a severe bite on his penis. It looked like human teeth marks, but the penis was so swollen that positive identification could not be made. It appeared that the penis had been hit with a sledgehammer after it was bitten. The patient was delirious with pain and could only mumble something about creatures.

In the following weeks, Richie's paranoia transformed his eyes into a scanning electron microscope that allowed him access to a secret world. Specks on the walls and imperfections in the woodwork were actually worms in disguise. The oak desk chair in Richie's study was their favorite hiding place. He saw every variety of worm in the grain of the wood. The most common type resembled long, thin black hairs. They were especially delicate and would break apart as soon as they were touched. Then each part would regenerate into a new worm. Other worms were as thick as pencils and stayed coiled in oval or teardrop shapes. Most worms were black, maroon, or red, although the ones that floated in the air were colorless. The coiled red worms were the most dangerous. Richie called them killers.

When he saw the worms on his chair, he would grab a towel or rolled-up newspaper and begin swatting the chair. The worms would try to dive into the leather seat cushion, so Richie had to keep beating them. The cameras recorded hundreds of such beatings, some lasting two hours. Richie experimented with a variety of sticks, rods, wires, and straps. His favorite weapon became a doubled-up electrical cord.

One day the worms attacked little Melvin's sweater. Richie ran to his rescue and brushed the worms away with his hands. He warned Melvin about the worms and snakes. Richie knew that Melvin understood. He was the only one in the house who ever admitted to seeing the snakes in the backyard trees. The next day Richie saw Melvin playing with the worms. Richie took a towel and gently swatted at Melvin's clothes. "Don't play with them," Richie urged as Melvin joined him in a game of brushing away the imaginary worms.

"How can you let your son be exposed to them? How?" Richie yelled at Robin that night. "Aren't you afraid they will hurt him? Tell me what they are and how to get rid of them." He could see that Robin was still too afraid to say anything. They really have control over her, he thought.

When the worms renewed their attacks on Melvin, Richie employed the same trapping technique he used on himself. First he pulled down the sleeves of Melvin's sweater and tied them. Then he tied the bottom of the sweater at the waist and began beating Melvin lightly with his hands or a towel. Melvin, thinking it was all a game, giggled and laughed. Richie was glad that the boy was too young to appreciate the evil conspiracy that was lurking in the house. I love him so much, Richie thought, like my own son, a son I always wanted.

In Richie's cocaine-blurred vision, the house became a portrait in black and white, a battleground between good and evil. The world had long since lost all of its color. Now the dark shadows were obscuring the light, leaving everything in shades of gray and out of focus like an old photograph in the family album. The thought kindled memories of his childhood. Richie could almost see the diamond ring on his father's fist as it pounded into his face. He cringed with the painful memory of the police belt whipping his back. After every beating he wanted to run away, but his mother always stopped him by tying his hands and feet to the bed. Now Richie's love for his own family was tying him down.

One night Richie detected an aged smell in the house. It reminded him of his father's body odor. Then he heard his father's voice: "I'll roast your ass. I'll roast your ass." Richie glanced in a mirror and realized that he was the one talking. He studied his face. It looked just like his old man's. He didn't understand what was happening. Maybe he was getting cabin fever. After all, it had been over a month since he'd gone outside the house. But he had to stay and protect his family. Little Melvin and Robin, who was now seven months pregnant with his baby, needed him. It was also breeding season for the snakes, which were beginning to mass in the backyard in broad daylight. Soon there would be hundreds more.

In May a new type of bug appeared on the front sidewalk. It was the shape of a kidney bean, with thin hairs protruding a good fifteen feet from one end. They started growing up the side of the house like ivy. Soon they would be pressing through the walls. Richie kept checking the peepholes. Every time he looked through the peephole in the front door, he saw a man wearing a green field jacket standing with a chimpanzee on the steps. And every time Richie opened the door, they vanished.

The day before Friday the 13th, May. Footsteps on the roof told Richie that the midgets were preparing an assault from above. He could see them as reflections in the windows of the house next door. They were wearing green field jackets and tactical harnesses. Then large brown snakes appeared outside the second-floor windows. They were thick as ropes and dangled from above. They are ropes! he thought. The midgets were rappeling down from the roof. They landed on a ledge and started running around the building. There are so many of them, Richie thought. He didn't know how to handle the invasion. When they started entering the house, he remained frozen in fear. He could only watch. And listen. A strange buzzing sound vibrated in his ears. The worms! They're in my ears! he thought.

DaDum DaDum DaDum DaDum. Now came the sounds of midgets running from room to room. The cats were right behind them, growling. The walls started to breathe as the bugs pressed against them.

Richie forced himself to look in on Melvin. He found the boy sitting on the living room floor, wearing only a T-shirt. Richie's microscopic vision saw a worm appear on Melvin's skin. One worm, then two, four, sixteen, multiplying at an alarming rate. They were the black ones. He pulled off Melvin's T-shirt. More worms. Richie heard himself screaming, "Oh, no! Oh, no!" He grabbed the electrical cord, doubled it, and started beating the worms. This only brought more worms to the surface. They were the coiled red ones. Killer worms.

"Oh, no! Oh, no!"

Every stroke brought more red worms to the surface. Richie concentrated on the worms, forgetting for the moment where they were coming from. Melvin remained as quiet as a desk chair.

Whack. Whack. Whack. Robin turned over in her bed. It sounded as though Richie were doing some carpentry work in the house. Jesus! It's the middle of the night, she thought. She got up and went into the living room.

Richie was standing over Melvin, who was lying on the floor.

"What are you doing?" asked Robin. She was still half-asleep.

He mumbled something about Mr. Discipline. "Stay out of here!" he yelled at her.

Robin knew how impossible he was to deal with during one of his worm attacks, so she went back to bed.

Whack. Whack. Robin ran back to the living room. Richie was hitting Melvin on the backs of his legs.

"Don't!" she yelled. "You're beating him, and you're hurting him. Please don't hit him anymore!"

Richie stopped.

Robin took Melvin into the bathroom and turned on the light. She freaked out. He was totally black and blue, with red marks all over his body.

"Thirsty . . . I want a drink," said Melvin. His voice was barely audible.

Robin gave him a glass of water.

"Thank you, ma'am."

Robin started to rub antibacterial cream into the open wounds, then slipped a clean T-shirt over his swollen body. He was moaning, and his eyes were closing.

"Stay awake, baby."

"Yes, ma'am."

"Don't go to sleep." She put some ice packs on his legs and stroked his short, curly hair.

Melvin's eyes started to flutter.

"Richie!" she screamed. "Something's wrong."

Richie ran to her. Melvin had stopped breathing. Robin called the paramedics.

Friday the 13th, May. 9:00 A.M. Office of the chief medical examiner. Autopsy room. The deceased, a three-year-old male, died of multiple blunt force injuries that involved the entire body surface except for the soles of the feet and the palm of the right hand. These injuries consisted of a whipping to the majority of the body and blows to the head. The whipping injuries had a pattern consistent with that performed by a narrow cord or wire. There was a loop at the end of several of these injuries, suggesting that the cord or wire was doubled over. The injuries caused bleeding around and swelling of the brain. There were no preexisting diseases that may have contributed to death. The manner of death was homicide.

I spread the autopsy photographs on my desk and started counting the contusions and abrasions. There were over one hundred on the back, sixty-five on the chest, sixty-five on the arms, sixty on the abdomen, fifty on the legs, eighteen on the head and neck, and ten on the buttocks. I saw others on the right and left eyelids, upper and lower lips, the armpits, the palm of the left hand, even on the base of the scrotum. There were burns around the shoulders. All the marks, even the burn marks, resembled the drawings of the worms that Richie had done for me. Some of the wounds consisted of linear abrasions resembling the letter *I* tattooed into the skin. Others were semicircular patterns in the form of the letter *C*. The most common abrasions were U-shaped. In a sense, the marks stood for Richie's "I see you" perception of the worms, which triggered the attack on Melvin's body. Each time an imaginary black worm was struck on the skin, it hemorrhaged into the very real red wormlike letters. The skin spelled out proof of Richie's paranoia in over four hundred such blood red letters. I found myself wishing Richie had used the Mauser 7.65-mm pistol he kept in the bedroom safe or the Smith and Wesson snub-nosed .38 that he kept fully loaded in a drawer only a few feet from where the vicious beating took place. A bullet would have been kinder than the half-hour nonstop beating of the child.

"I'm not a child beater," Richie had told one of the paramedics.

"What happened?" asked the shocked paramedic. He noticed a black wire cord with specks of red on a nearby bench.

"Don't be asking me questions. Can't you see he's not breathing? Help him. Help my son."

While the paramedics tried to save the child, Richie ran around the house talking to himself and pulling his hair. Nobody saw the midgets he was chasing or the worms he was pulling out of his hair. And Richie didn't tell them. He couldn't trust anybody, especially the paramedics. They're playing with the worms on my son's body, for Chrisakes! he thought.

The paramedics didn't trust Richie, either. They thought he might run away. So they called for the police. The police arrived and handcuffed him. He looked like just another wide-eyed frightened junkie. They searched the house and found empty plastic bags with white residue, a glass pipe, propane torches, and other paraphernalia associated with the smoking of cocaine. There were so many torches around the house, they thought Richie might be running a crack house where people came to smoke. All the television monitors, cameras, and expensive sound equipment suggested that he was accepting these goods in exchange for drugs. Pretty routine for the police. Coke addict, dealing, and child beating. Drugs are bad news.

"You beat Melvin," Robin told Richie before the police took him away. It was news to Richie.

"I beat him? I beat him?" Richie kept repeating it over and over. The police heard him. The paramedics heard him. Even a neighbor heard him.

"I beat him. I beat him. I beat him." Richie was saying it, but he couldn't believe it. "I don't believe I did this . . . I don't beat children."

The jury of seven women and five men believed he'd done it. They accepted his statements of "I beat him" as evidence that Richie knew what he did. They were right. But the intended victims, as I explained in testimony during the trial, were the worms, snakes, midgets, and other creatures created by his chronic use of cocaine. I tried to tell them how the world looked through Richie's paranoid eyes. It was a perspective that had started to form during Richie's childhood, when he was being beaten by a sadistic father.

His paranoid slant on life was further reinforced by the loss of his job and the humiliation of false arrest.

But it was Richie's descent into cocaine addiction that literally and figuratively opened the dimensional doors of his paranoid perception to the invasion of those killer creatures. Melvin was not even a target in Richie's eyes at the time of the beating. He was zeroed in on the killer red worms, flailing away in a cocaine rage that blocked all other perceptions and thoughts. The jury agreed that he had not intended to kill the child and convicted him of manslaughter rather than murder. The judge described the beating as "an egregiously brutal act" and sentenced Richie to serve eighteen to twenty years in prison.

After the trial, I flew back to Los Angeles. I was looking forward to a change in scenery after my trip to "Whackyland." On the plane I started reading *The Secret House* by David Bodanis. The book had several colorful micrographs of the subvisible world in which we spend our days and nights. There was an electron microscope photo of a dust mite showing serrated front claws for collecting flakes of human skin. It looked ferocious, and I read that my vacuum cleaner bag is probably full of them. I did not believe for one moment the author's claim that the dust mite is a gentle, passive creature. Another photograph showed a woodworm beetle emerging from a wooden chair. Magnified some one thousand times, it looked like a monster right out of a Japanese science fiction film. I made a mental note to check my wooden desk chair when I got home. Most disturbing of all was the photo of *Pseudomonad bacterium,* a bacteria that swims on kitchen tables and in damp sponges. The red body of this creature is shaped like a kidney bean with long, hairlike strands on the top. The strands spin like a twirling lasso. I opened my briefcase and took out Richie's drawings. His sketches of the bugs on the sidewalk and sides of his house were identical with this bacteria—only Richie's bugs were fifteen feet long!

I put away the book and ordered a drink from the flight attendant. As I sipped my drink and looked out the window, I knew that just on the other side of those dark clouds there were hundreds of dodo birds hooting at me.

8

BUNKERS

For a psychoanalyst, Joel Morgan is extremely defensive. At least that's how he plays chess. We were spending an evening at his house, conducting a postmortem on the case of Richie D. ("Richie in Whackyland") and playing a game of chess at the same time.

Joel likes to engage in heady conversation over the chess board. Perhaps it has something to do with listening to patients all day long while suppressing his natural urge to talk. Maybe it's a clever tactic used to distract his opponent. Whatever the reason, Joel seems to enjoy verbal jousting as much as the action on the chess board. This breaks my concentration, but I'm such an amateur that it really doesn't make a difference. I lose most of the time to Joel. It's frustrating because we are both ranked the same, although our strategies are very different. He tends to build a strong defensive blockade and wait for his opponent to make a mistake. I am more impatient and aggressive. My approach is to use rapid strikes at defenses, sacrificing a pawn here, reaching for a key position there, until I make the inevitable blunder. Joel is quick to turn my mistakes into checkmate. He does this with the same cold-blooded efficiency of my home computer chess game. Win or lose, my computer always thanks me for an interesting game. Joel simply strokes his bushy beard and grins.

Tonight Joel had me cornered. He stroked and grinned in antic-
ipation of the outcome.

"Your opening moves really surprised me," I said after tipping
over my king in resignation.

Joel reached for the last pieces of popcorn in the bowl next to the
board where the chess clock should have been. We never played
with a clock. After every move we grabbed a handful of popcorn
while waiting for the next move. Somehow the popcorn always
lasted until the final move of the game. "It was a modified Hun-
garian defense," he said, munching. "Not to be recommended. My
position was badly crowded."

But you still won, I thought.

Joel read my thoughts. "Still, I won. You had the opportunity
for the better game but blew it. Sad. You should read some of my
chess books."

And you should play my computer and learn how to win po-
litely, I thought. "So you really believe that Richie was schizophrenic at the end?" I asked, trying to get the conversation back on
track.

"Absolutely. His thinking exhibited the same curious discontinuities. His strange connections, or apparent absences of connections, are much like the knight's move in chess"—jumping over an
intervening square on the board. Joel picked up a knight and
started moving it around the board for emphasis. "There was an
apparent gap between where the thought begins and where it
ends."

Joel was referring to instances where Richie leaped to new associations. For example, when the emergency room physician told
him that "a stitch in time saves nine," Richie jumped to the conclusion that he had been mauled by a cat because a cat has nine
lives. The oblique connections can be seen, but they are not of a
kind likely to be used by a normal person.

I knew that such leaps occurred when my subjects were under
the influence of LSD or a similar hallucinogen, but Richie was using cocaine, a stimulant not associated with discontinuities of
thought. He had only a few such leaps, and they seemed relatively
minor compared to the major disturbances seen in schizophrenia.
In fact, Richie had improved since he'd stopped using cocaine. I

repeated the argument I had made at the trial, that Richie was suffering from cocaine paranoia that reached psychotic proportions, complete with delusions and hallucinations. It was schizophrenic*like,* not schizophrenia per se. I saw no evidence of such an underlying mental disorder.

"Even one instance of knight's move thinking can be a sign of a deeper underlying pathology," said Joel. "And all that stuff about Mr. Discipline? Come on, Ron. The pathology developed in his childhood. The sins of his father's abuse revisited him." Joel was now holding the knight and rubbing it. At any moment I fully expected him to start fondling the queen while telling me all about Richie's Oedipus complex.

"But he wasn't hitting little Melvin," I argued. "He was beating the hell out of the worms." Worms and snakes were classic cocaine hallucinations. The beating was a classic example of a cocaine rage.

"Part of him probably knew he was hitting the boy," replied Joel. "He sees the worms, sees the boy, even sees his father. But he can't see the connections. His mind jumps around like a knight and puts it all together in a schizophrenic, albeit paranoid, way." Joel grabbed a copy of the American Psychiatric Association's diagnostic manual from a nearby shelf and flipped to a section. "Here— 295.3x: Schizophrenia, Paranoid Type." He handed the book to me.

Joel was preoccupied with diagnostic neologisms. He was still ignoring the fact that cocaine caused the hyperexcitability that made Richie's thoughts jump around. Then Joel surprised me with some knight's move thinking of his own. "Freud once wrote a friend and asked him if he had ever seen a foreign newspaper after it had passed the censorship at the Russian frontier. Words, sentences, even entire paragraphs are blacked out. The result is that the remainder is unintelligible. Freud said that a 'Russian censorship' occurs in psychotic thinking. Paranoid psychotics like Richie are simply trying to fill in the gaps." He paused for a beat, then continued. "Hell, maybe that's why the Russkies are so paranoid"

The idea of "Russian censorship" was similar to my own opinion that paranoid thinking could be generated by the attempt to fill in gaps between anomalous experiences, inventing coincidences and significances. Thus Richie's hypervigilant brain saw Robin's silence as a sign of conspiracy and Melvin's imaginary play as evidence for the existence of the creatures. Richie was paranoid and psychotic all right, yet Joel was minimizing the role of the drug. I disagreed with his emphasis. It was the white knight of cocaine, not the black knight from a censored Freudian cellar, that carried Richie off to war.

Joel seemed lost in thought, once again massaging the knight in his hand. "You're forgetting that Freud did his own jumping to false conclusions under the influence of cocaine," I said. It was a direct attack on Joel's "king." More than one historian had linked Freud's theories about sex to the hypersexuality he'd experienced as the result of cocaine use. They'd even suggested that Freud's occasional episodes of paranoia, which coincided with periods of drug use, were the result of his addiction.

"You don't need coke to explain paranoia," said Joel. His voice was uncharacteristically loud. "I never met a chess player who used it, yet paranoia runs in their blood."

"Now you're going to tell me that they're all Russians," I said with a tinge of sarcasm. But I knew that Joel was right. While many of my contacts with paranoids were through my drug research, drugs were not necessary to produce paranoia. Drugs such as cocaine might evoke paranoia faster than other triggers, but all paranoids battled the same demon.

Joel launched into several tales of paranoid chess champions. They *were* all Russian. As he spoke I tried to remember if I had ever told him that my father was born in Russia.

In the 1972 world championship in Reykjavík, Iceland, the Russian champion Boris Spassky was playing Bobby Fischer. Russians had held the world title for forty-one out of the previous forty-five years. Now they were losing to the young American challenger. Spassky appeared distracted, his moves impulsive. His aides claimed that Fisher's team was irradiating Spassky with electronic devices, possibly microwaves or other radio-frequency energy. They suspected that chemical substances were also being used. The playing hall was examined by experts. They took scrapings, sampled the air, even X-rayed the chairs, testing everything for devices and poisons. Nothing was found, but Spassky was still suspicious. He kept peering at the lighting canopy over the stage, where two dead flies had been discovered. After he lost he confessed a lingering paranoia: "I still feel there was something in the hall which affected me. I am really convinced there was some curious thing in it." Prior to a later match, Bobby Fischer caught the paranoid bug, so to speak. He had all his dental fillings removed to insure that there were no implanted electronic devices that could influence his thinking. "I don't want anything artificial in my head," said Fischer.

The paranoia was particularly infectious during the 1978 title match between two Russians: Karpov, the defending world champion, and Korchnoi, his challenger. Karpov was accompanied by Dr. Vladimir Zukhar, a psychologist from Moscow's School of Medicine. Zukhar sat in the second row and stared at Korchnoi during every game. Aides to Korchnoi suspected that Zukhar was using the evil eye and other mind-control techniques. So Korchnoi put on a pair of dark glasses while his aides sat next to the psychologist and began staring back in order to break the doctor's evil glare. But neither the glasses nor the aides helped, and Korchnoi finally complained to the referee, who ordered Zukhar to a new seat in the back of the hall. Then two strangers arrived at the match and started staring at Karpov. Karpov claimed they were terrorists and members of a fanatical religious cult. The referee banished the strangers from the hall. When it was learned that these same strangers were hanging around Korchnoi's nearby villa, officials ordered them to leave the city.

Play resumed. Karpov kept swiveling on his chair. Korchnoi complained. Karpov said he would stop swiveling if Korchnoi took off his dark glasses. This provided an opportunity for Dr. Zukhar to move up to the fourth row and start giving Korchnoi the evil eye again. Korchnoi refused to continue. The match ended with Karpov still champion.

What was it about chess that provided such a nourishing environment for paranoia? The answer, of course, was right in front of me in black and white: Chess is war. The whole body is on guard. Senses are alert. The mind, trained by years of studying past battles, is ever suspicious, always looking beyond the present moves for hidden strategies and traps. Deception and distraction loom over the board like an enveloping fog. It blurs the boundaries be-

tween the battlefield and its surroundings. The player's entire
world becomes part of the struggle to protect his king and slay the
enemy.

Several weeks after leaving Joel's house with a stack of chess
books, I met an extraordinary knight of the game. Tall, skinny,
awkward, and paranoid as hell, Kenneth Jackson called everyone
"sir" and insisted you address him the same way. Yes, sir. The
public defender hired me to interview Jackson (who was charged
with murder) because he was suspected of being a cocaine user.
The arresting officers said Jackson acted paranoid and looked as
though he were under the influence of cocaine. Toxicological tests
were not performed at the time, but my subsequent analysis of his
hair revealed no prior exposure to cocaine or other stimulants.
This knight was no drug user. No, sir. Joel and I agreed this time.
Jackson was just a lifelong paranoid schizophrenic, a chess player
who found himself locked in a medieval mind-set where the stakes
of the game were nothing less than survival itself.

Kenneth Jackson always played with an extra piece up his sleeve.
The piece, a derringer pistol, was actually in the side pocket of his
corduroy jacket, the one he always wore when he played. It was
also his only jacket. The derringer was as necessary as the suede
elbow patches on the jacket. It was protection for when things
started to wear on him. The gun itself was made by American Derringer in Waco, Texas, just south of Dallas where Jackson grew up.
This was not some dainty lady's model with ivory grips that fired a
tiny .22-caliber bullet. Jackson's gun was a double-barreled .44
Magnum. Only four inches long and fifteen ounces, it was all business. He kept it loaded with Glaser cartridges. Jackson knew that
caliber for caliber, the Glaser cartridge delivered 3.5 times the stopping power of the best hollow-point bullet. The Glaser was pre-
fragmented, and when the soft nose hit tissue it released over 330
subprojectiles in a cone-shaped pattern. It has incredible knock-
down power, causing instant and total incapacitation. Jackson
liked the Glaser ad: "It's like being hit with a sledgehammer instead of an ice pick."

In fact, Jackson liked the Glaser cartridges so much that he kept his entire collection of derringers loaded with them. While he favored the .44 Magnum for big tournaments, he usually packed an ultralightweight single-barrel .32 or .38 derringer for everyday wear. Sometimes he took along a small .22 derringer he'd got as a birthday gift from Susan, the only girlfriend he'd ever had. It was engraved with beautiful scrollwork along the single barrel. He kept it loaded with a "Varminter" high-velocity fifty-grain soft-point bullet. His only regret was that an armor-piercing bullet was not available in that caliber. The bullet was meant for Susan, if he ever ran into her again. The bitch had a heart made of steel.

The other derringers in his collection were kept in a suitcase tucked away inside his small house trailer. Most of the guns were antique American makes that used black powder and fired small round balls. There was an unusual Remington made in 1863 that fired five shots from separate barrels. His pride and joy was a Philadelphia derringer made in 1860. This was the same model that John Wilkes Booth had fired at the back of Lincoln's head. Despite their size, the derringers were effective weapons, especially when the target was only a chess board's length away. Good enough to take out a president or a king. Yes, sir.

Kenneth, now forty-six, couldn't remember when he'd first started collecting derringers. But it was long before he had ever learned how to play chess. It had begun around the time he was having the bad dreams.

As a child he was considered unusually quiet. There were no brothers or sisters to play with, and there were no other kids his age in the neighborhood. His father was always working, and his mother, a drunk, had left when he was very young. She'd said that if she stayed, she would have had to kill Kenneth. Two prostitutes who lived nearby sometimes took care of little Kenneth. They embarrassed him by making constant jokes about his "teeny weenie." He had no friends at school. Even the teachers seemed to ignore him. One night, after learning about the Hindus in India, Kenneth dreamed that he was an untouchable and everyone was trying to beat him to death. He woke up shaken. Could it be true? After all, everyone seemed to reject him. People didn't like him because he had a crooked nose and crooked teeth. Some of the kids at school made fun of him and called him Ichabod because he looked so much like the cartoon version of Ichabod Crane in *The Legend of Sleepy Hollow*. Embarrassment, social isolation, and now humiliation gave rise to his first feelings of paranoia. Kenneth's world was becoming an increasingly hostile place. Kids and teachers not only rejected him, everyone seemed to be after him. He dreamed that the world was about to be destroyed. He started to prepare himself.

At first he collected all the weapons he could find and put them in one of his father's cigar boxes. It was an unimpressive collection even for a kid: a pea shooter, a slingshot, and an assortment of pocket knives. He threw in a rusted ice pick he'd found at the junkyard and buried the box in his backyard. Whenever he looked at the little mound of dirt covering the stash, Kenneth felt a little better. But he couldn't wait until he was old enough to put some serious weapons in the cigar box. A handgun would fit perfectly. The only guns in the house belonged to his father, and he knew better than to play with them without supervision.

His father started taking Kenneth shooting when he was only six. He displayed a natural talent and by the time he was ten became a crack shot with a .22 rifle and a .22 target pistol. That was the year he started to play chess and, immediately, displayed an equally uncanny talent. Kenneth read chess books the way the other kids read comic books. He collected chess columns from the newspaper and memorized the moves like statistics on baseball cards. By the time he was in high school, Kenneth was a junior chess champion, excelling in lightning-fast "blitz" games against all who dared sit across the board from him.

After high school he was drafted into the army. Nobody knew about Ichabod, and everyone called him by his last name. Finally Jackson was feeling like a real man. He went to Vietnam. His hair turned gray during the first six months. The dreams about the end of the world returned. He volunteered a lot for bunker duty. Here the sandbags muffled the sounds of war. The wooden ammo crates reminded him of cigar boxes. Jackson felt safe inside the bunker. Most grunts liked bunker duty because it was an opportunity to get wasted on marijuana, write letters, or just goof off. For Jackson it was an opportunity to work out puzzles and games on his pocket chess set. At night he did it in his head. Death was stalking outside the bunker. Inside, the world was reduced to sixty-four black and white squares. All he had to do was defend his squares from attack. As long as he didn't lose, he would survive. In a sense, he was living out a scene from Ingmar Bergman's 1956 movie, *The Seventh Seal*. In the film a knight returns from ten years in the Crusades. Death comes to claim him, but the knight challenges Death to a game of chess. "The condition is that I live as long as I withstand you," says the knight. "If I win, you will set me free. Agreed?" Death nods. By never losing a game, Private First Class Jackson tricked death and survived his tour. It was his proof that the strange link between his chess and his survival was not so strange. Call it knight's move thinking or schizophrenia, but for Jackson it worked.

Back in the States, Jackson resumed his chess career while working as a shipping clerk for a mail-order store. He played chess until all hours of the night and then rushed to work at six in the morning. He was always tired, so he made a little bunker among the stacks of cartons where he could take naps. Somehow he survived without getting fired. Now he knew that bunkers worked here as well as in Vietnam.

Jackson was advancing rapidly in the chess rankings. But he became bored playing the textbook attacks and defenses. He wanted something different, an edge. Then he discovered *The Art of War*, the classic Chinese text by Master Sun Tzu. If he was not the first chess player to read it, he was certainly the first to make it his playbook. He memorized it and could quote Sun Tzu or any of the ancient Chinese military leaders who wrote commentaries on the text. He stopped studying chess books and games. *The Art of War* was what it was all about. It was more than a handbook on military strategy. Kenneth saw it as an explanation of competition and conflict on every level from the interpersonal to the international. It would make him victorious as long as the people who were now spying on him didn't find out.

During the next local tournament, Jackson drew a bye in the first round. On the second day, his opponent resigned after only a few stupid moves. In the third and final round, his opponent forfeited because of illness. According to Jackson's developing paranoia, these coincidences had hidden meanings. He could almost hear his master's voice.

> To *win without fighting is best.*
>
> > Master Sun

But the victory frustrated him. He needed a more direct test of the military strategy. In a match several months later Jackson found himself behind in points and running out of time on the clock. He made an impulsive move, pressed the clock, and got up to visit the restroom. Master Sun Tzu was taking a shit in the stall next to his. His hallucinatory voice echoed off the tiles.

> *Use anger to throw them into disarray.*
>
> > Master Sun

Another voice whispered from the stall on the opposite side.

> *When the enemy is confused, you can use this op-portunity to take them.*
>
> > Du Mu

Jackson came back from the restroom smiling, his face streaked with makeshift camouflage paint. He took his seat and studied the board. His opponent stared in shock and utter confusion at this Ichabod Crane with shit on his face. Jackson won the game.

A few days later the boss discovered him sleeping in the cardboard bunker and started yelling. Jackson did not like it when people yelled at him. He had had enough of that in the army, with sergeants always barking orders. Now the boss wouldn't shut up. Jackson turned around, dropped his pants, and "mooned" the boss. That shut him up real good. He fired Jackson the next day.

Jackson was glad to be rid of the job. People had been spying on him at work, trying to learn the secrets to his successful chess strategy. The boss, an undercover agent for the Texas Rangers, had been part of the conspiracy. The Mafia were also part of it. That's why he had started carrying a derringer to work. There was only one time he had to pull out the gun. A black man asked him for some spare change. The Mafia sometimes used blacks as spies. He forced the black man to perform fellatio, and then gave the man

two dollars. "Don't report this. Report to me," Jackson told the
bewildered man.

> *You must seek out enemy agents who have come to*
> *spy on you, bribe them and induce them to stay with*
> *you, so you can use them as reverse spies.*
>   Master Sun

Losing his job at the mail-order house was the best thing that
ever happened to him. That's what he kept telling Susan. He met
her in the unemployment office, where she worked as a job coun-
selor. She was even taller than Jackson. Her long red hair and carefully applied makeup did little to change her beaklike nose and
misaligned features. It was a face that only Ichabod Crane could
love. She asked him out the day they met. That night she performed
fellatio. No girl had ever done that to him before. In fact, up till
now Jackson felt that he was homosexual, but he was shamed by
the feelings. Now he forced himself to stay with Susan. He said he
loved her and showed it the only way he knew. He began taking her
to chess tournaments. She thought he was brilliant.

Two months before their first anniversary, Susan gave him the
gun. She found it in a local pawnshop and couldn't wait to see his
reaction. Susan knew he collected derringers and was almost as
passionate about them as chess. She didn't mind the fact that he
always carried one. At least he wasn't hauling around the M-63
Stoner he claimed was his best friend in Vietnam. Susan heard endless stories from Kenneth about this gun. She could rattle off the
specs by heart. The M-63 could function as both an assault rifle or
a machine gun. It came with a 150-round box that allowed the
soldier to lay down sustained bursts of continuous fire. Rate of fire:
660 rounds per minute; muzzle velocity: 1,000 meters per second;
range: 800 meters; survivors: 0. But what Susan didn't hear was
that the U.S. Navy Seals were the only unit to use the Stoner. She
didn't know that Kenneth had never fired a shot during the war
even with his standard-issue M-16 rifle. She believed him when he
told her how he had used the Stoner to take out two VC mortar
positions. That's how he'd won the Congressional Medal of

Honor. Of course, he didn't have it anymore. He'd sent it back as a protest against the war. Susan really admired his politics.

When Jackson saw the derringer he smiled in appreciation. Silently he wondered what type of girl would buy a gun. Someone who's trained and knows what they're doing, he thought. Susan would have preferred a more enthusiastic thank-you, but she knew how hard it was for Kenneth to express his feelings. He immediately started cleaning the gun and reminiscing about the other derringers. It seemed as though he had been collecting them since he was a baby.

"Baby killers," Jackson said out loud.

"What?" asked Susan. Maybe he meant that derringers were baby guns.

No. Baby killers. That's what war protesters had called him and the men under his command in Vietnam, he told her. So what if he had to waste a village and some women and babies got greased? They were all Charlie anyways.

Jackson was laughing when he told her the details about how the bursts shattered bone and tore through soft flesh. The babies literally came apart. Susan realized that she had never heard him laugh before. Never! Now it scared her.

Susan called him a few days later to say good-bye. "It's not you, it's me," she said.

Jackson heard the nervousness in her voice. "It's the Texas Rangers, isn't it?" he asked.

"What are you talking about?"

"At first you are like a maiden, so the enemy opens his door; then you are like a rabbit on the loose, so the enemy cannot keep you out." Jackson was quoting Sun Tzu.

"What?"

He hung up.

Jackson knew there were spies everywhere. He quit his new job in the shipping room of a local factory. But he didn't want to worry about running into Susan again at the unemployment office. Instead he found a succession of part-time and temporary jobs in the classifieds. He lived that way for many years.

After the breakup with Susan, Jackson avoided getting close to women. One day he was eating at the lunch counter of a restaurant. A young woman sat down next to him. He thought it was peculiar because there were plenty of other empty seats at the counter. She was very attractive in a cheap way. He continued eating, trying to concentrate on a chess puzzle in the newspaper. He could feel her eyes watching him. She told the waitress she was not ready to order yet, just a cup of coffee, please. What is she doing here? he thought. Why is she staring at me?

"Are you having any luck?" she asked him. "I can never do those crossword puzzles."

"Chess," he said without looking up.

"Oh. I don't know anything about chess," she said.

Then why are you sitting here staring at me? he wondered. Jackson moved the newspaper to the opposite side of his plate, away from the woman.

The movement did not go unnoticed. "Oooh, afraid I might steal your answers?" she said.

"Why did you say that?" Jackson asked as he reached into his side pocket.

"Oooh, aren't we just a little touchy. You're not paranoid, are you?" The woman forced a laugh.

Jackson released the safety on the derringer and stared at her. Prostitutes came in all shapes and sizes. The ones that worked for the Mafia were easy to spot.

"Forget it, Mac. Just forget it." She got up and moved to another seat.

Jackson clicked the safety back on and returned to his chess puzzle. Mac! That has got to be McNamara, the ex–secretary of defense! he thought. The defense boys are in on this, too.

Over the years Jackson continued to wax his opponents on the chess board. But success was getting dangerous. He was attracting too much attention. Spies followed him to every major tournament around the country. He began traveling less and less, spending most of his chess time in local clubs and parks. However, few of the local players would sit across from him because of his bizarre behavior.

Jackson knew they were just afraid of losing. He denied accusa-
tions of annoying opponents by wearing clothes that smelled of
urine. This was America, right? Freedom of religion, right? That's
what he'd fought for in Vietnam, right? He was glad when the local
chess club burned down. Nobody there could beat him anyway.

> *When you use fire to help an attack, clearly you can*
> *win thereby.*
>
> Zhang Yu

The arson investigators found an incendiary device at the club
and came to interview Jackson. Their report noted that Jackson
was on crutches with both legs in casts. He had difficulty understanding their questions, telling them he was recovering from a car
accident. No, sir, he did not fire-bomb the club. How could he? He
said he had been in the hospital the night of the fire. They never
checked. After they left, Jackson threw away his casts and crutches.

> *A military operation involves deception. Even*
> *though you are competent, appear incompetent.*
> *Though effective, appear to be ineffective.*
>
> Master Sun

The last major tournament Jackson attended was held in a hotel
ballroom. He watched the players as they entered. Most were carrying chess bags holding their chess pieces and clock. The bags
were either small vinyl pouches or larger nylon "traveler" bags,
which had room for a soft roll board. Jackson was checking everyone's bags for telltale bulges. The vinyl bags could easily conceal a
handgun. Larger weapons could be concealed in the traveler bags.
Inside Jackson's own navy blue traveler bag was a Mossberg
twelve-gauge pump shotgun with pistol grip. It held eight shots
plus one in the chamber. Jackson kept a "birdbomb" shell in the
chamber. This shell, used to keep birds away from airports, traveled about 275 feet and then detonated with a very loud explosion.
Jackson likened the effect to tracer ammo—promise of things to
come. If that didn't deter the enemy, then the remaining fléchette
shot shells would do the job. Each shell contained twenty fléchette

darts resembling sharpened steel nails with tiny stabilizing tail fins. In heavy brush or close combat, the fléchettes were very difficult to deflect. Jackson had tested them on an old wooden chess board in the field behind his trailer. The fléchettes had torn through it like a baby.

After checking out the contestants, Jackson entered the ballroom and surveyed the scene. Players sat across from each other at long banquet tables covered with white linen tablecloths. There were hundreds of players, yet the only sound was the occasional mechanical click of a chess clock.

Jackson knew the silence betrayed the life-and-death battles being waged on those tables. Chess was war.

The air-conditioning units in the room kicked on, and the floor rumbled. Jackson heard and felt the distant mortars. His veteran eyes flashbacked. He saw blood spilling over the white linen tablecloths.

> *When you do battle, it is necessary to kill people.*
> Chen Hao

He squatted next to an empty table and scanned the battlefield. His eyes caught several blacks. They were all wearing the same baseball-style caps. Why? It was a dumb thing to wear. They should be wearing their helmets. Unless, of course, they were conspiring with the enemy. Jackson smiled and clutched his chess bag. A baseball cap would not stop the power he was packing.

Now he watched a young man with long blond hair playing at a table several yards away. The man had a habit of keeping his hands cupped around his neck as he pondered his moves.

More rumbling. Jackson looked up. The glass beads on the chandeliers reflected and refracted the light, turning it into colorful streaks of tracer fire.

He looked back at the blond guy. His cupped hands had moved from his neck to his mouth. It looked as though he were praying.

Suddenly an Asian boy stood up from the table and headed for the restroom. He looked Vietnamese. Jackson followed him. Inside the restroom the boy stood in front of an urinal. Jackson stood next to him and watched. He waited until the boy's penis was out.

When the opponent is just beginning to plan its strat-
egy, it is easy to strike.

Cao Cao

Jackson clamped his hand around the boy's penis. "Charlie?" asked Jackson as he squeezed.

"Please. No. I'm Harold," cried the boy.

"You're a sapper," said Jackson. It was the slang term for a VC soldier who infiltrated a camp for sabotage.

The boy was crying loudly now. Someone else came into the restroom, and Jackson pulled his hand away. The boy ran out before Jackson could demand a blow job. He followed the boy back to the ballroom. The boy ran up to a director and started pointing at Jackson. The director recognized Jackson, who was now heading out of the room. He would never be allowed to return.

Take three months to prepare your machines and
three months to complete your siege engineering.

Master Sun

Jackson listened carefully to the voice of Master Sun. He could hear it as clearly as the *whutt whutt whutt whutt* of the helicopters circling over the trailer park. He spent the next six months fortifying his trailer, turning it into a bunker. It was not a makeshift collection of lightweight arms stashed behind thin walls like the Branch Davidians would later assemble in his hometown of Waco. And it wasn't like the bunker with heavy steel doors and fifty-caliber machine guns that one survivalist constructed under his L.A. house. Jackson built a simple but effective bunker that took strategic advantage of the surrounding terrain. It was a bunker that would pass inspection by the master himself.

The house trailer was located in the back corner of a large trailer park. Behind the trailer, and surrounding it on three sides, was a large open field covered with brush. A small gulley snaked through the field. Jackson used the gulley as the perimeter for his defense. It marked the entrance to his side of the board. Any jeep or dirt bike approaching from the field would have to cross the gulley, so he seeded it with road stars. These four-pointed stars resemble the metal "jacks" used in the children's game. Jackson's oversize stars were no toys. They were sharpened steel spikes that would cause any vehicle to have an immediate blowout.

Jackson recognized that it was important to control the lines of attack to the trailer. The gulley formed an arc around his trailer. Brush separated the two. He ran barbed-razor tape, the same type used in Vietnam and around prisons, in crisscross patterns throughout the brush.

> *Induce them to adopt specific formations in order to know the ground of death.*
>
> Master Sun

The patterns he selected would force any attacker approaching on foot from the gulley into either a left or a right diagonal. These diagonals would be his kill zones. He placed a "bishop" along each diagonal. The bishops were spring-loaded ballistic knives he'd put together from kits. They were on small stands in the back of the trailer. He covered the stands with camouflage netting. When the projection springs were fired, they would thrust the sharp knives more than thirty feet along the diagonal at waist height.

Attacks at the front of the trailer would have to come from a small park road that provided the only other access to his bunker. The two-way road turned directly in front of the trailer. Jackson knew that this road was as important as the two center files on the chess board. Whoever controlled the center files usually controlled the game. He built two large birdhouses and put them on stands in the front of the trailer, facing opposite directions on the road. The front ends were hinged and could be swung open at a moment's notice. Inside each birdhouse was a ballistic mace. This device worked on the same principle as Jackson's bishops, only it fired a macelike piece of steel with tremendous knock-down power. The maces were powerful enough to drive through a thick wooden chess board at seventy-five feet! Jackson called the birdhouses his rookeries. The ballistic maces, of course, were the "rooks."

Next, Jackson buried several *punji* bear traps in the ground directly outside the trailer, especially around the windows. These V-shaped booby traps, invented by the Vietcong, consisted of two

boards with rusted spikes driven through them. They were designed to pivot when stepped on, thereby driving their spikes
through the leg. Jackson knew that combat boots, even those with
steel inserts, were useless against these traps. The traps didn't kill,
but they would cause nasty infections with the coating of shit he'd
put on the spikes.

There were two doors to the trailer. A wooden pallet covered the
ground in front of each door and served to keep out mud and dirt.
Jackson lifted up the pallets and buried several cartridge traps.
These simple booby traps consisted of a single rifle cartridge stuffed
inside a bamboo sleeve. Only the tip of the cartridge protruded
while the primer rested on a nail. Step on the bullet and you could
blow your foot off. The grunts called them toe-poppers, and Jackson recalled with pleasure how a black man in his outfit hopped
around in agony after stepping on one. After burying the traps, he
covered them with the pallets. He would remove the pallets each
night before going to sleep and put them back in the mornings.
Sometimes he sang a little ditty as he did this: "Eenee meenee
mainee, mo! Catch a nigger by the toe!"

The trailer doors had dead-bolt locks, peepholes, and gun ports
for his shotguns and rifles, which included a fully automatic AR-
15. There was a hatch in the roof that could be popped open, en-
abling Jackson to start lobbing his chemical arsenal. This
included a few bottles of his homemade napalm, which he had
tested at the chess club. It was a simple gelled flame fuel he had
prepared from a mixture of gasoline, lye, and castor oil. He preferred these fire bottles to traditional Molotov cocktails filled
with gasoline because his pasty fuel adhered more readily to the
target and produced a greater concentration of heat. Jackson also
made a number of urea nitrate pipe bombs. He called them piss
bombs because whenever he made the explosive mixture his
clothes would end up reeking of urine for days. The procedure
was simple. All he needed to do was collect his urine, boil and
filter it, add some nitric acid, then collect the urea nitrate crystals
and pack them into a pipe. Add a fuse and they were ready to go.
If I can't catch the niggers with toe-poppers, I'll piss on them, he
thought.

If anyone actually penetrated these defenses and entered the trailer, they would confront the awesome power of Jackson's end game. The entire trailer was one big bomb rigged to explode with the touch of an inside switch.

"I'm sick and tired of people messing with me," said Jackson when his employer called him at home. Jackson had not reported to work for several days. He told his boss he was quitting. He didn't explain. He didn't have time.

Everything was closing in on him. He felt events were sweeping him along toward a climax beyond his control. A black family had moved into the trailer park. The lights in their trailer flashed at night. A signal? Then he found a rifle bullet on the roof of his trailer. He couldn't remember being so careless. Besides, it didn't fit any of his weapons. The piece of fuse wire he found on the hood of his car one day was just as puzzling.

Now the local newspaper was running a series of articles on the CIA. They mentioned spies, the Mafia connections, and the KGB. KGB? That was Russian! They spied for all their chess champions! Jackson was really worried. A voice told him to check out the black family.

He waited until they left for the market one afternoon. It was easy to pick the lock on their trailer. He searched inside until he found a loaded revolver under a mattress. It's only a .22—a pea shooter, he thought. He took it anyway.

A woman was watering her plants outside an adjoining trailer when Jackson exited the black man's trailer.

"There's going to be trouble soon," warned Jackson.

A few hours later the black man was walking toward Jackson's trailer. Jackson watched him from a window. The black man looked mad. There was a bulge in his pocket. A chorus of voices clamored for Jackson's attention.

"Shoot the son of a bitch."

"He's KGB."

"Mafia."

"What is best is a quick victory."

"KGB Mafia."

"Victory is gained by surprise."

"Call him a son of a bitch before you shoot him."

Jackson walked out of his trailer to meet the man. He was holding the black man's gun by the barrel. The man smiled. Jackson went up to him.

"You're a son of a bitch," said Jackson as he twirled the gun around in his hand. He shot him once in the forehead, just above the left eye. The black man fell dead in his tracks, still smiling. Jackson put the gun in the dead man's hand.

The woman from the other trailer came running over.

"He committed suicide," said Jackson. She called the police. They were there almost immediately. Jackson knew they had been waiting for this to happen. The police were part of the conspiracy to get him. They were willing to sacrifice a black pawn to get what they wanted. Just like 'Nam. He didn't resist. The war was finally over.

Jackson was a model prisoner of war while awaiting trial for murder. He called everyone "sir" and did what he was told. He smiled at me when I took the witness stand.

I found myself sounding very much like Joel Morgan as I agreed with a defense psychiatrist who opined that Jackson was suffering from paranoid schizophrenia. All the major diagnostic signs were there, including the prominent auditory hallucinations of Master Sun's voice, the sounds of battle in the hotel ballroom during the chess tournament, and the sounds of helicopters flying over the trailer park. There were the bizarre delusions about blacks and KGB Mafia and, finally, the thought control by voices ordering him to shoot the victim. The minor associated features of paranoid schizophrenia were also present: anxiety, anger, argumentativeness, and violence. Kenneth's stilted and formal interpersonal relationships, symbolized by his "Yes, sir" and "No, sir" responses, were classic features. I was sad that drugs were not responsible. Then there would have been a way to detoxify Jackson and quickly close the gates on the demon. In paranoid schizophrenia, the gates might never close.

As I stepped from the witness stand, Jackson held a piece of paper high in the air. It was a crude drawing of the sun. I knew that for Jackson it was about to set for the last time. If he ever got out of the hospital for the criminally insane, he would probably spend the rest of his life in prison, behind barbed-razor tape.

9

THE FLOATING DOLLAR BILL

1

God woke up and stumbled into the bathroom. He flipped the switch on the wall. "Let there be light," he muttered as a bare overhead bulb came to life. It was too bright. Reflexively, God shut his eyes and hit the switch again. The darkness came back, only now clouds of purple and blue swirled in the void. It reminded him of the beginning, when cosmic gases first started to coalesce after the Big Bang.

He stood in front of the toilet, rocking back and forth on unsteady feet, trying to direct his urine. A pink neon "Vacancy" sign was flashing outside the tiny bathroom window. The flashes spilled into his eyes, filling his brain with ancient images. God saw that he was no longer pissing in the toilet, but on the wailing wall. Pious men, wrapped in prayer shawls, mumbled and rocked with him. Their tears streamed onto the wall. A thousand voices praised his name.

"Thank you," said God as he finished with a smile, then flushed. He stumbled back to the bed and stretched out on his back. There were mirrors directly overhead on the ceiling. He knew they were there. All the cheap adult motels had them. Although he couldn't see them in the dark, they still bothered him. Maybe because he was alone. He flopped over on his stomach, cupped one hand around his groin and the other on his chin with the thumb near his lips, just the way he liked to sleep since he was a child.

God farted. "Quiet, Harry," he said. God did not want to disturb the images now dancing somewhere between his eyes and the pillow. The men were still praying at the wall. He pointed to the righteous ones, and they rose slowly in the air, sprouted angel wings, then ascended to heaven. He pointed to the others, wiggled a crooked finger, and they sank slowly into puddles of burning urine. The judgments over, God drifted back to sleep.

Harry Balise woke up. He grabbed the bottle of cheap rum from the night table, rinsed his mouth with a slug, then swallowed it. Harry was no alcoholic—or drug addict, for that matter. But three weeks inside this sleazy motel room had left him a changed man. He still couldn't believe it. Harry knew he was no longer a man. He had become something special. The dream last night had confirmed it. Jeremiah, Job, and the other prophets of the Old Testament had to wrestle with the meaning of their dreams. Not Harry. He had reached a stage where he suddenly felt that he understood all that had been happening to him. In a flash of what is known as "paranoid illumination," Harry saw it all. He knew he was becoming a prophet of God. Harry greeted the thought with another shot from the bottle.

As soon as he stood up he knew it was too fast. He became dizzy and had to sit down on the edge of the bed for a few moments. The dizziness was more like a delirium and reminded him of when he'd huffed paint as a teenager and the world would spin. Now his world was spinning with the realization that over the past three weeks he had evolved into a being with knowledge and powers. He called the being a God prophet.

This was not exactly what Harry had been looking for when he checked into the Paradise Motel. He'd just wanted to get away from it all. Everything was bugging him. First, there was his job. He didn't have one. Sure, he used to have one, a good one. He had been a life insurance salesman, one of the best. He'd made salesman of the month more times than he could remember. Then the company let him go. They'd closed his local office—restructuring, they'd called it—and offered him no retirement pension, no transfer, no nothing. He couldn't even keep the "Salesman of the Month" plaque with his name engraved along with other past win-

ners. It went to the home office along with two of the white salesmen. Harry was black. He *knew* that was why he was unemployed.
After two decades of selling security to others, Harry was left without any of his own. That created the second problem that was
bugging him: his family. Actually, he was bugging them. His wife,
Margaret, resented the fact that Harry stayed around the house,
didn't look for a job, and was always underfoot. She was particularly territorial about the kitchen, roaring objections whenever
Harry came in for a snack. And Harry was always snacking. On
more than one occasion she found him sitting on a chair in front of
the open Sub-Zero refrigerator, fork in hand, eating his way
through the shelves. They started fighting, verbally at first, then
physically. The children didn't understand. Little Harry, five, and
Lynell, eight, took their mother's side.

"Daddy was always making Mommy cry," Little Harry told me
in an interview many months later. "He didn't want to work or
play with us anymore. Mommy called him lazy."

"A fat lazy ass," Lynell added with a giggle.

"Fat lazy ass," echoed Little Harry. More giggles.

Big Harry threw a butter dish at Margaret when she made the
remark. Then he stormed out of the house and went on one of his
long walks. Sometimes he walked all night, crisscrossing miles of
city blocks. The city was another thing bugging Harry. It was a
white city, hard on blacks. There were too many people, too
many cars, and too many taxes. Harry was beginning to notice
how much it cost to live in the city, and he didn't like it. When he
came home from his walks he wondered how much longer he'd
be able to hang on to the house. He owed money on everything,
even the Sub-Zero. The savings wouldn't last forever. They had
some income from part ownership of a commercial building, but
it wasn't much. He started complaining to Margaret. She spent
too much on this, too much on that. He ordered her to economize
on everything, even the toilet paper. Harry could hear the toilet
roll spin around and around as Margaret grabbed handfuls of it
at a time.

"Use one goddamn sheet at a time," he would yell through the
closed bathroom door. "That's why they put those goddamn per-
forations in it."

Harry took charge of the grocery shopping, but he ignored the lists Margaret gave him and used his own judgment. He bought the smallest packages of meat and fish and very little fresh produce. At a nearby wholesaler he bought soft drinks, cookies, and other snacks by the case. He got the kids a large tub of peanut butter but instructed Margaret to dispense it with a scoop used for making melon balls, two tiny scoops per sandwich. "We don't have the money for more," he complained.

"You have the power to change that, Harry. You have the power," she said. "Just get a goddamn job."

She said it often. It became her standard speech. The kids started to parrot her, making a game out of it.

"You're a good salesman, Harry," Margaret would say. "You have the power to sell anything."

"Get a job," the children would chorus, giggling.

"You have the power" was the only refrain Harry heard.

Finally Margaret did the unthinkable. She stopped having sex with Harry. Then Harry checked into the Paradise.

The motel was only a few miles from the house, and Harry parked the car where he was certain Margaret would see it. He thought he could make her jealous by pretending he was shacking up with someone else. Why else would he select an adult motel featuring waterbeds, mirrors, and X-rated films? Actually he would have preferred a nicer place, but $35 a night was Harry's kind of motel. The room included coffee, but there was none this morning. He made a mental note to tell the manager, then grabbed a dough-nut and washed it down with some flat Coca-Cola. He dressed and went outside for his daily walk.

The Paradise Motel was on Washington Boulevard in the Culver City section of Los Angeles. Culver City was home to most of the major studios—"The Heart of Screenland," as the local Chamber of Commerce liked to say. The city even named its streets after the stars: (Fred) Astaire, (Jackie) Coogan, and, of course, (Judy) Gar-land. For Harry the movies were a Technicolor escape from the black and white of city life. A sculpture in front of the local Vet-erans Memorial Building told it all. The sculpture, *Filmstrip U.S.A.*, was a gleaming seven-ton stainless-steel group of curling filmstrips rising out of a reflection pool. On the day Harry first visited it, he saw several cigarette butts and a used condom floating in the pool.

Harry started walking east on Washington toward the old MGM studio, the only local landmark he thought worthy of pointing out to visitors. It was where they had made *The Wizard of Oz,* one of his favorite movies. It was also the first movie he could remember seeing as a kid, and he'd made sure it was the first one his own kids saw. They'd enjoyed it, of course, although they were not affected to the degree that Harry had been as a child. Harry came out of the theater telling everybody he wanted to be a wizard. Later, after discovering the Superman series on television, Harry wanted to be Superman. He would tie a towel around his neck and jump off boxes in the backyard, pretending he was the caped hero himself leaping over tall buildings. Harry flew through the 1950s with his towel flapping in the backyard. Then in 1959 George Reeves, who played the television Superman, put a Luger above his right ear and blew his brains out. Superman was not as fast as a bullet after all. Harry was devastated. He desperately needed a different hero. Once again he wished he could grow up to be a wizard belching smoke and fire just like in the movie. That wish, tucked away in his memory, was now being awakened.

A bus belched black smoke and stopped ahead of him on Washington Boulevard. Harry wished it away just as the traffic light changed and the bus drove off. What this city needs is a good enema, thought Harry, recalling a Jack Nicholson line from *Batman.* He walked past several liquor stores, a bar called the Alibi Room, a couple of auto repair shops, and more liquor stores. When he got to the Seventh Day Adventist Church he stopped. Harry read the announcement on the bulletin board: "Worship service, Saturday 11 A.M." Why only worship then? he asked himself. You can kiss my ass anytime, just like I doted on all your underinsured white asses for twenty years. A few blocks later he came to the Culver Community Church. "Come and enjoy the spirit of God," announced the sign. Harry read it to himself, then added out loud, "At your service anytime," not as a pun, but as a promise to those who wished to praise his newly acquired prophethood.

Harry reached the Salvation Army Thrift Store and walked inside. Now here was a store that Margaret and the kids should know about. She had a charge card at Bullock's, which he had torn up. He wouldn't have to worry about her overspending on clothes here. Harry picked up two shirts at $.92 each and a pair of sweatpants for $2.47. He selected a black nylon nightgown for Margaret at $1.60 and a set of checkers for the kids at $.50. Harry didn't mind splurging on them. He had decided he was going home that day.

After walking several more blocks, Harry crossed the street to take the other side back to the motel. He passed a gun store. The parking lot was filled with police cars. Harry got nervous. This was the same store where a chess player named Kenneth Jackson ("Bunkers") once bought an antique derringer and ammunition. Harry didn't go inside. He wasn't interested in guns or ammo. He had the power.

He walked quickly now, heading west on Washington. Along the way he read signs out loud, something he always did when he was distracted by deep thoughts and needed to keep himself focused. No sense in getting killed at a crosswalk. He had the power, but he was still mortal—for now. Who knows what powers I'll have tomorrow, what secrets I'll learn? he thought. "Bun's Radiator," he announced. I'll have to study and get some books on crystals, he told himself. The secrets are in crystals. "Claude's Auto Painting and Collision Repairing." Got to learn about Kirlian auras, he thought. They're doing that stuff at UCLA. Maybe they want to study me. "Alibi Room. Cocktails, Sports and Games."

Harry could see the Paradise Motel up ahead, its faded turquoise-green roof barely visible through the smog. For Harry it was a site as inspiring as the glistening spires of Emerald City. Paradise Motel! What a perfect name for the birthplace of a God prophet! thought Harry. He hurried to his room and started packing. The bottle of rum was almost empty, but he put it in his suitcase anyway. He also packed a motel towel. He wouldn't need it for a cape—he had the power now—but a God prophet should have a towel stamped in Paradise. Harry took one last look around the room to see if he had everything. The place was clean. Well, not exactly clean. There were empty Coke and rum bottles on the bedroom floor, stains on the carpet, urine on the bathroom floor, a torn shower curtain, and paint peeling everywhere. Harry studied a spot high on the wall where large pieces of paint were curling. As he stared, a piece broke loose and floated down like a feather from an angel's wing. "At your service anytime," said the God prophet

Harry. He went to the motel office to get the five-dollar key deposit. The manager gave him six singles. God made him do it.

2

"Do drugs give you power?" asked the woman with a nervous voice on the other end of the line. Margaret Balise had called me for help. She was worried about her husband, who was acting very strangely. He had disappeared for several weeks, then returned, claiming he was blessed with a new energy and was learning to control it. He said he had power. Margaret wondered if drugs were responsible.

"Well, drugs can be very powerful," I answered cryptically, hoping to get more information from her. "What drugs does your husband do?"

She explained that he used to do cocaine, but he hadn't done any drugs since he was busted many months ago. He had been on a probation urine-testing program ever since, and all his tests had been clean. She was wondering if his past history of drug use could have changed him. While urine tests were easy to beat and Harry might still be using, I was willing to accept what she said at face value.

"How has he changed?" I asked.

"All he does now is read books on chemistry and crystals. He said he doesn't have to do anything else because he has power," she said.

"What kind of power?"

"He can levitate objects," she said with conviction. "He can levitate eggs, glasses, some plastics. He has trouble with metal."

Jesus Christ! I said to myself. I knew there was no drug that gave you that kind of power. Nitrous oxide and similar hallucinogens could produce negative hallucinations where objects such as a desk might seem to disappear, leaving the pencil and paper as if suspended in air. But Margaret had said Harry never used hallucinogens. My thoughts started drifting as I pictured scenes from René Magritte paintings with rocks, pipes, apples, even a locomotive, suspended in midair. When I came back to earth, Margaret was talking. I thought I heard her say "Jesus."

"I'm sorry," I interrupted. "Did you say something about Jesus?" Is she reading my thoughts? I wondered.

"He says he's a God prophet as real and true as Jesus," she repeated. She went on to explain that the family was Baptist and attended church regularly. Harry had stopped going when he came back from his three-week disappearance. He'd said Jesus had nothing on him anymore. He had the power.

"I'd like to meet your husband," I said. There's an abandoned car on the corner of my block. Maybe he could move it for me, I thought—a reflexive joke that betrayed my growing nervousness about this man.

"Harry's not here right now."

"Tell him I would like to see his powers. It would be of great research interest."

"Oh, he *can* do it," Margaret said. She described how Harry would put small objects in his hands and make them float.

"You saw them float?" I asked.

"I can see a small amount of light underneath them. Harry says this proves they rise above the surface," she replied. "Isn't that so?"

"Hmmm," I muttered, to encourage her to continue. I knew this also happened when objects rested on uneven surfaces like the palm of the hand. Silently I was planning on calling a tow truck to move the car.

"The kids love it," she continued. "Harry puts bits of Kleenex in their hands and makes them float." She paused for a beat. "He taught the kids how to do it."

"He taught the kids how to do it?" I repeated.

"Only with bits of paper. They're still working on other objects." Another beat. "I can do it a little," she added.

I decided to hold off on calling the tow truck until I got a chance to witness the Balise family in action. According to the antiwar protesters who tried unsuccessfully to levitate the Pentagon in the sixties, if you only have enough people, you can generate the power to do anything.

Margaret and I continued to talk. I kept emphasizing that I was a scientist, not a shrink. Harry can call or visit my lab anytime, I said. She promised to tell Harry about my offer. After she hung up

I thought I heard another click on the line before I put my own phone down.

I was excited. This sounded like a textbook example of paranoid delusions of grandeur, the rare flip side of delusions of persecution. In grandiose reactions the most prevalent themes are taken from the cultural milieu of the patient. Thus the patient may believe himself to be a brilliant scientist, inventor, philosopher, or prophet. Harry's delusions were undoubtedly influenced by his religious background. Although I didn't know it at the time, Harry was also influenced by his childhood. Joel Morgan had told me that delusions of grandeur represent a regression to the narcissistic feelings of early childhood. It is common for infants and very young children to experience feelings of omnipotence. In later interviews with Harry I learned that he kept these feelings alive with fantasies about the Wizard and Superman. The regression to these feelings can occur in the face of what is perceived as a hostile world. There is a tremendous need to free oneself from hostile aggression. In the case of religious grandiosity, the delusion is that you are a special person who can bring universal peace or universal destruction. In a sense, religious zealots and fanatics are often big kids waving holy books and flags instead of towels.

I didn't know which way Harry was going. Levitating eggs and pieces of tissue paper sounded like harmless parlor tricks. But when Margaret told me that Harry promised to teach the children how to fly over the freeway using a special "power towel," I got worried. I immediately flashed on Charles Manson, "a.k.a. Jesus Christ," as noted on his arrest report, another grandiose paranoid who convinced his followers he could fly.

As a young boy growing up in Utah, Manson acquired a make-shift cloak, climbed up to a low roof, spread his arms, and sailed through the air back to earth. It was a typical boyhood game to play Superman, to feel free and powerful. The experience was orgasmic, and Charlie never forgot it. According to his later followers, Charlie really did fly. Later in life Manson acquired other magical "powers from beyond." He convinced his "family" members that he could charm rattlesnakes and scorpions and levitate his magic bus, making it fly over boulders in Death Valley. His power to perform healing miracles was equally apocryphal. He claimed to have cured a case of clubfoot. Family members said he could bring birds and horses back to life. Perhaps Manson's greatest miracle occurred when a girl who was performing fellatio on him became overly excited and accidentally chomped his penis in two. Manson summoned "the power" and restored the penis to a condition "good as new." Five eyewitnesses under the influence of LSD swore it happened.

Throughout it all, Manson was as grandiose and paranoid as Hitler. Manson admitted he was a racist, disliked the Jews (who "run everything"), and hated "the rich piggies." He even carved a swastika into his forehead. It was not a Nazi swastika, but one Manson claimed was rooted in an obscure religious mysticism. He developed a violent hatred of the straight, clockwork society that used the word of God to make money. "You make fun of God and have murdered in the name of Jesus Christ," Manson once said. "The government of the U.S. is at war with their children and the powers of nature and God, and have grown so far above their own judgment that the Waffen SS are coming back from space." Manson saw himself as the divinely appointed agent for the wrath of God.

Charles Manson gathered an army of youths—children, really—who became his family. They literally worshiped him. He, in turn, kissed their feet—literally. Jesus Manson was going to save the world by destroying it, then emerge from the ruins to rule the new order. But don't call it murder. "There's no murder in a holy war," he explained. "The whole thing's a holy war." It was grandiose paranoia in the raw. Using a fleet of stolen dune buggies, Manson organized for desert warfare. He planned to copy the tactics of the Desert Fox himself, German Field Marshal Rommel. He even tried to recruit motorcycle gangs to supply the family with more military muscle. It was just a coincidence to everyone but Manson that the two biker gangs he befriended, the Satan Slaves and the Straight Satans, had the initials SS.

Manson knew he was paranoid, but so what? "Paranoia is just a kind of awareness," he told an interviewer for *Rolling Stone*.

"How does paranoia become awareness?" asked the interviewer.

Manson answered by acting terrorized, scrunching up his body into a ball of vibrating fear. Then he added a comment worthy of the shaman he had become in the eyes of his followers: "Have you ever seen the coyote in the desert? Watching, tuned in, completely aware. Christ on the cross, the coyote in the desert—it's the same thing, man. The coyote is beautiful. He moves through the desert delicately, aware of everything, looking around. He hears every sound, smells every smell, sees everything that moves. He's always in a state of total paranoia, and total paranoia is total awareness."

It was clear that Manson had learned an important lesson from observing coyotes. The quick head turns and darting eye movements he feigned for the interviewer were accurate portrayals of the paranoid streak's alarm call to action. In paranoid states the limbic system is on red alert. Senses *are* acute, and the brain *is* aware. It transformed Manson, not into a coyote, but into a monster from the id. Paranoia gave him a high. He instilled fear and paranoia in others, then fed on it in the same way he and his family drank the blood of their animal and human sacrifices. As Vincent Bugliosi, the district attorney who prosecuted Manson, summed it up for the jury, Manson was no longer a human being, he no longer had a heart and a soul. He was found guilty of conspiracy to murder seven victims, including actress Sharon Tate. The death penalty didn't matter to Charlie without-a-heart-and-soul Manson. "You want to kill me? Ha!" he screamed to the judge. "I'm already dead. Have been all my life!"

Manson was thirty-five at the time of the murders. His paranoid streak had been growing in the twenty-two years he had already spent in prison. In prison he had acquired the paranoid traits necessary for day-to-day survival. But something else happened to him. He looked upon prison as a good place, a monastic retreat that preserved him from the corruption of the world. It provided Manson with the opportunity to escape inside his imagination. His cell became a Platonic cave where he could imagine and project the entire universe. He mastered the art of transcending the reality of prison, reversing the inside for the outside. When he was released, he saw that the world outside the prison walls was equally illusory. This was verified by countless LSD trips wherein everything melted into everything else. Manson acquired the power to see everything as illusion, transcending and reversing opposites. God was Satan.

Good was evil. Hitler was Christ. Death was life. And he used this power to inspire others. He became Lord of his family. "There is no good, there is no evil. . . . If you're willing to be killed, you should be willing to kill," saith the Lord with the twisted cross on his forehead.

Manson predicted that black people would soon gain the power. Now Harry had it. Harry got in three weeks what took Charlie "Man Son—Son of Man," as he liked to write it, twenty-two years to get. Only the Son of God himself could do it as fast as Harry. Back in the days when Charlie was impressing people like Dennis Wilson of the Beach Boys, who called him "the Wizard," Manson worked for Universal Studios on a film story about Christ returning as a black man. Now Fast Harry the Black Wizard wannabe was back in town packing the power.

A few days later Harry called me.

"This is Harry Balise," he said. "You spoke with my wife the other day." There was a long pause. It sounded as though he were eating something.

"Yes," I said. "We spoke."

"Have you said the Lord's prayer today?"

"Yes," I said after pausing to rush through a silent version in my head.

"You want to see me?" he asked. The words were clipped and rushed.

"Yes. I do." Now I was sounding clipped.

"I don't have to prove anything," he said.

"I know," I rushed to say. What was I saying?

"I want to meet some physicists."

"I know ph-physicists. Physicists are m-my friends." I was getting too excited and told myself to slow down. "Perhaps I can arrange a meeting. I'm sure I . . . um . . . they'd be interested in seeing a demonstration of your power."

Harry wanted to know what Margaret had said to me. I told him everything. He asked if I believed her. I told him the truth: I wanted to believe. After all, there was still the matter of that abandoned car on the corner. Harry knew that I was a cocaine expert and volunteered that cocaine had nothing to do with his power, although his new feelings were just like being high on the drug. I told him I understood. We scheduled a meeting in my lab for the following week. I would arrange for a physicist to be there.

"You're a good boy," he said before hanging up. "Continue the good work." That night I found myself mumbling the Lord's prayer.

I contacted Bruno, a physicist who consulted with the parapsychology lab that was once housed next to my lab in the Neuropsychiatric Institute at UCLA. Together we prepared for Harry's visit. We set up several video cameras at different angles around the lab, some with special macro telephoto lenses for extreme close-up recording of any levitation effects.

Parapsychologists have investigated levitation supposedly caused by supernatural mental forces. On the other hand, physicists have studied several physical effects that allow true levitation of solid and even liquid matter. There's no way to measure the alleged paranormal mental forces, but the physical forces can be monitored. Bruno supplied an array of sophisticated equipment to detect intense sound waves, laser light, radio-frequency fields, alternating electric fields, and magnetic fields—all known physical forces that can produce true levitation phenomena. If Harry was using one of these sources, we should detect it.

Of course, magicians also use a variety of gimmicks to produce the illusion that objects are freely floating. If Harry's power was simply a magician's trick, then I might catch something the cameras and equipment could easily miss. While Harry was playing Superman in the 1950s, I was practicing magic tricks and performing for birthday parties and local schools. I was strictly an amateur, certainly not in the same league as James Randi, who had exposed Uri Geller and other alleged psychics. But I knew enough once to catch a local self-styled "mind reader" doing tricks available in any magic store. I had had the satisfaction of exposing him in front of television cameras. Since my repertoire never included "floating routines," I paid a visit to Hollywood Magic, a local shop for professional magicians, and purchased several books on the subject. I also picked up a few tricks to take home and practice. I had a hunch it might be necessary to show God a thing or two.

I came down with a bad case of stage fright as I waited for Harry to arrive at the lab. Bruno busied himself with equipment checks and calibrations. While we waited I showed him a few tricks. He saw or guessed how I did every one. I felt like the spastic, stuttering teenage magician in Woody Allen's play *The Floating Light Bulb*. After screwing up a magic trick, the boy cried, "I'm th-through! I c-can't do it." I was really nervous. But Harry never showed. Thank God. I had more time to practice.

We rescheduled the appointment with Harry, but he missed the next one as well. And the next one. And the one after that. By the time he finally materialized, many weeks later, I had lost my stage fright. I had also lost Bruno, who had to return to his own lab with all the equipment. Maybe God planned it this way? I thought.

Harry Balise shook my hand firmly and gave me a big toothy smile. He was wearing a dark blue suit with a subtle pinstripe, a white shirt, and a regimental tie. His shoes were polished to a mirror finish. Behind thick bifocals, his eyes were shifting constantly. He looked older than forty-nine, his thinning hair showing large areas of gray on the sides. I was startled by the resemblance to Supreme Court Justice Clarence Thomas. Even his voice sounded similar. It didn't exactly inspire trust.

"Did you say the Lord's prayer today?" he asked.

"Yes," I answered. I knew he'd ask, so I had.

"Good . . . but that traffic today . . . bad." Harry carried on for several minutes, complaining about the parking around UCLA, the deterioration of Westwood, the drive-by gang shootings, and, of course, the smog. He asked if I liked Los Angeles. In general, yes.

"If you could point your finger at something in the city and make it go away, what would it be?" he asked.

I thought for a moment. "Leaf blowers," I answered. They annoyed the hell out of me.

Harry gave a toothy smile and nodded. "Yeah, leaf blowers. Right."

"They drive me crazy," I added.

"Leaf blowers, yeah. They're bad," he said.

"I hear you have trouble with metal," I said. Otherwise I figured Harry would have fingered every leaf blower in the city.

Harry stopped smiling. "I don't have to show off," he said.

So we talked. First we talked about the good old days, the days before leaf blowers and smog, the days before the white man settled California. Harry knew his local history. He told me about the Gabrielino Indians, who were the first known inhabitants of the area that would become Culver City. They were simple, peace-loving people who did not believe in harming the environment or each other. They even let women become chiefs and shamans, but the high priest, a man, was the only one who possessed the "sacred power." I shuddered when Harry told me the priest tattooed his forehead with vertical and horizontal lines. Still, the Gabrielinos were not killers. In fact, while human sacrifice was practiced in much of prehistoric America, Southern California was spared. Until Manson and his family moved into the neighborhood.

"Then the Spanish came and mucked it up," Harry continued. "They're still coming in from Mexico."

"I came from New York, and my parents from Russia," I said. "Where were you born?"

Harry smiled again. "New York. But raised in Culver City."

He was relaxing enough to give me a bit of his family history. There were none of the usual sociological indicators of paranoid disorders. His parents were neither dominating, suppressive, nor cruel. They were both still alive and close to their children and grandchildren. While Harry had a "terrible" first marriage, he described his second marriage with Margaret as "happy." By this he meant sexual satisfaction, which had been lacking with his first wife. In later interviews with Margaret I learned that their marriage was a happy one until Harry lost his job. Then he changed. She accused him of brooding and quarreling. He showed a temper for the first time, she said, and refused to compromise. The marriage was full of turmoil. Harry changed again when he returned from his three-week trip. The God prophet came down from the mountain.

What happened during those three weeks in the Paradise? It took me a good six weeks of my own time and numerous interviews with Harry to find out. He was surprisingly cooperative and candid, perhaps because I never once asked for a demonstration of his power.

Harry was humiliated by the loss of his job. He felt like a failure.

His self-image was severely damaged. "It was difficult facing the kids when you're no longer their breadwinning hero," he told me. He was overwhelmed with feelings of distress, fear, and worthlessness. The crisis was immobilizing, his helplessness unbearable. He struck out at Margaret in anger. Harry checked into the motel, partly because he wanted to make her jealous, and partly because he was afraid of his own anger. He was having difficulty controlling it. Instead of looking up to their father, the kids were looking down, teasing him with their little "get a job" number. Part of him did hear them. And that part was getting very pissed off. The other part was afraid of what he might do. At least he had a heart and soul. He was still human.

These crisis conditions set the stage for Harry's psychotic episode in the motel. As he described his experiences in almost hour-by-hour detail, I recognized the onset of a classic religious paranoid reaction, the type that influenced many of the world's great prophets, who claimed they were able to communicate with supernatural forces, understand their intent, and even harness their powers. Levitation was one of those powers. Jesus walked on water. There were witnesses. Hundreds saw St. Joseph of Cupertino rise in the air as high as the spires of St. Peter's Cathedral. Saint Theresa, according to the nuns in her cloister, rose on her chair until her head literally touched the ceiling. But was Harry with the Clarence Thomas face full of divine power or something else?

Harry told me he communicated with the other great prophets who had apparently checked into the Paradise during his stay. He didn't actually speak to them—or see them—but he exchanged thoughts with them. It started when he got bored with the X-rated movies in the room and began flipping through the Bible, conveniently supplied by a management no doubt equally concerned about the spiritual as well as sexual needs of their guests. Between the biblical lines, the prophets spoke to him of secrets, of forces, of powers. He saw the hidden messages as clearly as Manson had found them in the book of Revelation and in the music of the Beatles.

In the middle of the night, when Harry couldn't sleep, he lay in his bed pondering the Bible, asking questions. The prophets in the next room gave answers through the plumbing. It wasn't clear at first, but over time he understood. The pipes in his motel room were noisy. They would vibrate, groan, and burp at the oddest hours. The sounds, nonsensical at first, began to punctuate his thoughts with distinct words: "power," "Harry," and "amen." Manson had a similar experience. At a recording session in a Santa Monica record studio, Manson was strumming his guitar and scat singing with nonsense syllables. "Digh-tu-dai, deigh-du-doi, di-tew-deigh." Words gradually evolved from the nonsense sounds, and Manson had sung them: "die-tew-dai, die-tu-day, die today, die today die today!" Harry's pipes had a nicer sound.

In addition to communicating with the prophets, Harry began to dream about them. Vividly. Lucidly. He remembered his dreams. The images kept flashing in his mind as if they were snapshots falling out of an old trunk in a dusty attic. Their lucid nature confused him. Were they memories of dreams or something else? What else? What did they mean?

He took long walks, looking for signs. He wanted—more than that, needed—answers. A series of anomalous experiences, coincidences, really, shaped the development of his grandiose delusions. He passed a stranger on the street. The stranger started to ask for some spare change. Harry waved a finger, and the stranger stopped in midsentence. Manson would wave his fingers at his followers, yell, "Die," and they all would lie down and pretend they were dead. One true-believing follower, Brooks Posten, went into a catatonic trance for three days. Harry was no Charles Manson, but the encounter with the stranger was a start.

Harry noticed that sometimes objects behaved oddly when he stared at them. A piece of paper flew out of a car window and caught Harry's eye. He stared at the paper as it was drifting toward the middle of the road. The paper executed an abrupt right-angle turn and flew to the side, coming to rest near the curb. Such events happened only a few times, but they impressed Harry and stuck in his mind. Back in the motel he saw a small spider start to descend from the ceiling on a barely visible strand of silk. Harry sent it back up the silk with a zap of mental power. The experience startled Harry as much as it must have surprised the spider. Harry *knew* this was not a coincidence. So he went around Culver City for three weeks, practicing his newfound power. It didn't work most of the time, but when he connected, it filled him with mystical feelings and a strange excitement. He was becoming a completely different person. He was becoming more than human.

He looked for other signs. Numbers, places, and dates held particular significance. Harry told me he was destined to be in a place called Paradise for these revelations. His first experience with the power occurred on the eighth day of his stay, which was also his eighth wedding anniversary. Harry chortled as he handed me a copy of the room bill as proof. Somehow he had not been billed for that night! Manson put similar mystical significance into coincidences of numbers and dates. His followers have continued the tradition, noting that Sharon Tate starred in the 1966 horror flick *13* (also released as *Eye of the Devil*). The movie is about a death cult, and in the film the Tate character is killed by a Manson look-alike. Manson was incarcerated in cell 13 on death row. The Tate murders happened on August 9, 1969, the anniversary of the bombing of Nagasaki. The Haunted Mansion ride opened at Disneyland that night. The LaBiancas were butchered the following night inside a house once owned by Walt Disney. Such associations were enough to send students of the occult on their own haunted rides into paranoia.

Harry's ride was enlightened by comparison, guided by the mystical illuminations of Buddha and Muhammad, among others. Of course, Harry was not the first human to claim audiences with such illustrious figures. Emanuel Swedenborg, an eighteenth-century scientist and philosopher, claimed he held repeated conversations with God, Jesus, Aristotle, Plato, Luther, and Calvin. Swedenborg recorded over a hundred volumes of the conversations in which he convinced these figures to change to a new theology he'd developed. A creative and productive scientist before his religious experiences, Swedenborg presented his new beliefs about contacting the spiritual world in an equally organized, scientific, and convincing manner. His thinking and routine behavior appeared entirely normal—a characteristic of paranoid disorders—and he attracted many followers. Among the converts to Swedenborg were Elizabeth Browning, Samuel Taylor Coleridge, Ralph Waldo Emerson, Johann Wolfgang von Goethe, Immanuel Kant, and Helen Keller.

Thus far, Harry had only his family behind him. I offered him the opportunity to convince me as well.

"I don't show off," he said for the zillionth time.

"Well, can you tell me *how* you levitate things?"

Harry smiled and shook his head. It was a secret, he said. I figured prophets probably had union rules just like magicians. But I persuaded Harry to explain the general theory.

"All matter is composed of atomic particles, right?" he said.

"Right," I agreed.

"And atomic particles are in constant motion, right?"

"Right."

"That's how," he said, flashing his Clarence Thomas smile.

"That's how what?" I didn't understand.

"I get in there and move them around," he confessed.

I flashed on Charles Manson and his family, who used to "creepy-crawl" through the wealthy homes in the Bel-Air and Brentwood sections of West Los Angeles, stealing and moving things around while the owners slept. That really rattled everyone who lived on the west side, including me. Did Harry somehow creepy-crawl through the molecules themselves? If this was possible, why was I wasting fifty bucks a month on an electronic security system for my house?

"You get in there and move them around?" I repeated. This was another way of asking him *how* he did it.

He took the bait. "Yeah, right. I do it with my mind," he said. "That's the only thing. That's how Christ did it."

That was similar to what Manson had once said about the power. "There is only the mind," he'd declared. "The mind is everything. It is Buddha. It is Christ. It is the Devil. It is God."

I had just the thing to test Harry's alleged mental powers. It was a modified "Schmidt machine" developed to test psychokinesis. Psychokinesis, or PK, refers to the movement of objects at a distance through the power of the mind. The machine uses radioactive strontium-90 as a random generator. As the isotope decays, beta particles are emitted randomly. A Geiger tube catches the particles and gates them to an electronic switch that operates either a red or blue light. The lights go on totally randomly once the subject presses the switch. All the subject has to do is use PK to influence the path of a single itsy-bitsy beta particle. Theoretically this should be easy for someone like Harry when you considered how many atomic particles were in a piece of Kleenex. Of course, the subject could cheat by using precognition—the ability to predict future events. But either way, better than chance performance on the Schmidt machine would suggest some paranormal power. I never met anyone who could beat the Schmidt.

Harry agreed to try. "I'm going to purposely try to miss," he announced, not realizing that significant deviations from chance either way meant the same. After one hundred trials Harry scored fifty-four misses. It wasn't significant, but I didn't want to discourage him. I told him it was promising. He complained about the difficulty of relating to a metal box.

"How about trying it your way, on some Kleenex or something?" I suggested.

"I'm as real and knowledgeable as Buddha," said Harry, "and I don't have to show off."

I was getting tired of this mantra. It was time to get Harry to show me his stuff. "I've met Buddha," I declared matter-of-factly. While I didn't explain, it was true. I had spent an afternoon inside a sensory isolation tank at John Lilly's ranch in the remote hills of Malibu. After several hours I'd had a hallucination of a tiny Buddha—not the Hindus' sacred Buddha, but a cartoon version that looked more like the Pillsbury Doughboy.

Harry was surprised. "Where?" he asked.

"In Malibu, a few weeks ago. I learned a lot from the experience." Harry seemed ready, so I piled it on. "He taught me secrets," I lied.

"Like what?" Harry was challenging me.

I was prepared. I asked him for a dollar bill, which I crumbled into a ball and placed in my open left hand. As I wrinkled my face in concentration, the bill started to rise about six inches above my hand. I let it hover just in front of Harry's wide-open eyes, then float slowly to my other hand. Then I reversed it, allowing the bill to stay suspended midway between my hands for a full minute as I pointed to the bill and passed my hands around it, showing that there was nothing there but empty air. The bill came to rest once again in my left hand. I handed it back to Harry.

The effect came off so cleanly, I almost believed it myself. But it was a trick called "The Floating Dollar Bill," and it was available at Hollywood Magic for $15. The price included a gimmick that can be used with any dollar bill at all and a set of simple instructions. Harry had never seen the trick. He said he accepted my explanation that Buddha gave me the power. Now it was Harry's turn.

He placed the crumpled dollar on his hand and stared. "Look! Look underneath!" he said, directing my attention to the space between the crumpled edges of the dollar and his palm. "Do you see light?" he asked.

"Yes, but that's only because—"

Harry cut me off. "Watch," he said as he tore the dollar into tiny pieces, placed them in both hands, and stared. The tremor in his hands caused the pieces to jiggle slightly, but they weren't flying the way he claimed. The movements didn't come close to my performance, and I said so. I was playing out the scene where Dorothy pulls the curtain aside and reveals the little professor, who pretends to be the Great and Powerful Wizard of Oz. Harry seemed nervous, almost panicked.

He pointed to my coffee cup and announced that it was moving across the table.

"No, it's not, Harry," I said as I picked it up to show him the wet ring that was still totally covered by the cup.

He pointed to my pencil and said it was rolling.

"I bumped the table going for the coffee cup," I explained.

I saw beads of sweat on the Clarence Thomas brow. Then Harry wiggled his finger at my bookcase and said it was starting to fall.

I ran to the bookcase. My books were as important to me as my coffee. "I don't see it moving at all, Harry," I said after examining it thoroughly. "It shook a little during the last earthquake. That's why I bolted it to the wall." I checked the bolts, and they were still tight.

Harry was in shock. It was as if Anita Hill had just slapped him across the face. A miniature earthquake traveled in rippling waves across his jowls. His lips were twitching.

"I—I don't have to show off," he stammered, then bolted for the door. After the door slammed, I could almost hear the Scarecrow as he yelled to the exposed Wizard: "You humbug!"

I didn't see Harry again. But I stayed in touch with Margaret. We met for several interviews. Margaret said he was still teaching her and the kids the power of levitation, although they hadn't advanced very far. He still said he had the power. They still believed him.

The Balise family was an example of *folie à famille*, the same type of shared paranoid disorder I had seen before in the Cliff Hill family ("Invasion of Bugs"). The Hill family recovered, but only after Cliff's suicide. I didn't want to wait around for something like that to happen again. But Harry Balise was avoiding me. In such cases, where the dominant family member cannot be reached directly, treatment has to focus on the rest of the family in order to minimize future problems in the children. I thought it was worthwhile to try the same tactic on the kids and Margaret that I had used with Harry. It would be treatment with magic.

The family arrived at my office in their Sunday best. Margaret was wearing a beautiful pink dress with matching shoes and purse. Lynell had on a yellow party dress, white tights, and yellow ribbons in her pigtails. Little Harry was absolutely adorable in his white shirt and Malcolm X bow tie.

We all talked for a while, then I asked Margaret and the kids for a demonstration of their power. Margaret refused to try. Lynell and Little Harry put balls of Kleenex in their hands, giggled, and said they were doing it.

"We're doing it," said Lynell. "There's light coming through."

"We're doing it, Mommy. We're doing it," Little Harry cried.

But they were not doing it. I hooked up their balls of Kleenex to sensitive string gauges and proved that they were not moving. The kids refused to believe the gauges. They didn't understand. Mommy jumped to their defense. "Of course you can do it," she told them.

I went after Mommy. I asked her to hold out her hand. Then I removed a single match from a book of matches and placed it on her outstretched palm. Slowly the match began to rise. I knew Margaret could not only see it happening, but she was feeling it. In a few moments the match was standing on its end. I faked disbelief and passed my hands all over and around the match to see if there were any threads or wires. There were none, I told everybody. I even picked up the match while it was standing, then put it back on her hand, where it resumed its standing position. Then the match slowly spun around and fell flat.

Margaret gasped and smiled. The kids cheered Mommy.

I took the same match, placed it in each kid's hand, and repeated the demonstration. Everyone was amazed by their power.

"It's the PK Factor," I announced with a smirk. That was the name of the trick I had purchased at Hollywood Magic. I explained how it was done. A steel splinter was embedded in the match stick, and I held their hands over a powerful magnet hidden under some sheets of paper on my desk. It was that simple. (The Floating Dollar Bill worked on a completely different but equally simple principle.) Magic tricks like this, I told them, were the only way people could make things seem to move by themselves. There was no secret mental power, only secrets of magic tricks. I spoke for quite a while, explaining principles of magic, illusion, and suggestion, but never once did I mention their father.

"Do some more," the kids begged.

I could never resist a kiddie audience. I excused myself for a moment and went to the storage closet for my trunk. Talk about regression to a state of childhood omnipotence! I opened the trunk and out popped Rondini, child magi who wowed tiny tots throughout upstate New York. His hands were faster than the human eye. He was more powerful than the miniature finger guillotine. He was able to restore cut rope with a single pass of his wand. Rondini!

So I did my entire shtick for Margaret and the kids. I performed the egg bag, the Chinese linking rings, the vanishing milk pitcher, and the cigarette-through-the-quarter trick. I stayed away from floating routines and any mental tricks because I didn't want to confuse the kids. But I did use a slightly frayed cloth hand puppet to pick the same card Lynell selected. For my finale I turned a match into a flower, which I gave to Margaret, pulled a silk handkerchief out of an empty tube for Lynell, then produced a "Thanx from Rondini" magic coin from behind Little Harry's ear.

I stayed in touch with Margaret after that wonderful day of magic. The kids couldn't stop talking about it. While Harry never mentioned the showdown between the Wizard and Rondini, he started changing again: he went looking for a job. Eventually he enrolled in real estate school, got his license, and started working for a small office in Culver City. Harry's new job gave him the self-esteem he needed so desperately, and it normalized his relationship with the family. I told Margaret that eventually Harry would lose his belief in the power just as she and the kids had.

"He's a good man," said Margaret.

"I know he is," I replied.

As the Professor told Dorothy, "I'm a very good man. I'm just a very bad wizard."

Weeks later a group of UCLA fraternity men carried off the abandoned car from the corner near my office. At least I think they carried it. As far as the leaf blowers go, they're still around. I wish I had the power to make them go away.

10

THE TENTH PLAGUE

1

"Before we start," said the detective, "let me advise you of your rights. I want you to understand that you have the right to remain silent and anything you say can and will be used against you in a court of law. You have the right to talk to an attorney and have him present with you while you are being questioned. If you cannot afford to hire an attorney, one will be appointed to represent you. Do you understand these rights?"

Linda Estrada looked around the room at the beat-up oak chairs, the desk cluttered with foam coffee cups, and the little fan humming away on top of the dusty file cabinet. Despite the fan, she felt hot, almost as if she were sitting under a bank of klieg lights. It all seemed like a movie. The cop sitting across from her could have been from Central Casting. She stared at the tape recorder on the desk. Why are they tape-recording? she wondered. She didn't want to be here. "No, no . . . oh, no! Please, please . . . I don't want to go in there, no . . . oh, no!" she had cried. They'd brought her anyway, almost by force. She thought they were going to kill her. Now they were asking questions. The movie kept going.

"Do you understand those rights?" he asked again.

"Um-hum," she said. Hyperventilation prevented her from saying more.

"Having those rights in mind, do you want to talk to me?" The detective, recognizing her fragile condition, was trying to be as soft-spoken as possible.

"Huh?"

"About what happened?" prompted the detective.

"Um . . . I—I don't know . . . um . . . what happened. . . . I'd like . . . to get a lawyer . . . first." The words were punctuated with audible inhalations as Linda worked to control her breathing.

The detective could see that Linda was on the edge of losing it totally. He understood. He remembered the scene he had walked into only hours earlier. It was hard to forget and even harder to talk about. "Okay," he said with relief, "I can't really ask you any questions or anything like that."

"I'd like to know what happened, though," Linda managed to say. "Like . . . if you could tell *me* anything . . . I just don't know."

"Well . . . it seems like . . . I don't know what happened there, but you remember that the police had gone out to your house earlier today?"

"Earlier today?" Linda didn't know what the detective was talking about.

"Yes. You were there," he said.

"I was there?"

"The fire department came out."

"The fire department came out?" Linda started hyperventilating again.

"Your daughter was hurt," the detective whispered.

"Oh, God! I . . . Oh, God," Linda whispered, almost as if she were praying.

"There is no gentle way to put this," the detective said gently, "but your daughter has passed away."

"Oh, God!" Linda was in full hyperventilation now. A chorus of primordial sounds, like the muffled cries of a newborn, came rushing out of her throat.

"Linda." A beat. "Linda." Another beat. "Linda. Linda," said the detective, trying to keep her from losing it.

"I want my daughter," she cried.

"I know you do. I know that."

"I love her so much."

The detective continued softly, "Your daughter had received some stab wounds."

Linda gasped sharply, as if in pain.

"We did a search warrant on your home and recovered some evidence," the detective was saying. "You are under arrest for Penal Code Section 187, which is murder. That being the murder of your daughter, Amy."

"No! That wasn't me! It wasn't. It wasn't me!" Linda said in choked cadences. She looked down at her hands. They were in handcuffs because she had been found beating them against the wall. She studied the bruised hands. They were not her hands. "It just wasn't me," she said. "It wasn't! It was not!" Linda started wailing. She couldn't control the sounds any better than her hands.

"It's really difficult to sit and listen to you," the detective said. He tried to distract her with details of the booking procedure. Maybe she should see a doctor.

Linda started calming down. "Can I have a cigarette?" she asked. She was a chain smoker.

"Well, unfortunately we can't give you one. This building is no smoking, and the facility that you're going to also is no smoking. So I guess we're going to have to help you kick the habit for a while."

It was turning into a very bad movie.

2

I reviewed the case file in my mind as I walked down the long corridors of the jail where Linda was taken after her arrest. Her public defender had hired me as an expert to investigate any possible drug connection with the murder. I had gone over everything, including the police reports, autopsy protocol, tapes of Linda's interview with the detective, crime scene photographs, everything. I didn't know anything. The case was as mysterious as the stab wounds on Amy's seven-year-old nightgown-clad body: six slit-shaped cuts in the shape of a question mark. The coroner had said that the wounds were made by a serrated knife thrust vertically from above. The knife had been plunged in almost to its full blade length each time. Each of the wounds were potentially fatal. There were no defensive wounds. The coroner thought that the victim was either asleep or overcome so quickly as to be unable to resist.

It all started with a call to 911 on a Saturday morning, just before Halloween. The operator heard a woman moaning, then she hung up. The operator called back. The woman cried for help, then dropped the phone. A police unit was dispatched. Linda let them in. She was hysterical. They found Amy's body in a pool of blood on the kitchen floor. The telephone was beeping. There was no other blood, no signs of a struggle. The house was clean and orderly, just the way you'd expect a woman who earned her living cleaning other people's houses to keep her own. Even the pictures of a smiling Linda and Amy, literally covering every wall in the house, were hanging perfectly straight. A half-eaten candy bar was next to the phone. There were two bags of Halloween candy on the kitchen table. The telephone book was open to the first page with the 911 information.

Linda told the police she didn't know what happened. Then she pointed to a closet in the bedroom. Inside the closet they found the knife. It had been cleaned and put away neatly.

Whatever happened that morning had been put away in some dark closet of Linda's brain. Thus far she had been unable or unwilling to open the door. There were only a few clues. Gil, her live-in boyfriend, told the police that the family had gone out to a Mexican restaurant for dinner around 6:00 P.M. on the previous night. Linda ate surprisingly little. They talked about plans for the upcoming weekend. Amy was excited about wearing her new Halloween costume. After dinner they rented a video movie and watched it at home. Linda complained of a headache and took some aspirin. Amy went to bed in her own room at 10:30 P.M. Before saying good night, Linda placed her hands on Amy's forehead and blessed her. Gil thought it was very strange. They continued watching the movie. Linda kept complaining about her headache. She sipped some wine, hoping it would help. Now her stomach hurt. Gil told her to relax and take it easy.

By 11:00 P.M. Linda was visibly upset. She had been getting up and looking out the windows all evening. Now she wanted to get out of the house. She didn't want to be there. Let's go for a ride, she said. Then she changed her mind and sat down to watch the rest of the movie. In a little while she wanted to go out again. Gil and Linda drove to a convenience store. She waited in the truck while Gil went inside. Then she started banging on the horn for Gil's attention. He came running out. Two men were walking into the store. Linda thought they were going to rob the store, and she insisted on leaving. They went home and climbed into their water-bed. It was midnight.

Linda didn't sleep. She kept getting up and checking the house. Noises, she said. They scared her. During the night she got a cigarette, a glass of water, even a glass of wine. She got everything but sleep. Gil's alarm went off at 5:15 A.M. Linda was lying in bed wide awake. He got dressed and left for work at 5:30 A.M. The 911 call came in at 10:20 A.M.

There were almost five hours of missing time. Was it still locked inside Linda's memory? Did I dare try to open the door?

I reached the end of the corridor and consulted the little map supplied by the officer who checked me through security. I was standing in front of the housing units on the women's side of the massive facility. Linda was in housing unit 9, cell F, bunk 6. Turn the 9 upside down, change the F to 6 for the sixth letter of the alphabet, add the bunk number, and you have 666, the devil's number! I thought. Coincidence? I pushed aside my paranoid musings and headed for the interview room.

Linda came in and sat down opposite me. Despite the tears in her eyes, she forced a smile. Long, dark curly hair cradled her angelic face. She was truly beautiful. I introduced myself. She told me I was not the first doctor to see her. Was I there to find out if she was crazy? No. I had seen one report from a court-appointed psychologist who spoke with her for a few minutes, judged her insane, and recommended that she be committed to a state mental facility. He suspected paranoia, but what type of paranoia could drive a mother to slay her firstborn? Another psychologist wrote that she was sane and did not require hospitalization. I didn't tell her about the reports because I didn't believe either one. After all, she'd told both psychologists she didn't know what happened. Then why was I there? To find out what happened, I told her.

How? I suggested I start by taking some samples of that long curly hair for analysis. It would tell me what drugs she might have been doing. Gil told the police that she might have used methamphetamine. Linda confirmed this by telling me that for two weeks prior to the incident she had been sniffing a little while cleaning houses. The subsequent laboratory analysis verified this, but the amounts were minuscule, less than what would be necessary to keep someone awake, let alone cause a violent rage reaction. Something else had kept Linda awake and on edge that night.

The medical history I obtained from Linda provided a clue. She had a prescription for thyroid medication, which can sometimes cause agitation. I had been on similar thyroid medication for many years and knew something about the adverse reactions. If I took a little more than I should, or I used a little too much coffee during the day, then I might stay awake for a few hours, listening to my heart pounding. I suspected that even a small amount of methamphetamine would do the same trick. When Linda told me that in addition to the thyroid medicine, she was taking daily doses of the stimulant phendimetrazine, a prescription drug used for diet control, I thought I was on to something. Before I could get carried away with this explanation for her all-nighter, Linda explained that she had been taking these prescriptions for seven years without one adverse reaction or one night's loss of sleep. She was tolerant to the drug. Later I confirmed this with the records from her physician.

The family history told me little that I couldn't deduce from the photographs in her house. She got along famously with both Gil and Amy. The three of them were very much in love with each other. They did everything together, including shopping. In fact, that Friday they went shopping for Amy's Halloween costume and a cordless phone for the house.

"As soon as we got home, we had to go back and return the phone right away," said Linda.

"Why?"

"Gil noticed the numbers on the box," she said.

"Yes?"

"Serial numbers, I guess."

"Yes?" Tell me already, I thought.

"They were six six six," Linda said. Her eyes were wide open. It was weird because I had been thinking about these numbers earlier.

I asked Linda if she was particularly superstitious.

"No, but it was the second weird thing that happened. The day before, I was looking through Gil's old high school yearbook. I noticed in one picture, in the background, there was a dead body hanging in a tree. When I looked again, it was gone."

One more weird thing and I'm outta here, I said to myself.

"Do you remember what movie you were watching that night?" I asked.

"I wanted to rent something the whole family could watch, a real family movie. We got *The Ten Commandments.*"

"A good family movie," I said. All about Moses and God. Nothing devilish about those characters. "I liked that movie," I added.

"Something seemed wrong with it," said Linda, twisting her face into a puzzle. "They were changing the words, trying to switch things. The movie really tripped me out. I had to stop watching it after a while."

Linda had seen the 1956 movie once before when she was a child. When I was a child I also saw it once. But the version she described watching that night did not resemble the one either in my memory or in hers. As I wrote down the lines and scenes she recalled, I had to agree that words had been changed and scenes switched. I suspected that the devilish editor was none other than the demon of her paranoia, triggered by the methamphetamine and other medication.

The movie is more than three and one-half hours long. Although Linda stopped it before the end, the movie continued replaying in her mind all night. It was still replaying in the morning when Gil left for work. These recurrent images became mixed with Saturday morning cartoons that Amy started watching on the living room television. I wrote down the lines and scenes she recalled from these as well. But everything stopped just before the stabbing of her daughter. "I don't know what happened," she said, once again slamming the door on her memory.

After a full day of interviewing Linda, I was anxious to rent a copy of the movie and compare it with the paranoid version I had scribbled on my yellow legal pad. It would be necessary to check with Gil to make sure when the movie tapes were stopped and started. I also wanted to check with the local television stations for copies of the cartoon programs for that Saturday. Then I would come back and help Linda through a replay of the revised and edited movie she saw in her head. I hoped it would open the door.

Before signaling the guard to open my own door and let me out of the interview room, I asked Linda if Amy had eaten any Halloween candy on Saturday morning. The police had found a half-eaten candy bar in the kitchen. Perhaps Linda's rage was triggered by Amy eating forbidden fruit. Although the autopsy found Amy's stomach empty, maybe she ate the candy on Friday but Linda didn't discover it until Saturday. It was a long shot.

"It was a chocolate-chip breakfast bar," Linda shot back. "I ate half, but Amy didn't want the other half."

"By the way, what type of Halloween costume did you buy Amy?" I asked. It was a throwaway question.

"Amy picked it out. She looked so cute," Linda said tearfully. "A little devil costume. It was bright red and came with horns and a little plastic pitchfork."

I'm outta here! I told myself.

I rented *The Ten Commandments* and viewed it several times. I also reread the book of Exodus. The movie is a faithful adaptation of the Old Testament story. Both are permeated by a violence that somehow slipped out of my childhood memory.

The Egyptian pharaoh, so goes the biblical story, feels threatened by the growing number of Hebrews. He decrees a policy of slave labor and even goes so far as to try to kill all newborn Hebrew males. The infant Moses is hidden by his mother and discovered by the pharaoh's daughter, who raises him as her son. Moses discovers his true identity and destiny as leader of the Hebrews. After a series of ten plagues, which climax with the slaying of Egypt's firstborn, the Hebrews are allowed to leave. They wander in the wilderness and finally arrive at Sinai, where God reveals his Law in the form of the Ten Commandments.

Like Linda, I remembered a version of the movie that was filled with the more spectacular images: the great Egyptian cities, the burning bush, the massive exodus involving thousands of movie extras, and the special-effects parting of the Red Sea. I also remembered the fog, which represented the Angel of Death. Curiously, I remembered a red fog, but in the movie it's green. Scenes of infanticide and murder are not something a child usually remembers from the movie. But they were there, from beginning to end. The Egyptians murder Hebrew children, Moses murders an Egyptian, God murders the Egyptian children, the pharaoh seeks to murder Moses, and so on. There are sacrificial slayings, too—both animal and human.

In my interviews with Gil, I learned that the scenes of infanticide and murder were the points at which Linda became visibly upset. She was especially bothered by the plague scenes. When the Nile turned to blood, Linda got up and started pacing. "She thought she heard things," said Gil. "She kept sliding open the blinds to check outside." By the time the burning hail was falling on Egypt, Linda was running out into the yard to check the weather conditions. The plagues may have hardened the pharaoh's heart, but they hammered Linda's head, upset her stomach, and fed her paranoia. Like the councilors to the pharaoh who whined like frightened children in the night, pleading with him to give in to Moses' demands, Linda cowered in fear. After the tenth plague, she turned off the movie.

I returned to interview Linda several more times over the next six months. Each time I obtained additional details about events as she remembered more and more of them. I also looked at the cartoons that were broadcast that Saturday morning, studied the local weather reports, and scrutinized every piece of evidence I could find. I even tried an impromptu experiment. On a Friday, when my wife and children were away for the weekend, I took the exact same dosages of thyroid medication, phendimetrazine, and methamphetamine that Linda ingested, then watched the movie in the evening. Memory images from the movie continued to entertain me throughout a sleepless night. In the morning I watched the cartoons and ate half of a tasteless chocolate-chip breakfast bar. I couldn't concentrate on the cartoons. The reverberating memory images from the movie were overshadowing everything. And I was overtired, hungry, and irritable. Then my answering service called me. I had missed an important meeting at the office. I snapped at

the operator, berated her for disturbing me at home, then slammed
down the phone. A smell caught my attention, and I turned to the
toaster and cursed it—I had forgotten about my bagel, which was
burned to a crisp. I was glad the children were not in the house.

The following week I went back to see Linda. The door to her
memory and the fatal stabbing finally opened. She was able to tell
me about the missing five hours in terms of recurrent images from
the movie mixed with actual events—a movie within a movie. Now
I could piece together the sequence of events that turned a family
movie into a horror show of biblical proportions.

As I walked through the script of Linda's movie with her, it got
to me in a way none of the previous cases had done. Perhaps it had
something to do with my love for movies and my tendency to really
get into them. Whatever the reason, I recognized how Linda's paranoia had turned the movie in her head into virtual reality. With the
help of the real images from *The Ten Commandments,* I felt I was
actually "seeing" her paranoid vision of the world. I was not alone.
I felt my demon was there with me. I tell it like a movie so that
perhaps you, too, will see and feel.

3

FADE IN. INTERIOR OF LIVING ROOM. It begins with Linda, Gil,
and Amy watching *The Ten Commandments* on the television in
their living room. The movie opens with a scene in the council
chamber of Rameses I, pharaoh of Egypt.

"Every newborn Hebrew manchild shall die," decrees the pharaoh. He turns to the scribe: "So let it be written. So let it be done."

DISSOLVE TO: EXTERIOR OF A HEBREW SLAVE'S HOUSE. A muffled
scream is heard. A woman is seated next to a broken, empty cradle.
She stares into space with a look of agony. An Egyptian soldier has
just killed her baby and now wipes the sword with a cloth. Another
woman, holding her child, tries to run from the soldier.

"No, no . . . oh, no! Please, please . . . no . . . oh, no!" screams
the woman in vain.

Linda sits in stunned silence. This is not the movie she remembered.

CUT TO: HEBREW SLAVES BUILDING THE TREASURE CITY.
"God made men—men made slaves," says Joshua.
"Which God?" asks Prince Moses.
"Which God, Mommy?" asks Amy. "There's only one God, isn't there?"
Linda is too confused to answer. They're trying to make me believe that Jesus is not the Son of God, she thinks. This is evil!
Gil explains to Amy that the ancient Egyptians believed in many gods, but there's only one.

CUT TO: THE GRANITE HEAD OF THE PHARAOH'S COLOSSUS.
"Let your own image proclaim my loyalty for a thousand years," says Moses to the pharaoh.
"You will sleep for a thousand years," hears Linda.

CUT TO: NEFRETIRI'S APARTMENT. Nefretiri has just killed her servant to protect the secret of Moses' true heritage.
"I love you. I killed for you. I'll kill anyone that comes between us!" she says to Moses.
The words *kill* and *love* echo in Linda's head.

CUT TO: MOSES STRANGLING BAKA, THE MASTER BUILDER.
"Death will bring death, Baka," says Moses.
"Death will bring death," mouths Linda in a whisper.

CUT TO: PHARAOH'S BEDCHAMBER. He is dying. His son, Rameses II, will sit on the throne of Egypt.
"May the gods bless you," chants the high priest, "as you go to join them in the Land of the Dead."
The pharaoh dies.

"Is he dead, Mommy?" asks Amy.

"He'll sleep for a thousand years," answers her mother.

"Is that forever?"

"Yes."

CUT TO: SHRINE OF THE RIVER GOD. Moses is about to launch the first plague by turning the Nile waters to blood. The high priest is chanting to Num, "great god of the Nile" and "praised of all gods."

No, no! Linda says to herself. They're changing things around. They're trying to get me to believe there's no Jesus. She gets up and starts pacing.

The water turns to blood. Linda goes to the kitchen and gets a glass of water from the tap. It is clear. She returns to the living room. Her wineglass is still sitting on the table. Linda stares at the red contents in disbelief.

CUT TO: THE PHARAOH'S BALCONY OVERLOOKING THE CITY. Moses calls for another plague: a hail that will burn as fire upon the ground and a darkness covering Egypt for three days. A low rumble of thunder is heard, and cries of awed fear are heard in the city.

Linda goes outside to the backyard. It is dark. Her eyes widen with fear as she rushes back inside.

CUT TO: THE PALACE HALL.

"If there is one more plague on Egypt, it is by your word that God will bring it," Moses says. He starts to leave, then adds, "So let it be written."

"The firstborn of each house shall die . . . beginning with the son of Moses," decrees Rameses II.

The councilors gasp. So does Linda.

She is speeding now, her heart beating rapidly, her brain racing with thoughts. The effect is to speed up the movie itself. Scenes start flashing across the television. Her darting eyes focus on selected images; her alert ears hear key words; her methamphetamine brain makes everything seen and heard important—a matter of life and death.

CUT TO: LINDA'S POINT OF VIEW AS THE MOVIE RACES BY ON THE SCREEN.

"Oh, God, my God—out of his own mouth comes Thy judgment," says Moses. "It is the power of God which uses me to work his will. . . . Around midnight the Destroyer will come into the midst of Egypt, and all the firstborn shall die." He is speaking directly to Linda.

"To set me free, death cometh to me," sings the beautiful Lilia. It is a simple yet hypnotic tune. Linda finds herself sitting next to Lilia, humming along.

"Tomorrow will bring a new world for us, Lilia," promises Joshua. He is looking at Linda as he says this.

"Those are Jesus' words," says Linda.

A greenish gray vapor is drifting down from the heavens, like a curtain obscuring the moon and stars. It resembles a ghostly hand. On the ground it becomes a fog, crawling through the streets and seeping under doors. The city is filled with distant death cries piercing the night.

Moses, his family, and Linda turn to face the door.

There is the sound of people running outside, then the thud of a body falling in its tracks. The thud jerks Linda's shoulders.

A terrified voice cries in the street: "Hold the baby high, keep him above it!"

Linda jumps up, bolts for the VCR, and starts beating her hand against the stop button, over and over again.

FADE OUT.

FADE IN. LINDA'S POINT OF VIEW INSIDE HER BEDROOM. Linda is lying on her back in the waterbed. Gil is sleeping. Water is heard running through pipes in the walls. In her overamped brain, Linda turns the sound of rushing water into the sounds of people rushing by on the streets outside.

They are running from the evil fog, she says to herself. I can hear their voices!

"It is some deadly thing."
"Go and get help."
"Too late—there is no help."

Now I hear voices from above, she thinks. Someone must be on the roof! The evil mist is all around the house! Now what? What are those noises coming from the attic? No, not noises—music!

[Lilia's song plays]

Linda is soothed by Lilia's hypnotic call for death. She starts humming and swaying in the waterbed. Gil wakes up.

"There's music coming from the attic," says Linda.

"We don't have an attic," says Gil as he turns over and goes back to sleep.

No attic! Linda thinks. My God, what's happening?

FADE OUT.

FADE IN. MORNING. LINDA'S POINT OF VIEW CONTINUES. Gil has left for work, and Linda has gone back to bed. But she still can't sleep. The voices have kept her up all night. Now she hears President Bush's voice coming from the television in the living room. Is the government behind this? she wonders.

Linda goes to the living room, where Amy is sitting on the floor watching cartoons. Amy has the remote control in her hand. Linda sits on the couch behind her daughter. A bunch of little cartoon characters are running across the screen. Suddenly President Bush pops up on the screen and starts talking directly to Linda.

"They're watching," says the president. "The children of the world are watching."

Linda gets up and turns off the TV. It comes back on all by itself. Of course, Amy is doing this with the remote, which she's been using to click through channels.

A sudden chill surrounds Linda. She goes to the bedroom and comes back with a blanket wrapped around her shoulders. It looks like a cape an Egyptian soldier might wear. She walks past the TV. Coincidentally one of the cartoon characters has a blanket around his shoulders. He is keeping pace with Linda. She stops. He stops.

"We're talking to you," he says. "We're watching you."

Linda turns off the set again. It comes right back on. President Bush is on the screen. He is talking about . . . a guitar? She turns off the TV. This time it stays off. Linda needs a cigarette and heads for the kitchen. Amy follows her.

When Linda goes to the stove to light her cigarette, she discovers that the oven knob has been turned up all the way. There is no heat, but there is a strong smell of gas. Immediately Linda turns off the oven and opens a window. Outside there is a dark overcast sky, and it is starting to drizzle. Linda starts munching a breakfast bar. Amy isn't hungry.

"Mommy, I had a dream," Amy says. "I dreamed I was going to sleep forever."

"Don't say that! You're scaring me." Linda is shaking.

"Why, Mommy? Because you're going to be all alone?"

"Yes," Linda cries, then drops to her knees and starts praying.

Amy reaches up and puts her tiny hand on her mother's forehead, blessing her. It is the same blessing her mother gave her last night.

Suddenly Linda is aware of a terrible smell filling the kitchen. She looks at the open window. The green fog is pouring over the sill. It didn't pass over last night, screams Linda's mind. The evil is still here! The evil is here!

Linda runs to the telephone. She calls her brother.

"The AntiChrist," she yells, then hangs up.

"Who should I call for help?" asks Linda as she frantically flips through the telephone book. She notices listings for the FBI, for missing children, for TV cable repair. They distract and confuse her.

Amy picks up a card with her baby-sitter's telephone number and hands it to her mother. Linda ignores it.

"Too late—there is no help," cries a voice from the movie.

The smell is getting stronger. The green fog starts crawling across the kitchen floor.

"Hold the baby high, keep him above it," screams another movie voice.

Linda picks up Amy and holds her close. The fog is moving up Linda's legs. She can feel it. Pure evil. Linda is hyperventilating. Amy is very frightened. Linda puts her down.

"You were chosen to take the sword of God unto your hand," says Joshua to Moses to Linda.

"May the gods bless you as you go to join them in the Land of the Dead," says the high priest to Linda to Amy.

Amy is standing motionless, frozen in fear. She puts her hands together and starts praying.

"Who are you praying to?" asks Linda.

Amy looks up and points with a finger to heaven.

The knife comes down.

Linda, still wearing the Egyptian soldier blanket, wipes the sword with a cloth and puts it away in her scabbard in the closet. She goes to the telephone and calls for help. Whatever evil killed her daughter is now locked inside the closet. Later, when the police recover the knife, they also find a small plastic Baggie with traces of white powder. They put the powder through a narcotics field test. Mandelin's reagent is added to the powder and shows the presence of methamphetamine by turning green.

FADE OUT.

4

Linda was too emotional to go to trial and accepted a plea bargain: eleven years for voluntary manslaughter. The small amounts of methamphetamine she had used, in combination with the thyroid medication and diet pills, had put her inside the movie and, now, inside prison. When Linda gets out, Gil will be waiting for her. They exchanged marriage vows in the courtroom just after the sentencing. Like Joshua, Gil promised that tomorrow would bring a new world for them.

So let it be written.

So let it be done.

11

THE HUNT FOR THE LAST DWARF

Lou Levin clawed the air in front of his face and gritted his teeth. He was showing me how the dwarf reacted after being shot. The possibility that the dwarf might have died did not bother me as much as the fact that Lou had taken both hands off the steering wheel to gesture. He grabbed the wheel again, just in time to negotiate a sharp curve. The Porsche 911 hugged the road impressively.

It was my first time in Lou's new car. He told me matter-of-factly that he'd worked an entire week to earn the eighty grand for it. I thought that if I said I liked it, maybe he'd give it to me matter-of-factly. So I told him I loved it. He only offered me the gearshift and ordered me to shift as we toured through the hills of Bel-Air, an exclusive residential area in Los Angeles. The car impressed me more than the real estate. Words like *comfortable, balanced,* and *superbly stable* came to mind—all the things Lou was not. But the Porsche and Lou did share one characteristic—both had impeccable style.

Lou wore beautifully tailored clothes from Bijan in Beverly Hills. He favored shirts without jackets, slacks without pleats, and loafers without socks. "Einstein didn't wear socks," explained Lou, who considered himself a genius in the world of big-time drug dealing. But when we got into the car Lou removed the loafers and put on a pair of slipper socks, the kind that the shuttle astronauts wear as they zip around the earth at thousands of miles per hour. Lou said the soft leather soles of the slippers gave him a better feel for the car, almost as if he were wearing it.

I feared we might achieve orbit ourselves as Lou raced through the hills. The top was down, and the rushing wind exaggerated our speed. I wasn't wearing a hat, and my hair, which was heavily matted down with hairspray to hide my bald areas, was flapping around in one embarrassing piece like a flag. It kept hitting me in the face, reminding me that I was losing the war against my genes.

Lou wore his baldness as confidently as his clothes and his car. He had a little horseshoe of jet black hair that was pulled into a short ponytail. It looked like a black knot. He was handsome, and his smooth skin belied his sixty years. Lou said he worked out every day in his gym at home, which was where we were headed. He glanced at his watch, a gold Piaget, once again taking both hands off the wheel to point out the time. The gesture seemed unnecessary since the car's computer displayed the time as well as the temperature. It was late afternoon and still eighty-one degrees, even hotter in other parts of the city. August was the hottest and bloodiest month for the City of Angels. When the heat was on, the murder rate soared. The city averaged eighty-six homicides in August. In just one sweltering twenty-four-hour period that week, there had been seven murders—eight if you counted the dwarf Lou said he'd killed.

He was anxious to get home before sunset so we could look for the body. Lou promised to take me to a working dinner afterward. His attorney had hired me as an expert witness to help in his defense against federal racketeering and drug charges. The government was charging Lou with operating a large cocaine distribution ring. They had plenty of evidence to prove it. A conviction seemed certain. The attorney was counting on me to find psychological grounds for reducing the sentence.

Lou was now taking me on a sightseeing ride through the grounds. We were driving not just around Bel-Air, but through a secluded area of Lou's mind known as a "paranoid pseudocommunity." The pseudocommunity is an imaginary organization of both real and imagined persons who seem to be united in some plot against the paranoid patient. Lou's pseudocommunity was inhabited by the very real DEA agents who had shadowed him for years, as well as by an imaginary army of dwarfs who had been recruited by equally imaginary Mafia neighbors. It was the oddest pseudocommunity in the psychiatric literature.

We drove in circles around Lou's block as he pointed out the mansions that were owned by the Mafia. He kept looking for DEA surveillance vans but saw none. While Lou's paranoid pseudocommunity certainly had some strange bedfellows, like all such pseudocommunities, it represented the final crystallization in severe paranoid thinking. Prior to this stage, the paranoid is bewildered by suspicions, ominous threats, and referential ideas. There is massive fear and confusion as to what is happening. "They" are out there. But who are "they," and why are "they" threatening? The paranoid searches and speculates and finally comes up with the answer. Everything becomes crystal clear. The existence of the pseudocommunity explains the massive fears and all that has been happening. When Lou told me about his community, he seemed relieved now that he *knew* who "they" were.

I knew that it was not unusual for a drug dealer like Lou to have the massive paranoia necessary to construct such a pseudocommunity. For years paranoia had helped Lou avoid busts and rip-offs, just as it had helped a long succession of dealers who suffered from this occupational hazard. In the early part of the century, narcotics police were known as "bulls," and people who had a morbid fear of them were said to have the "bull horrors." Lou had a morbid fear of DEA agents, but a bull by any other name was still a persecutory horror. His dealing created this horror, and to the extent that Lou had been involved with organized crime, his fear of the Mafia was also understandable. But who or what were the dwarfs? I wanted to meet one—even a dead one—and see for myself.

We pulled up to a large Tudor house in a secluded section of Bel-Air. A beat-up white car with a "U.S. Mail" placard stuck in the window was parked in the circular driveway. Lou took me around to a side door and into the kitchen. It was a splendid country kitchen full of pine cabinets, tile counters, and gleaming copper pots and pans hanging from the ceiling. I stood there and admired the collection of cookbooks while Lou went into another room. He spoke with a woman I assumed was his wife, then returned with a stack of envelopes and invited me to join him while he took care of some mail.

"I thought we were going to look for the dwarf," I said. It was getting late, and there was a new moon that night. I was worried it would be too dark to see anything.

"You wanted to know how I know about the dwarfs," said Lou.

"Yes."

"Follow me."

He led me into a small office off the kitchen. This was Lou's "mailroom." I saw a small electric teakettle, an electric iron, and a photocopy machine. There was a large glass worktable holding petri dishes and cups filled with an assortment of tongue depressors, camel's-hair brushes, cotton swabs, and small tools. A fluorescent magnifier lamp and an infrared lamp were mounted on the sides of the table. A bottle labeled "carbon tet" gave away the secret of this room. This was carbon tetrachloride, a chemical used to loosen cellophane tape and glue on envelopes. In the parlance of intelligence services, Lou's mailroom was a "flaps and seals" operation used for the clandestine entry into mail.

Lou sorted through the pile of envelopes and selected one. It was addressed to a neighbor but had been intercepted by his wife, who posed as a mailwoman. He inserted a small tool that looked like an ivory spatula and carefully separated the glue sealing the envelope. He took out the letter, read it, then put it back and resealed the envelope. The whole operation took only a few minutes. Such dry openings, he explained, were best because they were quick and nearly impossible to detect. Next he demonstrated a wet opening by carefully steaming open another neighbor's telephone bill. He had some trouble but finally got it open with no apparent damage. Lou pointed to one of the long-distance numbers on the bill. "That's a number with Mafia connections," he said. Then he photocopied the bill, resealed the envelope, and passed it to me. I looked it over and noted that there was no evidence of his tampering.

As Lou continued opening and closing the mail, he explained that several neighbors were members of the Mafia and acted as control agents for the dwarfs. During the day, the dwarfs stayed inside their houses, but at night they ventured out for forays on his property. I glanced at some of the addresses. There wasn't one Italian or Sicilian name. Most were Jewish. Was Lou certain the Mafia was involved?

"Who's got all the money?" he asked with a smug expression. I didn't answer.

"Who's got the smarts?"

I shook my head.

"Who would be most envious of me?"

I shook my head again as Lou went on to answer the question. "Israeli Mafia," he said with conviction.

"Come on, Lou, in Los Angeles that's more often myth than fact," I protested. Years before, I had testified as an expert witness in a so-called Israeli Mafia case. Jehuda Avital and Joseph Zakaria, two Israeli citizens, shot and killed Eli and Esther Ruvens, ringleaders of an L.A. cocaine business. Then the killers raped Esther and dismembered both bodies. They took breaks from the chopping and butchering to eat a little fruit. The case was horrific, and the notion of an Israeli Mafia complete with enforcers made good press. But I saw no evidence of a Mafia-style criminal organization. Two Israelis hang out together and the prosecution calls that a Mafia. Hell, it's not even a minyan (the minimum of ten adult males required for Jewish worship). There was no denying the defendants had conspired in the murders. You can call them ganefs (criminals), but not necessarily Mafia. "It's unlikely to be an organized Mafia," I repeated to Lou. I was the *mumchech* (expert), I should know.

"Who else?" he asked, turning to look at me with sparkling blue eyes. "Who else doesn't want to see another Jew like me make it? Who else would hire a *shvartze*"—black—"dwarf to do their dirty laundry?"

"The dwarfs are black?" I asked.

He nodded. "Niggers with little green beards."

"About the size of a small child?" I asked, trying to ignore his racist comments. I was searching for a real stimulus that could have triggered Lou's misperception. Maybe there *were* black families in the neighborhood. A small child hiding behind a bush might even appear to have a green beard. Silently I formed a plan to survey the households in the immediate area.

"Smaller," Lou said. He held his hand about eighteen inches above the top of the table. That was much too small for a human dwarf or child and too big for one of the hallucinatory creatures who torment cocaine abusers like Richie D. ("Richie in Whacky-land"). Some L.A. coke fiends coined the word *dweef* to describe the tiny dwarfs who play hide-and-seek games with their visual perception. But Lou's dwarfs were no dweefs. They were killers. Besides, as Lou continued to describe his dwarfs in detail, I realized they were not the typical blurred black-and-white figures produced by the cocaine brain.

Lou told me they had coarse dark hair and large bushy eyebrows and walked around in a deformed stooped position. Gee, I thought, give them glasses and a cigar and you got miniature Groucho Marxes.

"They got a wide mouth and two long crooked teeth, like tusks," Lou said as he continued to work on the mail. "And big Mr. Spock ears," he added. This guy can't be serious, I thought. He doesn't even sound afraid.

Lou's dwarfs reminded me of the gang of Smurfs that terrorized Houston schoolchildren in 1983. Smurfs, of course, are cute little cartoon characters. The Houston Smurfs were anything but cute. They were described as wearing blue body paint and black jackets and carried little knives and machine guns. The school kids believed the Smurfs were lurking in toilets, waiting for an opportunity to attack. It was rumored that they had already killed one principal. The paranoia became so severe that children refused to go to the bathroom, attendance dropped, and at least one family took their child out of school and moved to Philadelphia. (I was sure it was just a coincidence that Lou spent his own childhood in Philadelphia.) It turned out that the panic was nothing more than fanciful exaggeration of a news story about a juvenile gang called "the Smurfs" who had committed a series of petty thefts around Houston. Perhaps Lou's dwarfs were fanciful incarnations of his old fears about the Israeli Mafia mixed with the antics of very real children in the area.

"Are the dwarfs Israeli?" I asked. If the neighbors were Israeli Mafia, why not their dwarfs?

"Name a Jewish dwarf," he challenged. "Name one."

I quickly ran through my memory of dwarfs. There were Snow White's seven dwarfs, including Dopey, my favorite. But they were fictional, as were the dwarfs in Tolkien's *The Hobbit*. There was General Tom Thumb, the twenty-seven-incher who was exhibited by P. T. Barnum, but he was Christian. I couldn't think of one dwarf, imaginary or real, who was Jewish.

"See," said Lou when I failed to come up with a single name. "Then what are they?" I asked.

Lou held up his empty hands and shrugged. All he knew was that the Israeli Mafia had been watching his house for almost two years, passing information on to the DEA. Then they sent in their dwarfs about a year ago. There were thirteen dwarfs, he insisted, which was unlucky for them. Lou said he was able to scare away all but one. This was the only one he really saw close up, the one he thinks he killed the other night, the last dwarf. That explained his light-hearted attitude: he figured they were gone for good. But why thirteen? Was there some occult significance to the number? Lou explained that the Israeli Mafia was run by people who had the brains of a child. They couldn't think higher than thirteen, the age when Jewish males became men. "Their collective IQ is probably thirteen," Lou said sarcastically. Lou may not have seen occult significance in the number, but his thinking about it was significantly paranoid.

When Lou finished with "his mail," we went outside to look for the body. He showed me a small tree where the dwarf was last seen. Lou had fired two shots from his .22-caliber target pistol. He recovered one bullet from the tree. "The little fucker ran off with the other slug still in him. Should be dead," he said.

How could he be so sure? The grounds to his house were enormous. A gardener could get lost here, let alone a .22 bullet.

"I used a Walther OSP Match pistol—costs over two grand," added Lou in his braggart manner. "I never miss with it." I was sure the tree would agree.

We searched without success until dark, then left for dinner in Lou's car.

Everyone at the Italian restaurant seemed to know Lou. He pressed a bill into the hand of the maître d', who led us to a table on the side. Lou sat with his back to the wall, commanding a full view of the room. A bottle of his personal wine was brought to the table. We clinked glasses, then Lou offered suggestions on the menu. When we ordered, he told the waiter to have the chef use plenty of garlic on our food.

I like garlic, so I didn't object. But why extra?

"They hate it," said Lou, referring to the dwarfs. He didn't like to use the "d" word in public. "They can't stand anything smelly, especially garlic breath."

"Hmm . . . like vampires," I mused. I was watching Lou for some hint of humor, which would tell me he wasn't as delusional as he sounded.

"Who knows. Who knows." Lou shrugged with open hands.

Since it was a working dinner, I pulled out my pocket tape recorder and placed it on the table. Lou didn't object. He pulled out his own and placed it next to mine. While the machines would be recording the same conversation, I wondered if Lou would ever hear things the same way I did.

Lou filled me in on his history. His parents were still alive and in their nineties, which probably accounted for his belief that his genes would enable him to outlive any prison sentence. He had had a normal childhood and graduated near the top of his class from a junior college, then he'd gone into the gambling business. I was right. He did have past connections with organized crime. Lou claimed he was smarter than anyone else, including the police, who eventually busted him with evidence that added up to only a fraction of what he was actually doing. The secret, Lou said, was flash paper. Lou recorded all his bookkeeping on special paper that had been chemically treated. When touched by a match or cigarette, the paper burned instantly and completely in a "flash," leaving no ash or residue. Lou said all the old-time bookies used this trick, but modern gamblers and drug dealers seemed to have ignored it.

I pulled out a piece of flash paper from my wallet. Lou was surprised. I explained that I had used flash paper in my amateur magic act since I was a kid. There was nothing better for startling audiences or distracting their attention. I carried it because I was always entertaining my children with it at dinner. The little munchkins, as my wife and I affectionately called them, were delighted.

Lou took the paper, removed a solid gold Cross pen from his briefcase, scribbled the number 13, then made it disappear with the touch of a match. It was just a magic trick. Did Lou really believe that the army of dwarfs could vanish so easily? How about the Israeli Mafia? They were still living in the area. Lou's delusional thinking had worked it all out. According to Lou, the kids who ran the Israeli Mafia had no balls, that's why they used "them." Cut off their balls—in other words, get rid of "them"—and the problem would disappear. Tonight Lou was celebrating the last castration.

I turned the conversation back to Lou's perception of the dwarfs. He had given me some details during interviews at my office, but I wanted more. Lou accepted the dwarfs as real, not the paranoid hallucinations I suspected them to be. But real or imaginary, why this hatred? It sounded more like racism than fear.

Actually, it was both. Lou confessed that the hatred was rooted in his mistrust of their movements. He saw them as deformed bandy-legged cripples who moved with a gait that was something between a hop and a shuffle. It was a movement that he couldn't understand, alien to his experience, therefore it was not to be trusted. Lou's survival in the world of cocaine dealings was based on trust, a trust you sensed almost instinctively. Every instinct in his body told him not to trust creatures who hopped and shuffled in the night. They conjured archetypal images of an underworld even more vile than the one Lou ruled.

Lou never saw the cocaine slaves and crack babies his empire created. His underworld was filled with beautiful people. He spent his days on his car phone talking to other beautiful people sitting in their own expensive homes or cars. No one walked with a hop and a shuffle or hid behind trees and rocks like a troll from a children's fairy tale. Misshapen creatures who couldn't walk the straight line of Lou's beautiful world didn't belong. Such creatures could not be trusted any more than a mischievous child. Indeed, Lou said he didn't believe in having children. He didn't like them. Did he ever consider guard dogs around his property? No, he didn't like dogs, either. He was the kind of guy W. C. Fields would have said was not all bad.

It was around the time Lou learned the feds were starting to investigate him that he spotted the first dwarf on his property. He recognized how difficult it was for them to hop and shuffle around. They moved so awkwardly, they must be in constant pain. This was the key to his scare tactics: make it more painful for them. How? Lou refused to discuss it further tonight. He reached for the tape recorders and turned them off. Another bottle of wine appeared on the table. Party time.

We left in a giddy mood and headed back to my office, where I'd left my car. It was still a warm night, even with the top down. Feeling flushed with wine, I relaxed and enjoyed the Porsche's magnificent ride.

"Munchkins," I barked, shattering the silence of the drive.

"What?"

"Munchkins. There were over a hundred of them in *The Wizard of Oz*. Fictional, of course, but played by real dwarfs. Some of them *had* to be Jewish. I'm sure."

Lou laughed. "I hated the Munchkins," he said. "Those squealing voices singing all the time." He was smiling and shaking his head.

I leaned back and watched the night sky. "I liked them," I said, reminiscing.

Then I started singing. " 'Ding dong, the Witch is dead . . .' "

Lou picked up the next line without missing a beat. " 'Which old Witch?' " he said in a singsong voice.

" 'The Wicked Witch,' " I sang.

" 'Ding dong, the Wicked Witch is dead," we sang together, then cracked up with laughter. Lou almost spun out on a curve, and we laughed even harder.

We continued singing the song over and over, stumbling over forgotten verses, until he dropped me off at my office. As I waved good-bye I realized Lou was probably singing a victory song over the death of the last dwarf. Little did I know that in a few nights he'd be changing his tune.

I spent the following days working with the private investigator hired by the defense attorney. Together we surveyed Lou's neighborhood and determined that there were no black families and no families with small children living nearby. So much for my theory of

mistaken identity. Next I interviewed Lou's friends. They described
how Lou got up from dinner parties to run around the backyard
with binoculars and a flashlight. On several occasions he'd forced
them to look at the dwarfs through his binoculars. No one saw anything. Then there were the famous car rides. People who had been
in Lou's car during the dwarf era got a completely different run-
around from mine. Lou took elaborate measures to avoid a tail. He
would never drive directly to his destination. He varied his speed,
watching for cars that were keeping pace with him. He pulled into
driveways at night, turned off his lights, and waited for cars to pass
before continuing. Sudden U-turns with the Porsche were his spe-
cialty. And throughout it all he was nervous, edgy, and irritable. The
description of his behavior sounded like that of someone under the
influence of cocaine. Yet no one saw him do any. Money was his
narcotic, they all said. Well, maybe he didn't have a monkey on his
back, but thirteen dwarfs didn't seem much better.

This information agreed with the toxicological hair tests I ran on
Lou. Lou had not used cocaine for several years. He admitted to
use earlier in his career but never saw cocaine dweefs when he was
high. His use stopped completely when he started big-time dealing.
"I didn't want to snort my bottom line," he quipped. Lou's dwarfs
were kept alive by his paranoia from cocaine dealing and were not
born out of any past or current cocaine use. In this sense, the dwarfs
were like the Houston Smurfs, images borrowed from some other
source and embellished by his own paranoia. He had lots of real
reasons to be paranoid, but why did it take the shape of dwarfs?
The presence of Jewish neighbors provided a template for his delusions about the Israeli Mafia. But how did the dwarfs come into
the picture?

"Not another dwarf case," said Joel Morgan when I stopped by
his office. He remembered Ed Tolman's ("Dr. Tolman's Flying Influence Machine") recurrent images of angry dwarfs. In that case,
Joel believed the dwarfs were symbolic of the pet hamsters Tolman
had killed as a child. It turned out that Tolman's dwarfs were from
his memories of a movie, not a murder. Where did Lou's L.A.
dwarfs originate?

"Maybe the Israeli Mafia is really using them," said Joel as he
stroked his beard. It was clean for a change.

"Come on, Joel," I said.

"Historically dwarfs and midgets have been used as spies, sometimes impersonating babies," he said.

"But these dwarfs are impersonating killers."

"The dwarfs are a symbol for the dark forces from the unconscious. They represent the parts of the self that are imperfect, deformed, hence dwarfish. It's a classic archetypal conflict." Joel smiled, obviously pleased with his instant Jungian analysis.

"But even so, why should such conflicts be represented by dwarf images?" I asked. "Why not images of hamsters or turtles or whatever?"

"Dwarfs are part of the collective unconscious," Joel replied. He argued that the dwarf was a universal image representing the myth of a base and grotesque creature. The myth, he said, was perpetuated in fairy tales, folklore, even art.

I suggested a more mechanistic explanation, one that was consistent with the fleeting nature of Lou's dwarfs. In the midst of his massive paranoia about the federal investigation, Lou's senses detected minute movements of leaves and bushes, as well as changes in background sounds. His brain exaggerated these stimuli while searching for an explanation to fit the data. Perhaps the cluster of small movements and sounds were best explained by a small person—a dwarf. Lou's brain then pulled out a dwarf image from memory and overlaid it on the data. It would fit! This was how dwarfs were created for cocaine users, so why shouldn't the same mechanism apply to Lou's dwarfs created by the paranoia of cocaine dealing?

"You're in denial," said Joel. "The dwarf images were there first in the unconscious. Conflict caused their outward projection."

I kept shaking my head, even after I left Joel's office. I refused to accept that our collective unconscious is filled with diminutive creatures ready to fight it out in our backyards. The brief visit with Joel did not deter me. I still wanted to believe Lou's dwarfs were triggered by his occupational paranoia. But where did such detailed images come from? Perhaps his wife knew.

She called me in the middle of the following night. Lou was freaking out. Could I please come over? I met her in the circular driveway. Marilyn was wearing a bathrobe and heavy makeup.

But I recognized her as the same woman who had delivered Lou's mail. They had been in bed when Lou heard some noises in the backyard. He flipped on the yard lights, but nothing happened. There was no power to the lights. Lou didn't know that the gardener had put the lights on an automatic timer. He started screaming about the dwarf and ran into the yard with his gun. Marilyn handed me a flashlight.

Why me? I kept asking myself as I walked onto the rear patio. The underwater pool lights were still on, bathing everything in an eerie glow. I moved to the edge of the lawn just beyond the pool. The yard was dark. I held the flashlight so that the light illuminated my face, then called Lou's name.

"Over here," he said. Slowly I inched toward the voice, careful not to hop or shuffle. Then I froze.

Snow White emerged from the darkness. The long, flowing white nightgown was almost transparent as it shimmered in the pool light. The apparition came closer and turned into an aberration.

Lou stood in front of me in his bare feet and his wife's nylon nightgown. He clutched the target pistol in his hand, cursing. Snow White was armed and mad. I would not ask questions.

"The fucker's back. He's not dead," said Lou as he walked back to the house. He asked me to wait while he changed into some clothes. Something more comfortable? I said to myself.

While I waited in the kitchen with a cup of coffee, Marilyn tried to explain. "We were getting ready for sex. Lou sometimes likes to dress up."

There was no need to explain. I really didn't think that Lou was trying to lure the dwarf by masquerading as Snow White. Actually I thought he probably looked better in the nightgown than the mailwoman.

Lou appeared dressed in jeans and a sweatshirt, carrying two large duffel bags. I helped him take them to the back, where we unpacked an assortment of dwarf-busting gear. Lou had it all: binoculars, night vision scopes, even parabolic microphones for pulling in a whispered voice three-quarters of a mile away. He handed me something that looked like a pocket radio with headphones. The device was a personal audio amplifier, which Lou had purchased from The Spy Shop, an outfit that equipped secret agent wannabes. They also sold the amplifier to hunters with the advertised promise that "now you can hear your quarry before you see it and, more importantly, before it sees you!" Lou told me it was just what I needed to monitor the east side of the property. He motioned me with a wave of the gun to take my position. I sat on the east lawn for the next two hours, trying to remember if it was the Wicked Witch of the East or the West.

At breakfast Lou and Marilyn agreed that I could move into the house for a few days to help. Everyone had a different agenda. I still wanted to help Lou's defense, and I needed more data. Lou wanted the last dwarf. Marilyn just wanted an end to all this *meshuggass* (insanity) on the part of her husband. "He's not the sharpest tool in the shed," she told me privately.

Lou felt safe inside the house. After all, he had spent a fortune making it dwarfproof. All exterior doors were steel or copper. All interior doors, including closet doors, were solid wood and equipped with locks. Windows were barred and never opened. Two sets of stairs led to the second floor. The main staircase had an iron gate that was kept closed and locked at night. The other staircase, located near the kitchen, led to a dead end in a tiny room. The room was too small for any practical use but irresistible to a prying dwarf. It was actually an elaborate trap. Once someone entered the room, the door closed automatically and could not be opened from the inside.

There were also cubicles hidden behind false panels and at least two hidden closets where Lou had once stashed his money, rare coin collection, and probably his drugs. These items had been replaced with dwarf bait: sweets laced with rat poison. Lou believed that dwarfs could no more resist sweets than crawling into cubbyholes.

Perhaps the most paranoid constructions were the "dwarf doors" scattered around the house. They resembled commercial dog doors, large enough to accommodate a medium-size dog or a full-grown dwarf. The usual rubber flaps were replaced with doors made of inlaid wooden panels arranged in beautiful mosaic patterns. The designs spelled DEATH. Once opened, the doors snapped shut and locked. Some doors led to disconnected ventilation shafts with lethal drops to the basement. Others led to blank walls. A dog might know enough to stay away, but then a dog has an IQ higher than thirteen.

Lou's paranoid remodeling reminded me of Sarah Winchester's mansion in San Jose. Sarah, heiress to the Winchester rifle fortune, inherited twenty million dollars and enough paranoia to match. She believed that the untimely deaths of her baby daughter and husband were caused by the evil spirits of Indians and others killed by "The Gun That Won the West." Sarah knew she was next unless she could keep away the evil spirits. She did this by keeping carpenters and craftsmen hammering twenty-four hours a day for the next thirty-eight years. The result was a bizarre, rambling estate of 160 rooms with staircases leading to nowhere, doors opening into blank walls, a window built into a floor, and a chimney that stopped just below the ceiling. Some parts of the "Winchester Mystery House" may have been constructed with a dwarf in mind. There was a hallway only two feet wide, a storage cabinet that opened to a half inch of space, and a stairway with two-inch steps.

Sarah was even more obsessed than Lou with the number thirteen. There were thirteen coat hooks in the closets, thirteen windows in a room, thirteen panes of glass in the windows, thirteen bathrooms, thirteen panels in a wall, thirteen lights in the chandeliers, and thirteen steps in a staircase. The main driveway was lined with thirteen palms, while the greenhouse was adorned with thirteen glass cupolas. Sarah signed her will thirteen times and died at the age of eighty-two.

Lou was not dead yet, but neither was the dwarf. That belief changed Lou. He was no longer the happy-go-lucky singer who drove with the top down. I watched him go through a startling transformation. It was no coincidence that his trial was scheduled to begin in a few days. Days as well as nights became pure agony for him. A bird would circle over the lawn. It was no accident. Marilyn and the maid were stopped in the hallway. They were not talking. Why not? Someone called on his private unlisted line. They said they had the wrong number. He knew they didn't. The pool man came by to clean the drains. He mumbled while he worked. Lou knew he was talking to the dwarfs in the drains.

Each night Lou organized Marilyn and me into dwarf patrols.

We alternated shifts every three hours so that each of us got a reasonable amount of sleep. Nothing else about those nights was reasonable. Lou showed us how to patrol. First he scanned the trees and bushes in the back with a night scope and the parabolic microphone. Then he walked the perimeter of the property while lobbing stink bombs into the neighboring yards in order to flush out the dwarf. The stink bombs were tiny glass ampoules of ammonium sulfide that broke apart with an audible *pop!* The first time I heard the pop I was several yards behind Lou. I rushed ahead to see what it was. Before I got to him I ran through a cloud of fine talcumlike powder drifting in the air. By the time I got to Lou, I was scratching my face. Lou explained that in addition to the stink bombs he was dusting the area with itching powder and sneezing powder. These were the secret tactics he'd developed for giving pain to the dwarfs. He had purchased the stuff in the same joke shop where he'd bought the flash paper. I don't know what was in the itching powder, but it worked so well that I had to run into the house and shower. I couldn't understand how they sold that stuff in a *joke* shop.

Neither Marilyn nor I would have anything to do with Lou's chemical warfare. But we agreed to monitor the surveillance equipment and walk the perimeter at regular intervals. If there was a dwarf sighting, we would call Lou, who would keep custody of the gun. Throughout the next few nights there was our own occasional scratching and sneezing, but the dwarf stayed away.

I realized it might be impossible to do away with Lou's imaginary dwarf using conventional weapons. Perhaps I could attack it on the mental grounds where it was running amok. If I could show Lou that dwarfs were not so evil, if I could replace his unbridled fear and hatred with understanding, maybe his delusions could be reined in. This would not kill off the dwarf, but it might diminish Lou's paranoia, which was now out of control and becoming increasingly dangerous. While I knew that any effort to win an intellectual debate with a paranoid was likely to bomb, it seemed no worse than lobbing those glass ampoules.

One day I managed to slip away from Lou's castle for a few hours and make my way to the library. I researched the subject of dwarfs, from Aesop to Zep, the dwarf assistant to famous Danish astronomer Tycho Brahe. Finally, in an eye-opening study of freaks by Leslie Fiedler, I found what I needed.

"Lia Schwartz," I blurted at dinner that night in Lou's house.

"Do we know her?" Marilyn asked Lou. He had his mouth full and simply shook his head.

"Her professional name was Lia Graf. She was a Jewish dwarf, Lou." I could tell I had his attention, so I continued with the story. Lia performed in the Ringling Circus during the 1930s. She once sat on the lap of J. P. Morgan, a contrived act that brought her instant publicity. But the publicity took on a negative tone when Morgan described the experience as "unusual and somewhat unpleasant." According to some reporters, the incident prompted Lia to leave the United States and return to her native Germany. The year was 1935. Her career was doomed because in two more years Germany banned freak shows. The Nazis arrested Lia as a "useless person." In 1944 she was shipped to Auschwitz, where she joined other dwarfs who were being purged from the Aryan genetic pool. The Nazis employed an artist to sketch their skulls, noses, and limbs before execution.

"There may be few Jewish dwarfs today because of Nazi racism," I said to Lou. I was hoping to drive a wedge between Lou's hatred of Nazis and his fear of dwarfs.

"They *are* useless," said Lou. His mouth was full with food, and he actually spit the words.

"No, Lou," I spit back. Marilyn started to motion to me, but I ignored her. I began to repeat Fiedler's argument that dwarfs were actually the most successful, the most conspicuous, the most articulate, and the most intelligent of all freaks. Yet because of folklore and mythology and prejudice, they were the most feared and reviled. In a sense, dwarfs were the Jews of the freaks.

Lou would hear none of this. He stood up from the table and pulled the target pistol out of his custom-made shoulder holster. He demanded to know why I was defending dwarfs when I was hired to defend him.

I stood up. The table was hiding my shaking legs. "Right, Lou. What are we waiting for? Let's go get the fucker." I headed for the backyard.

The beads of sweat on my forehead mixed with raindrops as

soon as I stepped onto the rear patio. Despite the drizzle, the air was hot and sticky. It ain't a fit night for man or dwarf, I thought, paraphrasing the W. C. Fields line.

We patroled for several hours until Lou started sneezing, not from any powder, but from a developing head cold. On our way back to the house we all heard a motorcycle roaring down a nearby street. It seemed to stop just behind Lou's property. We rushed to the perimeter bushes and peered through the leaves with our binoculars.

"Nigger dwarf," Lou whispered.

"Don't jump to a concussion, Lou," said Marilyn.

I saw a figure getting off the motorcycle. At this distance anyone would look small. And in the darkness race could not be determined. The night vision unit, which displayed everything on a phosphorous screen in shades of green, could not resolve the question.

"Nigger dwarf," repeated Lou. "Betcha."

Whatever it was disappeared into the neighbor's house for a few minutes, came back out, and drove off. Whatever hopes I had to win the bet with Lou or dispel his paranoia drove off with that ghost rider in the night.

The trial was over in a few days. Lou was convicted on all counts. I prepared a presentencing report telling the judge all about Lou's paranoia. His hypervigilant brain detected small movements and sounds. He rushed to the conclusion that small people—dwarfs—were responsible. The delusion was supported by others, like his wife, who never challenged him. While the source of the detailed dwarf image was still a mystery, Lou's fear and loathing were not. I had learned that his attitudes were shaped by a childhood rich with scary stories of evil elves and dark dwarfs. In a sense, Joel Morgan's explanation of the dwarf as an unconscious representation of evil was partially true in this case.

If the report had any impact, it was difficult to decipher from the sentencing. Lou was given a dwarfproof cell for the rest of his life. On the whole, I'm sure Lou would rather be in Philadelphia.

After the trial I visited Lou's parents to return a family photo album I had borrowed. They showed me more baby pictures of Lou. I was more interested in the collection of engravings and woodcuts hanging in the living room. One beautifully framed picture caught my eye—an engraving of Bertholde, a seventeenth-century Italian prime minister. He had a very large head, coarse hair, little eyes overshadowed by large eyebrows, and a wide mouth with two long, crooked teeth. He also had a short beard and Mr. Spock ears. Bertholde was a dwarf.

12

THE PARANOID EXPRESS

1

Mario N. reminded me of the cartoon character in "Super Mario," the Nintendo video game. He was taller and thinner, but with the same dark hair, mustache, and large, expressive eyes. The electronic Mario was always getting into trouble, either falling into pipes crawling with bad guys or trying to jump from one moving beam to another as he attempted to avoid pits and traps. If he got hit by a bad guy or knocked off a beam, he always had another electronic life with which to try again. When Mario N. jumped on an Amtrak train, he fell into a world that the Nintendo programmers could not have imagined even in their worst nightmares. It was kill the other players or die. And Mario N. had only one life. No replays. It was no game.

On a Thursday in October, Mario boarded Amtrak train number 82 in Jacksonville, Florida, en route to New York. He was accompanied by his sister, her infant son, her three-year-old daughter, a Browning 9-mm pistol, and an MAC-10 .45-caliber submachine gun.

The family entered compartment A at the end of a sleeping car. Mario went to sleep in the top bunk Thursday night and was awakened early Friday morning. The train had stopped. The window shade was moving. Fingers were reaching under the shade. The compartment door opened. There were flashes of colored lights.

Someone came into the room. Mario *knew* that the intruder was an armed commando. He shot the commando. But there were others who had surrounded the train. They had automatic weapons and a helicopter. He recognized the voices of old friends. Some friends. Now they were part of the commando unit. Mario hid in the top bunk, flattening himself against the wall like a frightened animal.

More commandos invaded the train. Mario heard footsteps and heavy breathing outside the compartment. He fired shots at the door and warned the commandos not to shoot back: "Be careful! If you shoot, I have the machine gun at the boy's head."

On Monday, after seventy-nine hours, Mario left the train. Like Dorothy returning to Kansas from Oz, Mario stepped from his Technicolor commando-infested compartment into the black-and-white train station at Raleigh, North Carolina. The police SWAT teams—Mario's "commandos"—took him into custody. Inside the compartment were the decomposing body of his sister, with a bullet in her forehead, and the dehydrated remains of the infant. The daughter survived.

During his train ride, Mario had killed his sister, probably early Friday morning. After he'd fired the first shots, the train was halted in Raleigh. When police approached, Mario fired from the machine gun. His sleeping car was then isolated on a siding, where the three-day hostage siege took place. While he cowered in the top bunk, the infant was dying of thirst in the berth just below him. The district attorney charged Mario, who had once done time for cocaine dealing, with murder and kidnapping.

The stakes in the trial were as high as they had been on the train: Mario's life or death. The prosecution was going for the death penalty. The defense was prepared to argue that Mario was an insane paranoid and should be excused from responsibility. But under North Carolina law, paranoia, even paranoid schizophrenia (as the defense would argue), was not enough by itself to show legal insanity. Legal insanity was not a medical diagnosis, but a question for the jury to decide. The jury would have to determine whether Mario knew right from wrong. However, if Mario had used cocaine, which rendered him paranoid, as the prosecution believed, then the insanity defense would be weakened, if not lost. At the request of the prosecutor, the judge appointed me to investigate and determine if the "insane" behavior actually occurred because of cocaine use.

The first thing I wanted to know was how much cocaine Mario used. I examined all the police, psychiatric, and evidence reports, looking for clues. Mario had told one of the defense psychiatrists that he sniffed cocaine only three or four times at the beginning of the train ride so he would not fall asleep. Less than half a gram, Mario said. This was hardly enough to generate the wild paranoia he exhibited. But was this all? One of the evidence reports listed a used Kleenex that had been found under the driver's seat in the car Mario abandoned at the Jacksonville train station. When I had it analyzed, large amounts of cocaine were found in the folds of the tissue. Now I knew Mario probably used even *before* he got on the train. He was more of a regular user than he pretended. I confirmed this by a most unusual urine test. Mario had been so afraid to leave the top bunk that he was forced to urinate in his pants. I sent those pants to the FBI lab, which found massive amounts of cocaine metabolite, much more than would be expected following just three or four sniffs.

How much more? I turned to an unusual set of audiotapes for answers. The police had wired Mario's compartment with sensitive microphones and tape-recorded all sounds during the entire siege. When I listened to these tapes, I heard gunfire, Mario yelling and screaming at the commandos, the children crying for water, and the noise from a news helicopter overhead. The microphones also picked up several distinct sounds: "chop, chop, chop . . . sniff, sniff"—the telltale sounds of cocaine use. These occurred no less than sixty-four times. After the sniffing, Mario's rate of speech jumped from 108 words per minute to 188. It sounded like more than half a gram. In fact, based on the amounts Mario told me he usually sniffed in each inhalation, I calculated he might have used as much as 6.75 grams in round-the-clock sniffing on the train. This would explain his remark to the police on Saturday evening: "I have coke in here with me. I be a-snorting all the fuckin' time."

While such continuous cocaine use could trigger paranoid reactions, Mario was definitely fearful before he even got on the train. He described his life in Miami, where he was an illegal immigrant and ex-con subject to deportation if arrested, as filled with constant fear and suspicion. Mario admitted to occasional use of cocaine, which could have magnified these feelings. This was further complicated by a history of betrayal by his wife, who had a child with another man. But there was more. "I have other problems," said Mario. He had been working with some nasty people in Miami. "These people kill people. They kill children. They kill women. They kill everything," he explained. "And now they want to kill me." Mario insisted these things really happened. "Believe me, that's the way it is," he said, "I'm not lying to you. Don't go and believe that I'm crazy or something."

In an interview with one of the defense psychiatrists, Mario spoke of becoming so afraid of these people in Miami that he finally escaped on the train. The psychiatrist saw this as evidence of Mario's delusions and insanity, predating any use of cocaine on the train. But I knew that it could also be evidence of the occupational paranoia associated with the cocaine trade. I had reviewed Mario's rap sheet, listing convictions for distributing cocaine. Was he still involved in dealing as well as use?

Mario described his business in Miami as transporting "packages" from one place to another. The police asked Mario about these "packages," knowing that the word was a euphemism for the football-shaped packages of cocaine distributed by Colombian cocaine rings. Mario's response: "Maybe, it's very possible. I don't know, understand?" No drug packages were found in the compartment, but Mario did bring with him the accoutrements of the trade: the guns, two pagers registered to a fictious name, and over $8,000 in small bills. He purchased the train tickets in a false name and identified his sister and her children as his wife and children. Mario's explanation for this secrecy was his belief that his friends now wanted to kill his family as well as him.

I flew to Miami, where I spent several days tracking down Mario's friends and talking to agents on a special federal task force that was investigating narcoterrorists. The agents told me about Mario's friends. If you betray them, they kill your family and give you a "Colombian necktie." First they spread-eagle you on a vertical board and slit your neck vertically, from the chin to the collarbone. This severs the larynx and prevents you from screaming. Then they pull your tongue through the slit and watch as you slowly strangle.

The tongue ends up looking like a blue necktie. Friends like that would make anyone want to catch the next train out of town. So there was at least one kernel of justifiable fear for Mario's paranoia. Were there others?

During the train siege, Mario said commandos were invading the train, surrounding him, trying to kill him. Hallucinations and delusions, said a defense psychiatrist. I studied the crime scene photographs, then read newspaper articles and watched videotapes of television news reports that had monitored events at the time of the hostage drama. Everyone called it a hostage situation because of the family held inside the compartment. There were "commandos" all over the place in the form of military-attired SWAT teams and snipers who took up positions in, under, over, and around the train. I interviewed several other passengers who occupied compartments near Mario. They saw the commandos, too. While it was beginning to look as though Mario were correct when he'd said, "I'm not crazy," I still could not explain many of the experiences he'd had on the train. The commandos may not been hallucinations, but what were the fingers reaching under the window shade or the flashes of colored lights?

After 472 hours of investigation and analysis, including three days of interviews with Mario, I still had many unanswered questions about what really had happened on the train. I was convinced that cocaine played a major role. But there was more to Mario's runaway paranoia on the train than cocaine use or trouble with traffickers. I listened to the audiotapes again, hoping to find more clues. The tapes told a story of hunger, thirst, sleep deprivation, sensory isolation, and life-threatening danger during the more than three days he spent besieged inside the train compartment. Mario's own words spoken during the incident painted the scene: "I've gone many days without eating or sleeping—without even drinking water—and drenched in sweat up to my ass. And I have my sister dead on the floor and the children are full of shit and piss. My sister smells bad . . . and now the children smell of pee and shit. No one has eaten. Everyone's thirsty . . . what goddamn heat . . . not even informers have I kept this way." The conditions of confinement were humiliating to Mario. He couldn't stand it. "I don't humiliate men," he cried, "I kill them."

As I listened to the tapes, I tried to visualize the scene. Mario must have been under massive stress. The police added to the pressure. Snipers trained their high-powered rifles on the window of Mario's compartment and waited for him to appear. They wore earpieces, listening for the words *green light,* the signal to take out the terrorist. Mario peeked through the window and saw what was happening.

"Get the commandos off the roof," he yelled. "They're aiming at me. They'll kill me."

It was not bad reality testing. The police identified themselves. Mario called them commandos, explaining that in his country he called them commandos. But "if you are police, suck my motherfuckin' dick, police," Mario said. "You will have to fight with me to the end." Then, in a line right out of Al Pacino's coke-crazed mouth in *Scarface,* Mario yelled, "War! War! I want war!"

In Raleigh, coke-crazed cowboys were seen only in the movies, not in the streets. Raleigh was not Miami. The police didn't know what they were up against. They responded with a war of words. Loudspeakers and bullhorns were aimed at Mario's compartment. A negotiator tried to reason with Mario in Spanish and English. A doctor and a priest also tried. They pleaded. They sympathized. They even called themselves commandos. They said anything to avoid saying "green light." The verbal assault was almost nonstop. In the background sirens wailed, trains rushed by, blowing whistles and horns, and helicopters fluttered overhead. The little girl cried for water 290 times and screamed another seventy times. The baby did not stop whimpering. It was too much for Mario. He started yelling, *"Silencio! Silencio!"* He yelled it over and over, eighty-eight times. He threatened to shoot the children, the trains, the police, even himself.

It seemed like enough to make anyone irritable, short-tempered, perhaps even violent, with or without coke. Mario didn't have to be insane to act the way he did. But how did I know? I could almost hear the defense attorney cross-examining me: "How do you know, Dr. Siegel? You weren't there, were you? You weren't on that train with Mario, were you?"

I thought about the Nintendo Mario again. Whenever I played the game, I really got into it. The outside world vanished as I grew totally absorbed in the game. I surrendered willingly to the experience, whispering words of encouragement to the cartoon Mario or cursing the bad guys. Hours, dinners, sometimes entire evenings went by as I moved through this fantasy world. When I did tire, and tried to sleep, scenes from the game continued to scroll across my bedroom ceiling for hours. The video game was good, although not nearly as convincing as that promised by future developments in virtual reality. Computer scientists working on the "Oz Project" at Carnegie Mellon University were trying to build computer characters and virtual worlds so convincing and engaging that you would actually feel as though you were skipping down the yellow brick road with Dorothy and her friends.

I couldn't wait. I realized that the materials available in this case gave me a once-in-a-lifetime chance to pursue my dream of creating the virtual world of a paranoid, then jumping into it. I decided to play Mario N. in a simulation I dubbed "The Paranoid Express." As it turned out, it was no game.

2

The plan was to duplicate Mario's train ride from Jacksonville. Amtrak donated use of train number 82, including a sleeper car identical with the one used by Mario. When the train arrived in Raleigh, the sleeper car would be uncoupled and isolated on a siding. The Raleigh police would play their original roles as "commandos," only this time they would guard me inside the sleeper car, preventing any disruption of the "experiment." A generator would be hooked up to my car to regulate the temperature and power a sound system that would play the original tapes of the entire incident.

Inside the compartment I would try to relive Mario's experiences with him. Although I knew it wasn't for real, there were some real dangers. In addition to duplicating the conditions of Mario's hunger, thirst, sleep deprivation, and sensory isolation, I would be listening to the tapes of him going through the same experience for real, with all the amplified sounds of yelling, screaming, crying, and dying. This was certain to add to my confusion and increase the risk of sharing his paranoia in a type of contact *folie à deux*.

Of course, I wasn't an illegal immigrant, coke dealer, or coke user in fear of the authorities. But, unknown to the Raleigh police and the Amtrak personnel supervising my experiment, I carried with me a considerable quantity of cocaine. My license to conduct laboratory studies with the drug back at UCLA did not extend to transporting or using it on a train. I could lose my license—maybe more than that. The paranoia was beginning.

And, while I was not fleeing from narcotraffickers in Miami like Mario, I had enemies—real enemies. Mario's three defense attorneys were certainly going to be gunning for me in court. They had vehemently objected to my appointment. Once the judge appointed me, all three attorneys were present during my interviews with Mario in Raleigh. They guarded him as closely as any commandos, ordering him not to answer some questions and answering others for him. It was a hostile environment. I sensed everyone in the interview room was conspiring against me. When the interviews were completed, Mario asked me where I lived, hinting that he might want to visit me. Well, he didn't use those exact words. When I refused to give him my address, what he actually said was: "If my lawyers can find you, then I can find you and get to you if I have to." He was smirking.

Back in Los Angeles I began to receive threatening telephone calls. Direct from Miami and Medellín. From public pay phones. Collect! The garbled voices spoke in a mixture of Spanish and English. The accents sounded Cuban or Colombian. My life was in danger. I went to the FBI, who told me that their own agents on the case had been threatened. They said I should take the threats seriously because Mario had some nasty friends. I knew all about his friends. The FBI said they torture people. I knew all about torture. After all, because of the limits placed on my services by the court, I was going to make only about $11 a hour. That wouldn't even cover one of those collect calls from Colombia. Don't tell me about torture, I said to the FBI. Give me protection. They refused. So I loaded my shotgun and kept it under the bed. And I stopped answering the phone. I was actually looking forward to hiding out for a few days, even on a train.

So there I was in Jacksonville on a Thursday night, trying to enjoy my dinner, knowing that there were all these people running around wanting to give me a necktie. I was eating the same steak-and-lobster dinner that Mario had eaten. I hate steak and lobster almost as much as I dislike greasy fast food. Then I boarded Amtrak train number 82 and stepped into the end compartment of a sleeper car.

3

The first thing I do is inspect my surroundings. Like Mario, I have never been in a sleeper car. There is a sitting room and a bathroom. The sitting room has a small couch that converts to a lower bunk. An upper bunk can be pulled out of the wall above. A sliding door connecting to the next compartment is locked. Here and there are small panels resembling hatch covers, too small for anything other than dwarf commandos. The tiny bathroom contains a steel toilet and a sink that flips down from the wall.

A porter comes in and prepares the bunks. I give him the same three-dollar tip Mario had given. Then I take off my shoes but keep my clothes on and crawl into the top bunk, where I go to sleep with the light on, as Mario had done.

I discover that trains are full of mechanical noises, and a loud one jerks me awake at 5:30 A.M., the same time Mario was awakened. The train had made a stop outside Raleigh. Now it is clunking along to the city. My compartment is vibrating so hard that the flesh-colored window shade, which does not fully cover the window, starts to move. As I reach over to grab it, I see a reflection of my fingers in the glass. When Mario reported a similar perception of fingers reaching under the shade, the psychiatrist called it a hallucination. I recognize it as a simple illusion. My door is also rattling. I'm not paranoid enough—yet—to believe someone is trying to enter my compartment.

This was about the time that Mario's sister goes to the bathroom. He hears her tearing a package, then flushing the toilet. Was this one of his "packages"? If so, Mario should have been really pissed, and he was. The people in the next compartment start hearing loud arguing and yelling. They bang on the wall and shout,

"Shut up!" The arguing and yelling continue from inside Mario's compartment. A baby starts crying. A single shot is heard. It is probably the 9-mm shot that kills Mario's sister, although Mario would later claim he thought he was shooting a commando entering his compartment. Then the call for breakfast from the loudspeaker in the hall. It is 6:30 A.M. for both Mario and me.

As the sun rises in a hall window outside the door to my compartment, bursts of colored light dance through the cracks. One of the defense psychiatrists had called this an example of schizophrenic hallucinations. Now I know he was mistaken. Sometimes a sunrise is just a sunrise. The conductor comes through and announces Raleigh. This is when Mario fires the first burst from the machine gun. The bullets go through the compartment door. The conductor sees one of them on the hall floor. The train is stopped. Mario smashes the lights in his compartment.

My train stops. The lights in my compartment are turned off by the Raleigh police. Mario and I are in darkness. Our cars are uncoupled and moved to a siding. I hear the generator kick over. It will keep the heat in the compartment at the same sweltering temperature Mario had experienced.

I listen to the footsteps and heavy breathing of the Raleigh police as they move through the hall, setting up the other equipment for the simulation. When these same officers moved through Mario's car, evacuating passengers, Mario fired at the sounds. It is Friday, 7:41 A.M. I wait in the top bunk. I know that Mario is also waiting. He is checking his weapons. The 9-mm pistol has jammed, but the submachine gun is working, and Mario has a new clip with thirty-five bullets. "This son of a bitch hits hard," he later shouts to the police.

At 9:50 A.M. the police attempt to open the door to Mario's compartment. The door handle to my compartment starts to turn. Although I knew this was coming, I didn't have a watch, and it takes me by surprise. I had locked the door last night just as Mario had done. Nonetheless, he fired a burst at the door. My commandos back away.

I feel a sudden urge to urinate. I do it in my pants. The smell of urine quickly fills the small compartment. I am certain the officers in the hall can smell it, adding to my humiliation.

At 10:30 A.M. the sound system starts broadcasting the tape of the incident through a ventilation duct. The first shots startle me. Then come the sirens, voices of police, more shots, and, through it all, the incessant crying of the baby and the little girl. The audio quality is incredibly realistic. The sounds bounce around the metal compartment with an intensity that borders on a migraine. Then I realize I am suffering a headache from caffeine withdrawal. Mario, who was also a heavy coffee drinker, must have experienced the same problem. It makes the noises seem even more irritating. Then, at twelve noon, I hear the first of many repeated sounds: "sniff, sniff . . . aaah." Mario has started snorting coke. I pull out my own vial and sniff along with Mario. I will do this sixty-four more times before I am done. My headache soon disappears.

The drug snaps me to attention. I become hypervigilant. The police who are changing the tapes are not so alert. There is a delay of several minutes as they fumble with the equipment. The silence is ruining the experiment.

"Tape! Tape! Tape!" I yell, punctuating each word with a bang on the wall. "Change the fuckin' tape!"

After what seemed like an eternity, but was only three minutes, the tape starts again.

"Is everything all right?" asks a voice from the hall.

They're not supposed to talk to me. Don't they know that? I think. It's going to ruin everything. I feel like screaming one of Mario's lines: "If you are police, suck my mother-fuckin' dick, police. I don't deal with the police."

However, I did have to deal with them. So I grit my teeth and snap, "I'm okay." But I know that I'm not. I'm on the edge, barely hanging on.

I decide to write a note to the police, asking them to be more diligent about changing the tapes. It is important that there are no seams in my auditory environment. I place the note in the small cupboard above my bunk and close the cupboard door. Passengers who need their shoes shined can place them in this cupboard and the porter can retrieve them from the hall side. The police know to look here for communications from me.

Mario and I sniff again. It makes me horny. I can no more stop the drug from exciting the sexual areas in my brain than I can halt the other effects. Being alone with a corpse under such conditions is no fun. I retrieve the note and add a personal request: "Call Jane and tell her I'm having a wonderful time. Wish you were here."

On the tapes the police identify themselves sixteen times throughout Friday. I count at least fifteen shots fired by Mario. By Friday night the police stop trying to enter his compartment. But neither Mario nor I can relax. The coke makes it impossible. I'm not accustomed to such heavy sniffing. Mario blows his nose several times. The Kleenex I am using becomes spotted with blood.

"I'm hearing footsteps and everything," Mario says for both of us. I hear him trying to fix the jammed pistol. My eyes and ears are constantly scanning the compartment, checking out everything. I must work hard to separate the recorded sounds from what is really happening. The tapes would be the perfect cover for Mario's friends to launch their own commando assault on my train. In the evening, as the shadows lengthen inside my compartment, I know this is likely. It becomes impossible to sleep and ill advised to do so.

I stare at the night.

The police give Mario a time check. It is Saturday morning. I am still alive.

There are more screams, threats, and shots throughout the day.

If the drug had once turned me on, the corpse is now turning me off. Canisters of putrescine and cadaverine, two noxious chemicals produced by decaying flesh, are released in my compartment to mimic the smells from the corpse of Mario's sister. The stench gets to me. My eyes burn, and I become weak and dizzy. Somehow I find the odors themselves ghoulishly attractive. Is this what you smell just before you die? I wonder.

I'm not hungry, but by early Saturday night my thirst is so intense that I start seeing dolphins and sharks swimming on the ceiling of the compartment. The cries for water from the kids don't help. Then, on the tape, I hear Mario slip into the bathroom and take a drink. I do the same—only I discover that the water in my bathroom is not connected! It is a glitch in the simulation. Did someone really want me to die in here? I feel justified in taking two swallows from my emergency water bottle. I find myself repeating Mario's comment about the people who were determined to kill him: "Those people don't know me. They're surprised."

The two sips of water only make my thirst more pronounced. I can't get my mind away from it. I start hearing more bathroom sounds on the tapes. These are sounds I had not noticed before when I'd listened to the tapes in my office. I definitely hear water running in the sink. Is this wishful thinking or really on the tape? Is it live or Memorex?

I try to think of other things. Perhaps I should have packed a book in my duffel along with the rest of the gear. Of course, Mario didn't read anything, and the light was not really good enough. But it is something to think about besides water. Let's see. If you were going to be held hostage on a train for three days, what book would you take? I decide on *The Little Engine That Could*.

My reverie is interrupted by a loud noise. "Excuse me," I say to the pocket tape recorder I am using as a notebook, "but the Colombians are knocking on my door." It is a nervous joke. I turn off the recorder and listen. I am getting very experienced at identifying every creak and groan in the train, as well as the sounds on the tape. I click the recorder back on: "Correction. Mario just belched."

If he belched, he must be drinking again, I think. But I didn't hear the water running in the sink. He must be drinking from the toilet like a dog. Yeah, I can almost see him smirking at me, wiping his lips. He knows there's no water in my toilet!

The thoughts renew my thirst. I don't know if there is water in my toilet or not, but I decide not to check. The last time I climbed down I discovered the putrescine and cadaverine smells were strongest near the floor. I decide to stay on the top bunk, where the smells don't burn my eyes as badly. I turn on my tape recorder again: "Addition to book list: *As I Lay Dying* by William Faulkner." Then I cackle like a madman.

The tape finally runs out, and I reach into my duffel, feeling around for another. Something stabs me! I pull out my hand and discover that my finger is bleeding. I dump the contents of the duffel on the bunk and find the culprit: the open pin of a large lapel button. The button, a promotional giveaway from Federal Express, reads "Don't Panic." One of my assistants in Los Angeles must have slipped it into the duffel as a joke. Some joke. Didn't she realize she was messing up a really important scientific experiment?

I know it is wrong, but I can't help picturing her lying on the compartment floor with a bullet hole in her forehead.

I have to urinate again. My pants can't absorb any more, so this time I do it in the portable urinal I packed. At almost the same time I hear Mario urinating in the bathroom again! Our bodies are in sync! What about our brains?

There is no time to ponder the question. More pressing matters are demanding my immediate attention. The police are making too much noise. I bang on the compartment walls, screaming for them to be quiet. I find myself using Mario's words: *"Silencio! Silencio!"*

There is a lull in the activity on the tapes. Now it's easy to hear the sounds of *my* train without the interference from Mario's ride. Wait! There are rustling noises in the next compartment! A flash of light from the crack in the sliding door, then an eyeball winks at me! The fuckin' police are spying on me, I think, trying to catch me masturbating or something. I don't know if it's legal to masturbate in a train in North Carolina. I decide it's probably like flushing the toilet: illegal if the train is in the station, but legal if the train is moving. My train is not moving. The police will have to play with themselves if they want to catch someone.

So I lay on my bunk, snorting with Mario. We are sniffing up a real snowstorm. The blood on my Kleenex says so. I know there is no way I will be able to sleep. Well, at least the hunger and headache are gone. The temperature in the compartment must be near the 100 degrees it was for Mario. I am drenched in sweat and urine. Mario took his clothes off at this time, so I strip. I am happy to get out of my wet pants.

"Hey, Tato or Juan Carlos or *Ronaldo!* One of you, man. Have a dialogue with me so we can end this thing right." It was Mario talking on the tape, calling to see if any of his business associates were among the commandos. I had heard this tape before, but I didn't recall hearing my name. Was it really there? I can't be sure. The only thing I am certain of is my thirst.

And the smells. The heat is bringing them up to my bunk. They seem to be getting stronger. Now they smell like something burning. *Tobacco!* One of those cops in the hall is smoking!

"Put out that fuckin' cigarette!" I yell. "Put it out! Put it out!" I keep yelling until I can't smell it anymore. Mario was right about police. They can't be trusted.

I listen to the little girl crying for water. The little baby is no longer crying. Is he dead already? Will she be next? She won't shut up. "Soda . . . water . . . please," she cries over and over. I can't stand it.

"Listen to me," Mario says on the tape. "If you open your mouth one more time, I will shut you up for good."

She stops crying for the moment. I am thankful for such moments.

I lay on the top bunk as Mario did, away from the window where the police snipers have trained their rifles. The ceiling, only inches from my face, seems to be pressing down on me like the lid of a coffin. The oppressive weight binds my lungs. The smells clog the air. My throat constricts. It is hard to breathe. My heart is pounding. I close my eyes and try to escape the claustrophobia.

Now I see *angel* fish. Am I dead? Flashes of other tropical fish and underwater images tell me that I'm not dead, only dying of thirst. I hear Mario drinking in the bathroom again. That little cheater! I am too stubborn to use my emergency water bottle again. I might be stuck by the pin. I can't seem to remember where I put it.

Aichmophobia! A newfound fear of sharp and pointed objects is haunting me. Where did it come from? Why now? Maybe my psychoanalyst friend Joel Morgan would say it was sexual frustration. The aichmophobiac fears sharp instruments because he does not trust his own power to resist their appeal. He is fascinated yet terrified by instruments that release a surge of blood—a symbol for orgasm. The best way to avoid such phobias is to avoid suppressing sexual expressions. I can picture Joel handing me a prescription that reads "Masturbate now." But the police are watching me, waiting for this to happen. Joel is working with the police. I decide he cannot be trusted.

A police negotiator who sounds uncannily like Joel Morgan is talking to Mario, trying to win his trust. Mario will have none of it. "We're talking a lot of shit. . . . The object of this operation is me, only me." Mario is right. Neither one of us will surrender to this shit.

Mario starts talking about suicide. He doesn't want to give up. He'd rather kill himself. An FBI negotiator, fresh out of the FBI training program, arrives and starts talking to Mario. Mario won't listen. "You're giving me butts and queer talk. . . . I don't want to speak anymore, please."

I am lying in my bunk, listening to trains passing in the night, real trains and recorded ones on tape. Mario climbs down and checks the baby. "Ay, ay, ay," Mario cries. He realizes the baby is dead. "Oh, dear God . . . Holy Mary."

It is time to take my vital signs, something I have been doing periodically. But now I decide it's unnecessary. I no longer care if the signs are there or not.

I am still counting train cars rolling through the Raleigh station when Ray, the FBI negotiator, calls to Mario with the bullhorn. It is now early Sunday morning. I hear Mario climb down and urinate in the bathroom. This is verification of the water he drank last night but always denied. Now I hear him stepping over the crushed glass from the overhead light he smashed. I hope he cuts his cheating little feet, I think. He climbs back into the bunk and does three quick breakfast snorts. I start to feel better.

The drug heightens my senses as well as my mood. The smells are stronger than ever. Overpowering. I grab my emergency emesis basin and vomit. Just as I finish retching, I hear Mario vomiting! Our bodies are really in sync!

I lean back in the bunk, close my eyes, and try to suppress the continuing nausea. A helicopter is hovering overhead. For a moment I forget it is the sound of the news helicopter on the tape. The sound is totally believable. I entertain the possibility that it is from Mario's defense team, which has discovered my secret ride and is bent on stopping me. In my mind's eye Mario is licking his lips and smirking at me again.

Ray is talking with Mario, trying to be compassionate, friendly, even brotherly. His voice is very slow. It gets even slower. Then it stops. I realize that the generator has stopped. The sound and heating systems are dead. Outside, it is winter. I can freeze to death. Did Mario's commandos sabotage the generator? The tapes are more important than the heat.

"Get a battery-powered tape recorder, you fucks!" I yell to the police in the hall. I hold an imaginary machine gun in my hands and spray the door for emphasis.

The generator starts again after an hour. Lucky for the police.

Ray is sweet-talking Mario, offering him Gatorade. Mario refuses. No, Mario! Say yes so I can have some, too, I tell him. Mario
doesn't want to listen to me or Ray. "I don't deal with the fuckin'
government," he says. Does Mario know I'm a government consultant? I wonder. Did his lawyers tell him? Is that why he's trying
to get me?

Now Mario and I are yawning together.

I hear Mario going into the bathroom several more times to
drink. Finally I decide to take a few swigs from my emergency
water bottle. I do this without impaling myself on the pin, which
proves some psychoanalytic point, but I am unsure as to what it is.

Then someone starts banging on the window. I freeze!

That isn't on the tape. Another bang on the window. Then another. Oh, my God! Someone's really there!

"Is that you?" I yell to the police commando in the hall outside
my compartment.

"Is that you?" he echoes.

Someone is running down the hall. Train doors open and close.
Any minute I expect the commandos to break into my compartment. Mario's commandos. More noises. The door moves. Now it
is happening. I think I see someone come inside. I freak and throw
a pillow at the door. But you can't win a pillow fight with a commando. I clutch the only weapon I have—my portable urinal—and
position myself to throw it at the next thing that moves.

Nothing moves. After an eternity the policeman yells, "Everything's okay."

Later I learned that an Amtrak worker had heard about the experiment and wanted to check out the crazy doctor. He was the one
who had banged on the window. The police stopped him before he
could enter my car. They questioned him, then let him go. That was
a mistake. The "worker" was Cuban. There were many Cubans
who worked with Mario in Miami.

I start to calm down again. My headache is back. I am weak and
dizzy. My energy is draining. The smells are making me sick again,
but I have nothing left in my stomach. My vision is very blurry. It
is Sunday afternoon. I am waiting for a signal that will come at
2:32 P.M.

"Pop the window, Doc," a police commando yells. It is my signal to remove the window to the compartment as Mario had done. I discover this cannot be done. The design of my window is slightly different, and it doesn't pop out. When Mario took out his window, the stifling temperature of his compartment dropped suddenly and the fresh air diluted the smells. It was also through the open window that he received food and drink.

I rush to improvise. First I open the shade and signal to the police that I cannot open the window and we were to go to an alternate plan, which I scribble on a note. This plan calls for adjustment of the heating system to maintain a relatively cool 63 degrees during the day and 56 degrees at night, the temperature of Mario's compartment during the duration of the siege. Next I open several outside air vents to help disperse the smells. Then I wait for the food and drink to be delivered in the cupboard.

Mario and I snort a few more times. It helps the waiting game.

The cupboard is bare each time I check it over the next few hours. I feel like a dog sniffing its bowl, waiting for din-din. "Don't put poison in it," says Mario. My fears exactly. Finally, at 4:50 P.M. I hear the cupboard door on the hall side open. I reach in and literally grab the food out of the hands of a commando. I really don't care who he's working for.

I chug the sixteen-ounce bottle of Coca-Cola, then wolf down two soggy toasted bacon-cheese-ham sandwiches. This is the same greasy fast-food meal delivered to Mario. I love it. Sandwiches never tasted so good. I wash them down with two bags of dextrose IV fluid that were in the package delivered to Mario. Then I start on the apple. Mario and I burp together. We share a snort for dessert.

At 7:32 P.M. Mario and I receive a penlight. He uses it to find his identification cards and other papers to burn in the toilet. I do the same thing with the business cards his lawyers have given me.

Sunday, 8:53 P.M. Another sixteen-ounce bottle of Coca-Cola is delivered. I empty it by 8:54 or 8:55 at the latest. "That's good, that's good," says Mario, belching again. Right on, man.

I discover that I'm not very good at calculations. My brain is definitely slowing down. I give up trying to remember how long I've been in here.

I search my duffel with the penlight, looking for new batteries for my tape recorder. Thank God I packed them. I consider other things I could have packed, such as a set of camouflage fatigues, a Castro beard, and an AK-47. Then I could emerge tomorrow morning looking like a commando coming out of Mario's hallucination. I thought it would be very funny. The police would probably shoot me. I'd die laughing.

The negotiations continue. Mario is bonding with Ray. "You've been quite sincere with me," he tells Ray. "It's a pleasure to talk with you. I'm going to turn over the child to you . . . to you personally, but please, Mr. Ray, don't go and kill me afterward."

Mario hands the little girl to Ray through the window. Ray is holding a blanket between his arms to catch the girl. Underneath the blanket he is holding a gun. Mario sees the gun and reaches to shake the hand that is holding it. Ray drops the gun and shakes hands. "I admire very much your bravery and your sincerity," says Mario. Not to mention your stupidity.

Now Mario is ready to surrender himself. "Yes, I'm ready. You can tell me right away what I have to do."

The next thing I realize, it is 5:45 A.M. on Monday morning. Mario and I exit our compartments, seventy-nine hours and three minutes after entering.

4

I testified for four days on the witness stand, trying to get the jury to understand in words what Mario had experienced. I knew what I was talking about because I had been there. While my ride was just a simulation, and I *knew* that I was well protected, it was enough to scare the demon out of me and give me the experience of paranoia. At times I doubted the certainty of my safety and the loyalty of my police guards. I couldn't always trust my senses, let alone my thoughts about Mario and his friends and lawyers.

For both Mario and myself, real stimuli such as the shade moving and the door banging were misinterpreted and embellished with paranoid thoughts, then images. Neither one of us had a clear window to the real world outside the train, and we were forced to construct our own versions based on limited sensory data and our own projections. The isolated conditions combined with the drug to produce another reality inside the compartment. This reality was full of suspicion, distrust, irritability, illusions, hallucinations, and delusions. I knew what was happening, but the conditions were so powerful that I couldn't stop them from influencing my behavior. I couldn't stop the runaway paranoia. So I reacted in the same way I always did, a pattern dictated by my past experiences and personality. I yelled and swore, banged on the walls, wrote a note of protest, and even pulled out a nervous joke or two. Mario also knew what was happening. So he pulled out his guns and started shooting, the way he always had done in the past.

My verdict was that under the right conditions—the cocaine, the confinement, and the "commandos"—anyone could become paranoid like Mario or me. Our brains were in sync, after all.

The jury decided that Mario was not insane, which could have meant commitment to a mental hospital. They convicted him of killing his sister and nephew, but they spared him from the death penalty and gave him a life sentence instead. Mario stood and blew a kiss to the jury. A Mafia kiss? I wondered.

Their judgment about me was not recorded.

13

NIGHT ON HEMINGWAY'S GRAVE

On a moonlit night in June 1992, I broke into the Ketchum Cemetery at the foot of the Sawtooth Mountains. It was easy. I walked the short distance from the Sun Valley Lodge, where I was staying with a group of FBI agents who had gathered there for a week of lectures and workshops on drugs. Trespassing on hallowed ground right under the noses of sixty federal officers gave me an extra special thrill.

I stopped at the gate to the tiny cemetery and looked around. To the south I could see the outskirts of Ketchum, a small town in southern Idaho. Looking north across the valley, I saw the house where Ernest Hemingway lived and died. I turned to the gate to see where he now rested. The gate was locked, but I managed to find a gap between the bars and a stone wall where I could squeeze through. I made my way to a group of pines, where I found a marble slab flush with the ground. The inscription was simple:

ERNEST MILLER HEMINGWAY
JULY 21, 1899—JULY 2, 1961

I sat on the soft grass at the foot of the grave.

The slab was covered with a sprinkling of pine needles and two pinecones resting side by side. A lone ant crawled across the inscription. Nearby was Mary Hemingway's grave. Her slab was clean—no needles, no cones, no ants. Mary always was a good housekeeper. Ernest was the messy one, leaving lots of unfinished manuscripts and empty bottles around their house. He certainly had an appetite for alcohol, and critics have suggested there was a causal connection between the unfinished works and the finished drinks.

Hemingway once wrote, "I'm no rummy," but, of course, he was a master at writing fiction. In the nonfiction world he was an alcoholic from a family filled with depressive and manic-depressive illness. He drank everything from beer to whiskey. Hemingway had a special fondness for absinthe, the outlawed drink with brain-rotting hallucinogenic effects that he first discovered in Spain. In *For Whom the Bell Tolls* he described the green liquor as a "brain-warming, stomach-warming, idea-changing liquid alchemy."

There is little doubt that alcohol changed Hemingway's life as well as his writing. The characters in his early short stories and novels drink heavily, reflect deeply, and defend their creator's use. Eventually Hemingway suffered discernible damage. His liver and kidneys started to go, and there was a frightening loss of weight as well. A series of accidents added to his misery. Meanwhile his characters became banal, even boring, in a twisted self-parody of their creator. Friends and doctors warned him of the dangers. Then he ceased to create believable, living characters. Everyone saw the connection between his alcohol use and his declining productivity. Everyone, that is, except Hemingway. As far as he was concerned, his drug of choice had nothing to do with his words. In "A Train Trip," a chapter from an unfinished novel, a young boy asks his father about dope fiends.

"I don't know whether they use dope or not," says the father. "Many people use it. But using cocaine or morphine or heroin doesn't make people talk the way they talk." Or write the way they write.

Hemingway felt that way right up to the end. "Drinking is fun," he wrote a friend even after it stopped being fun. Continued drinking exacerbated a lifelong depression. The writing went badly, then stopped altogether. His mental and physical health deteriorated. Surprisingly, it wasn't alcohol that killed Hemingway, but a train trip of sorts, a wild yearlong ride on the paranoid express.

The first signs of paranoia were noticed by his friend A. E. Hotchner in 1960. Hemingway appeared nervous and suspicious. He abruptly hurried his friend out of a bar and made a fast getaway in someone else's car. What was he afraid of? The feds, said Hemingway. They were tailing him. Why?

"It's the worst hell. The goddamnedest hell," complained Hemingway. "They've bugged everything. That's why we're using Duke's car. Mine's bugged. Everything's bugged. Can't use the phone. Mail intercepted."

Throughout the drive, Hemingway watched and studied every strange car, every unknown person. Passing a bank, he thought he spotted two IRS auditors who were out to get him, and he drove in another direction.

No place was safe, even the sanctuary of the bar. When he told his wife and Hotchner that two men standing at a nearby bar were FBI men, Hotchner got up to check. He returned with the good news that the men were salesmen who had been coming to the bar for years.

"Of course they're salesmen," scoffed Hemingway. "The FBI is noted for its clumsy disguises. What do you think they'd pose as—concert violinists?"

Hemingway's core delusion was that the FBI wanted to arrest him for not paying taxes. Later he added another fictitious crime: attempting to corrupt the morals of a minor. Believing that the FBI was following him everywhere, Hemingway took circuitous routes in his travels, kept his name off passenger manifests, and spoke in cryptic phrases on the telephone. He began to suspect that old friends were part of the conspiracy against him. The doctors recognized that Hemingway had retreated to an impregnable prison in his own mind. They tried to break him out of it with electric shock treatments. It didn't work. Hemingway found his own way to escape. He put a shotgun to his head and pulled both triggers.

Damn you, Hemingway! I thought. What happened to guts? Where was your grace under pressure? Then I remembered that sometimes there is no way out from the pressures of paranoia—if it is strong enough or goes on long enough. What Hemingway wrote about the world in *A Farewell to Arms* could have been written about paranoia:

"The world breaks everyone and afterward many are strong at the broken places. But those that will not break it kills. It kills the very good and the very gentle and the very brave impartially. If you are none of these you can be sure that it will kill you too but there will be no special hurry."

The passage was an apt description of what happened to the paranoids I had known and studied. The cemetery setting moved me to remember.

Mark Steiner, the creator of the Adolf program ("Interview with Hitler's Brain"), dropped out of UCLA. He took the Adolf program with him. The rumors about Hitler's brain died around the same time. I heard that he studied veterinary medicine, dropped out again, and was taking care of attack dogs for the South African police. Several years later I went to South Africa to testify in a trial, then visited the South African Police Dog School at Kwaggaspoort, west of Pretoria. The officer in charge was dressed in a Nazi-style outfit. I asked about Mark. His clipped response: `I don't remember Steiner.`

Hitler's skull was finally discovered in a cardboard box inside a Moscow archive. The box also contained bloodied fragments of wood from a sofa in the bunker. The other remains, including the brain, were rumored to be in the hands of the KGB.

Edwin Tolman ("Dr. Tolman's Flying Influence Machine") returned to Los Angeles and started on a program of antihypertensive medication. It seemed to be helping. I asked him to lecture on his experience to my undergraduate class. In a show of hands, most of the students thought the satellite was real. That got to Tolman. He stopped his medication and left town. I never heard from him again.

Miss Lillian Rush ("Whispers") passed away in her sleep. Miss Louise, Dr. Rose, and I were the only ones at the funeral.

Leroy ("Whispers") is out of prison and traveling around the country. He is interested in contacting other people who are victims of the conspiracy.

Victoria Torto ("Shadow Dancing") was given an early release from prison. She wants to find a new boyfriend.

Cliff Hill ("Invasion of Bugs") was buried in Los Angeles. Mary read passages from Shakespeare at the memorial service. A quote from *Romeo and Juliet* appears on Cliff's headstone: "These violent delights have violent ends."

Matthew Nichols ("Invasion of Bugs") called me after his release from prison. The bugs were back. I referred him to someone else.

Richie D. ("Richie in Whackyland") is still serving eighteen to twenty years in prison. When he gets out he wants to earn enough money to buy state-of-the-art equipment to prove the existence of something no one else in the world knows about.

Kenneth Jackson ("Bunkers") is in a hospital for the criminally insane. He studies the Bible in the same fanatical way he studied *The Art of War*. Recently he asked his attorney to get in touch with Madonna. She wants to have his baby, and he's ready.

Harry Balise and his family ("The Floating Dollar Bill") disappeared.

Linda Estrada ("The Tenth Plague") reads her Bible every day in prison. There has been a good sign. Recently she saw *The Ten Commandments* on television. It didn't upset her.

Lou Levin ("The Hunt for the Last Dwarf") was transferred from prison to prison. I lost track of him. I hope the dwarfs did, too.

Mario N. ("The Paranoid Express") is still serving his life sentence. When he walks down the prison corridors, the inmates make sounds like a train whistle.

These were not happy endings for most, but their stories, like Hemingway's, were not fiction. The pressures may have been imaginary, but the experiences were all too real. Before returning to the lodge, I cleaned the pine needles and cones from Hemingway's grave. He had endured enough.

The next day I departed from my prepared lecture and told the FBI agents the story of Hemingway's paranoia. I suggested that they might want to visit the nearby grave and pay their respects. After all, they were part of the tragedy. Perhaps they might want to say they were sorry, that they really didn't mean to bug him.

The FBI men sat in their seats like a bunch of salesmen, staring at me with those sneaky we-always-get-our-man expressions, thinking I was crazy. I just stood there. It was the worst hell. The goddamnedest hell.

BIBLIOGRAPHY

GENERAL REFERENCES

Fried, Y., and J. Agassi. 1976. *Paranoia: A Study in Diagnosis.* Dordrecht-Holland/Boston: D. Reidel.

Keen, S. 1986. *Faces of the Enemy: Reflections of the Hostile Imagination.* San Francisco: Harper & Row.

Kraepelin, E. 1921. *Manic-Depressive Insanity and Paranoia.* R. M. Barclay, trans. Edinburgh: E. & S. Livingstone.

MacGregor, J. M. 1989. *Discovery of the Art of the Insane.* Princeton: Princeton University Press.

Matos, J. X. de, 1898. *A Paranoia: Ensaio Pathogenico Sabre Os Delirios Systematisados.* Lisboa: Livraria Editora Tavares Cardoso & Irmao.

Meissner, W. W. 1978. *The Paranoid Process.* New York: Jason Aronson.

Meissner, W. W. 1986. *Psychotherapy and the Paranoid Process.* Northvale, N.J.: Jason Aronson.

Oltmanns, T. F., and B. A. Maher (ed.). 1988. *Delusional Beliefs.* New York: John Wiley & Sons.

Retterstöl, N. 1966. *Paranoid and Paranoiac Psychoses.* Springfield, Ill.: Charles C. Thomas.

Retterstöl, N. 1970. *Prognosis in Paranoid Psychoses.* Springfield, Ill.: Charles C. Thomas.

Swanson, D. W., Bohnert, P. H., and J. A. Smith. 1970. *The Paranoid.* Boston: Little, Brown and Company.

CHAPTER REFERENCES

PROLOGUE

Kafka, F. 1971. "In the Penal Colony." In *Franz Kafka: The Complete Stories*, ed. N. N. Glatzer, 140–167. New York: Schocken. (Originally published 1919.)

1. THE DEMON OF PARANOIA

Cantril, H. 1940. *The Invasion from Mars*. Princeton: Princeton University Press.

Chekhov, A. 1988. "Ward Number Six." In *Ward Number Six and Other Stories*, ed. and trans. R. Hingley, 23–69. Oxford: Oxford University Press. (Originally published 1892.)

Dick, P. K. 1987. *Radio Free Albemuth*. New York: Avon Books.

Gogol, N. 1985. "Diary of a Madman." In *The Complete Tales of Nikolai Gogol*, ed. L. J. Kent, 239–259. Chicago: University of Chicago Press. (Originally published 1835.)

MacLean, P. 1969. "The Paranoid Streak in Man." In *Beyond Reductionism: New Perspectives in the Life Sciences*, ed. A. Koestler and J. R. Smythies, 258–278. Boston: Beacon Press.

O'Brien, B. 1960. *Operators and Things: The Inner Life of a Schizophrenic*. London: Elek Books.

Rancour-Lafferiere, D. 1988. *The Mind of Stalin: A Psychoanalytic Study*. Ann Arbor: Ardis.

Rheingold, H. 1991. *Virtual Reality*. New York: Simon & Schuster.

Waite, R.G.L. 1977. *The Psychopathic God: Adolf Hitler*. New York: Basic Books.

2. INTERVIEW WITH HITLER'S BRAIN

Bezymenksii, L. 1968. *Death of Adolf Hitler: Unknown Documents from Soviet Archives*. New York: Harcourt, Brace & World.

Colby, K. M. 1975. *Artificial Paranoia: A Computer Simulation of Paranoid Processes*. New York: Pergamon Press.

Colby, K. M. 1981. "Modeling a Paranoid Mind." *The Behavioral and Brain Sciences* 4:515–560.

Ellinwood, E. H., and A. Sudilovsky. 1973. "Chronic Amphetamine

Intoxication: Behavioral Model of Psychoses." In *Psychopathology and Psychopharmacology,* ed. J. O. Cole, A. M. Freedman, and A. J. Friedhoff, 51–70. Baltimore: The Johns Hopkins University Press.

Ellinwood, E. H., A. Sudiolovsky, and L. Nelson, 1979. "Behavioral Analysis of Chronic Amphetamine Intoxication." In *Origins of Madness,* ed. J. D. Keehn, 159–171. Oxford: Pergamon Press.

Faught, W. S. 1978. *Motivation and Intentionality in a Computer Simulation Model of Paranoia.* Basel and Stuttgart: Birkhäuser Verlag.

Fleming, C. 1988. *If We Could Keep a Severed Head Alive: Discorporation and U.S. Patent 4,66,425.* St. Louis: Polinym Press.

Galante, P., and E. Silianoff. 1989. *Voices from the Bunker.* New York: G. P. Putnam's Sons.

Heston, L. L., and R. Heston. 1980. *The Medical Casebook of Adolf Hitler.* New York: Stein and Day.

Heymann, C. D. 1989. *A Woman Named Jackie.* New York: Lyle Stuart.

Hitler, A. 1943. *Mein Kampf,* trans. R. Mannheim. Boston: Houghton Mifflin. (Originally published 1925.)

Irving, D. 1983. *The Secret Diaries of Hitler's Doctor.* New York: Macmillan.

Langer, W. C. 1972. *The Mind of Adolf Hitler: The Secret Wartime Report.* New York: Basic Books. (Original manuscript 1943.)

Lavater, L. (c. 1800). *Of Ghostes and Spirites Walking by Nyght, and of Strange Noyses, Cracks, and Sundry Forewarnynges, Which Commonly Happen Before the Death of Menne, Great Slaughters, & Alterations of Kyngdomes,* trans. R. Harrison. London: Henry Benneyman for Richard Watkyns. (Original work published 1572.)

O'Donnell, J. P. 1978. *The Bunker: The History of the Reich Chancellery Group.* Boston: Houghton Mifflin.

Payne, R. 1973. *The Life and Death of Adolf Hitler.* New York: Praeger.

Randrup, A., and I. Munkvad. 1979. "Stereotyped Activities Produced by Amphetamine in Several Animal Species and Man." In *Origins of Madness,* ed. J. D. Keehn, 69–77. Oxford: Pergamon Press.

Rauschning, H. 1940. *The Voice of Destruction.* New York: G. P. Putnam's Sons.

Schwaab, E. H. 1992. *Hitler's Mind: A Plunge into Madness.* New York: Praeger.

SS Werwolf Combat Instruction Manual, trans. M. C. Fagnon. 1982. Boulder: Paladin Press. (Original work published 1945.)

Trevor-Roper, H. R. 1947. *The Last Days of Hitler.* New York: Macmillan.

Waite, R.G.L. 1977. *The Psychopathic God: Adolf Hitler.* New York: Basic Books.

Zalampas, S. O. 1990. *Adolf Hitler: A Psychological Interpretation of His Views on Architecture, Art and Music.* Bowling Green: Bowling Green State University Popular Press.

3. DR. TOLMAN'S FLYING INFLUENCE MACHINE

Becker, R. O. 1990. *Cross Currents: The Perils of Electropollution.* Los Angeles: Jeremy P. Tarcher.

Becker, R. O., and G. Selden. 1985. *The Body Electric: Electromagnetism and the Foundation of Life.* New York: William Morrow.

Brodeur, P. 1977. *The Zapping of America: Microwaves, Their Deadly Risk, and the Cover-Up.* New York: W. W. Norton.

Brodeur, P. 1989. *Currents of Death: Power Lines, Computer Terminals, and the Attempt to Cover Up Their Threat to Your Health.* New York: Simon & Schuster.

Cheney, M. 1981. *Telsa: Man Out of Time.* New York: Dell.

Haslam J. 1810. *Illustrations of madness: exhibiting a singular case of insanity . . . with a description of the tortures experienced by bomb-bursting, lobster-cracking, and lengthening the brain.* London: Rivingtons.

Niederland, W. G. 1974. *The Schreber Case: Psychoanalytic Profile of a Paranoid Personality.* New York: Quadrangle/The New York Times Book Co.

O'Neill, J. J. 1978. *Prodigal Genius: The Life of Nikola Tesla.* Hollywood: Angriff Press. (Originally published 1944.)

Porter, R. 1989. *A Social History of Madness: The World Through the Eyes of the Insane.* New York: E. P. Dutton.

Rokeach, M. 1964. *The Three Christs of Ypsilanti: A Psychological Study.* New York: Alfred A. Knopf.

Schreber, D. 1988. *Memoirs of My Nervous Illness,* trans. I. Macalpine and R. A. Hunter. Cambridge: Harvard University Press. (Originally published 1903.)

Tausk, V. 1933. "On the Origin of the 'Influencing Machine' in Schizophrenia." *The Psychoanalytic Quarterly* 11:519–56.

4. WHISPERS

Bates, E. S., and J. V. Dittemore. 1933. *Mary Baker Eddy. The Truth and the Tradition.* London: George Routledge & Sons.

Brodsky, L., and J. Zuniga. 1975. "Nitrous Oxide: A Psychotogenic Agent." *Comprehensive Psychiatry* 16:185–188.

Davidson, M. J., and D. D. Peters. 1990. "Dental Treatment Responsibility for the Delusional Patient." *General Dentistry* 38:143–146.

Harris, D. 1982. *Dreams Die Hard.* New York: St. Martin's/Marek.

Peel, R. 1966. *Mary Baker Eddy. The Years of Discovery.* Boston: The Christian Science Publishing Society.

Pickering, G. 1974. *Creative Malady.* New York: Oxford University Press.

"Radio Transmission Through Fillings." 1959. *The Journal of the American Medical Association* 169:1271.

Steinberg, H. 1956. "Abnormal Behavior Induced by Nitrous Oxide." *The British Journal of Psychology* 47:183–194.

Stoudemire, A., and A. M. Riether. 1987. "Evaluation and Treatment of Paranoid Syndromes in the Elderly: A Review." *General Hospital Psychiatry* 9:267–274.

5. SHADOW DANCING

Lonsdale, S. 1982. *Animals and the Origin of Dance.* New York: Thames & Hudson.

Revitch, E., and L. B. Schlesinger. 1981. *Psychopathology of Homicide.* Springfield: Charles C. Thomas.

6. INVASION OF BUGS

De Leon, J., R. E. Antelo, and G. Simpson. 1992. "Delusion of Parasitosis or Chronic Tactile Hallucinosis: Hypothesis about Their Brain Physiopathology." *Comprehensive Psychiatry* 33:25–33.

Elpern, D. J. 1988. "Cocaine Abuse and Delusions of Parasitosis." *Cutis* 42:273–274.

Evans, P., and H. Merskey. 1972. "Shared Beliefs of Dermal Parasitosis: Folie Partagée." *British Journal of Medical Psychology* 45:19–26.

Gieler, U., and M. Knoll. 1990. "Delusional Parasitosis as 'Folie à Trois.' " *Dermatologica* 181:122–125.

Hopkinson, G. 1973. "The Psychiatric Syndrome of Infestation." *Psychiatria Clinica* 6:330–345.

Lyell, A. 1983. "Delusions of Parasitosis." *British Journal of Dermatology* 108:485–499.

Marshall, M. A., R. F. Dolezal, M. Cohen, and S. F. Marschall. 1991. "Chronic Wounds and Delusions of Parasitosis in the Drug Abuser." *Plastic and Reconstructive Surgery* 88:328–330.

McAndrews, J., R. Jung, and V. Derbes. 1956. "Delusions of Dermal Parasitosis (Acarophobia) Manifested by Folie à Deux." *Louisiana State Medical Journal* 108:279–286.

Partridge, M. 1950. "One Operation Cures Three People: Effect of Prefrontal Leukotomy on a Case of Folie à Deux et Demie." *Archives of Neurology and Psychiatry* 64:792–796.

Shelley, W. B., and E. D. Shelley. 1988. "Delusions of Parasitosis Associated with Coronary Bypass Surgery." *British Journal of Dermatology* 118(2):309–310.

Siegel, R. K. 1978. "Cocaine Hallucinations." *American Journal of Psychiatry* 135(3):309–314.

Siegel, R. K. 1982. "Cocaine Smoking." *Journal of Psychoactive Drugs* 14(4):271–359.

Skott, A. 1978. "Delusions of Infestation." *Reports from the Psychiatric Research Centre, St. Jorgen Hospital, University of Goteborg, Sweden, No. 13.*

Stark-Adamec, C., R. E. Adamec, J. M. Graham, J. M., S. E. Bruun-Meyer, R. G. Perrin, D. Pollock, and K. E. Livingston. 1982. "Analysis of Facial Displays and Verbal Report to Assess Subjective State in the Non-Invasive Detection of Limbic System Activation by Procaine Hydrochloride." *Behavioural Brain Research* 4:77–94.

Trozak, D. J., and W. M. Gould. 1984. "Cocaine Abuse and Connective Tissue Disease." *American Academy of Dermatology* 10(3):525.

Wilson, J. W. 1952. "Delusions of Parasitosis (Acarophobia)." *Archives of Dermatology and Syphilology* 66:577–585.

Wilson, J. W., and H. E. Miller. 1946. "Delusions of Parasitosis (Acarophobia)." *Archives of Dermatology and Syphilology* 54:39–56.

Yaffee, H. S. 1968. "Dermatologic Manifestions of Cocaine Addiction." *Cutis* 4:286–287.

7. RICHIE IN WHACKYLAND
Bodanis, D. 1986. *The Secret House*. New York: Simon & Schuster.

8. BUNKERS
Benko, P., and B. Hochberg. 1991. *Winning with Chess Psychology*. New York: David McKay Company.

Byck, R. (ed.). 1974. *Cocaine Papers by Sigmund Freud*. New York: Stonehill Publishing.

Nack, W. July 29, 1985. "Bobby Fischer." *Sports Illustrated* 63:70ff.

Thornton, E. M. 1983. *Freud and Cocaine: The Freudian Fallacy*. London: Blond & Briggs.

Tzu, S. 1988. *The Art of War,* trans. T. Cleary. Boston: Shambhala. (Original manuscript sixth century B.C.)

9. THE FLOATING DOLLAR BILL
Allen, W. 1982. *The Floating Light Bulb*. New York: Random House.

Bonner, H. 1950. "Sociological Aspects of Paranoia." *American Journal of Sociology* 56:255–262.

Brandt, E. H. 1989. "Levitation in Physics." *Science* 243:349–355.

Cerra, J. L. 1992. *Culver City: The Heart of Screenland*. Chatsworth: Windsor Publications.

Glassman, J.N.S., M. Magulac, and D. F. Darko. 1987. "Folie à Famille: Shared Paranoid Disorder in a Vietnam Veteran and His Family." *American Journal of Psychiatry* 144:658–660.

Kelsey, M. T. 1974. *God, Dreams, and Revelation: A Christian Interpretation of Dreams*. Minneapolis: Augsburg.

Madden, R. R. 1857. *Phantasmata or Illusions and Fanaticisms of Protean Forms Productive of Great Evils*. Vols. 1 and 2. London: T. C. Newby.

[Rolling Stone, ed.]. 1972. *The Age of Paranoia: How the Sixties Ended*. New York: Pocket Books.

Sanders, E. 1971. *The Family: The Story of Charles Manson's Dune Buggy Attack Battalion*. New York: E. P. Dutton.

Schmidt, H. 1970. "A PK Test with Electronic Equipment." *Journal of Parapsychology* 34:175–181.

Schreck, N. 1988. *The Manson File*. New York: Amok Press.

Steinberg, H. 1956. "Abnormal Behavior Induced by Nitrous Oxide." *The British Journal of Psychology* 47:183–194.

Zaehner, R. C. 1974. *Our Savage God: The Perverse Use of Eastern Thought*. New York: Sheed and Ward.

10. THE TENTH PLAGUE

De Mille, C. B. (producer and director). 1956. *The Ten Commandments.* Screenplay by A. MacKenzie, J. L. Lasky, J. Garcia, and F. M. Frank. Hollywood: Paramount Pictures.

Williams, J. G. 1991. *The Bible, Violence & the Sacred: Liberation from the Myth of Sanctioned Violence.* New York: HarperCollins.

11. THE HUNT FOR THE LAST DWARF

"Attack of the Killer Smurfs." April 4, 1983. *Newsweek:* 35.

Fiedler, L. 1979. *Freaks: Myths & Images of the Secret Self.* New York: Simon & Schuster.

Harrison, J. M. 1975. *CIA Flaps and Seals Manual.* Boulder: Paladin Press.

Thompson, C.J.S. 1968. *Giants, Dwarfs and Other Oddities.* New York: Citadel Press.

12. THE PARANOID EXPRESS

Peterson, I. 1992. "Wizard of Oz: Bringing Drama to Virtual Reality." *Science News* 142:440–441.

Vassos, J. 1931. *Phobia.* New York: Covici, Friede.

13: NIGHT ON HEMINGWAY'S GRAVE

Bellavance-Johnson, M. 1989. *Ernest Hemingway in Idaho.* Ketchum: The Computer Lab.

Dardis, T. 1989. *The Thirsty Muse: Alcohol and the American Writer.* New York: Ticknor & Fields.

Hemingway, E. "A Train Trip." In *The Complete Short Stories of Ernest Hemingway: The Finca Vigia Edition,* 557–570, New York: Collier Books, 1987.

"Hitler's Skull in Moscow Archive, Izvestia Says." February 19, 1993. *Los Angeles Times,* A6.

Hotchner, A. E. 1966. *Papa Hemingway.* New York: Random House.

Jamison, K. R. 1993. *Touched with Fire: Manic-Depressive Illness and the Artistic Temperament.* New York: The Free Press.

ACKNOWLEDGMENTS

The people in this book represent a small fraction of the hundreds of medical and legal cases I investigated in the course of my research on paranoia. I am indebted to the many psychiatrists, psychologists, public defenders, district attorneys, private attorneys, investigators, and police who contributed to these cases. I learned from all of them.

These are true stories, but some names and identifying or circumstantial details have been changed. In a few instances I have grafted minor but relevant aspects from other individuals onto a central character. Actual transcripts are quoted whenever possible. However, because of the difficulties in tape-recording conversations with paranoids, some dialogue has been reconstructed from written notes. The transcript of the interview with the Adolf program in chapter 2 has been edited from the actual printouts.

I extend my appreciation to the faculty and staff at the UCLA Center for the Health Sciences, who provided support services for several of the clinical cases. For helpful discussions along the way, I thank Werner Baumgartner, Ph.D.; Kenneth M. Colby, M.D.; Murray E. Jarvik, M.D., Ph.D.; and Louis Jolyon West, M.D.

I also want to thank Reid Boates, my literary agent, and Joyce Engelson, my editor, for advice and support. Bethany Muhl provided valuable research assistance and comments on the manuscript. Paula Berinstein provided excellent assistance in library research.

The bulletproof vest that I sometimes wore during the writing was supplied by Martin B. Retting, Inc., Culver City, California.